LAWYERING

PRACTICE AND PLANNING
Third Edition

By

Roger S. Haydock
Professor of Law
William Mitchell College of Law
Director, Academy of Court Appointed Masters

Peter B. Knapp
Professor of Law
William Mitchell College of Law
Co-Director, William Mitchell Law Clinic

AMERICAN CASEBOOK SERIES®

WEST®

A Thomson Reuters business

Mat #41046157

TO

SOPHIE WOJCIK HAYDOCK

AND

SHARON PETERSON KNAPP

WHAT WE OWE YOU IS
BEYOND EVALUATION

Acknowledgements

Ann Juergens, David Herr, and Jeffrey Stempel co-authored the first edition of this book and deserve our great thanks and deep appreciation. Without their contributions, ideas, and work, you would not be reading and using this third edition. They are very good friends in addition to being very good colleagues, and what we owe them is also beyond evaluation.

We are grateful for the support we have received from our colleagues at The William Mitchell College of Law. We want to especially thank Dean Eric Janus and Associate Deans Niels Schaumann and Nancy Ver Steegh for their assistance and encouragement. Our colleague Mehmet Konar-Steenberg made helpful suggestions for this new edition. Another valued colleague, John Sonsteng, has promoted many of the ideas expressed in this book in his Legal Education Renaissance efforts at http://renaissancereport.wordpress.com/. We also want to thank Jean Backes, Sue McKenzie, Darlene Finch, and Jennifer Miller for their support. Our research assistants, Bhupesh Pattni and Adina Florea provided valuable help in the preparation of this edition.

This book promotes and continues the development of lawyering courses at law schools throughout America and abroad. Law professors who teach these courses have provided us with suggestions for this new edition. We hope this book inspires the addition of lawyering and related courses to other law school curriculums, as recommended in the MacCrate Report and once again in the Carnegie Foundation's report, Educating Lawyers, and CLEA's Best Practices for Legal Education. Law students need this essential theoretical and practical education to succeed in life after law school.

Many lawyers and judges have influenced us and contributed to ideas contained in this book. We especially want to thank the Honorable Michael Davis, Ed Anderson, Bradford Colbert, and all the adjunct professors at William Mitchell who teach with us. Roger also wants to thank members of the faculty and Associate

Dean Mary Jo Wigins of the University of San Diego School of Law where he has taught as a visiting law professor and the staff at Forthright who provide dispute resolution services. The "Think Twice" feature of this edition adds a new dimension to the scope of this book, and allows us an opportunity to express ideas others have suggested.

Our families have always been sources of inspiration and aspiration for us. Our wonderful wives, Elaine Haydock and Lucinda Jesson, have taught us how best to negotiate, many times. And our charming children – Marni, Marci, Jeffrey and Brad, Chris, Nathan, John – have experienced our counseling efforts. All have witnessed our attempts at advocacy.

This book is primarily devoted to helping clients and parties who have legal needs and problems. We thank the many law students who have taken our courses and read the earlier editions, especially those who made constructive comments. We further acknowledge all of the clients we have represented, who provided the wide range of examples illustrated in this book. It has been—and continues to be—a privilege and honor for us to teach, practice, and write.

Preface

This book explains the fundamental lawyering skills, values, and relationships involved in the practice of law. There are three parts to this text: Part One explains how to interview and counsel clients. Part Two describes how to negotiate transactions and resolve disputes. Part Three explains how to prepare for advocacy. This text analyzes the theories, strategies, and tactics involved in client representation.

Chapter One begins with an explanation of professional relationships and the work of the lawyer. Chapter Two explores the business of practicing law successfully. Chapters Three and Four describe effective practices for interviewing and counseling clients. Chapters Five and Six focus on proper planning and preparation for transactional work and dispute resolution, and Chapter Seven discusses the process of obtaining information needed for effective planning and representation. Chapters Eight, Nine, and Ten cover successful negotiations and mediation. Chapter Eleven explains how to initiate claims effectively. Chapter Twelve discusses the scope of discovery and disclosure during dispute resolution, and Chapters Thirteen and Fourteen describe depositions and other effective discovery methods. The Epilogue concludes this book with the sometimes necessary transition to advocacy.

When the first edition of this book was published in 1996, the American Bar Association and the Association of American Law Schools had recently issued recommendations about teaching practice skills in law schools. The ABA MacCrate Report identified ten lawyering skills and four critical values essential for the competent representation of clients. The Wahl Commission recommended that law schools provide their students with training in these lawyering relationships. Since that time, the call for more practice-oriented education has grown louder. Two of the most important recent assessments of legal education are The Carnegie Foundation's report, Educating Lawyers (March, 2007), and the Clinical Legal Education Association's best practices project, Stuckey et al., Best Practices for Legal Education (2007) and http://bestpracticeslegaled.albanylawblogs.org/.

We reprint here the MacCrate Report's list of those ten fundamental lawyering skills and four critical values. The breadth and depth of these values and skills is a reminder of just how challenging it is to represent clients effectively and responsibly. Acquiring these skills and honing these values is the work of a career. This book has been created and designed to explain these lawyering values and to help law students and novice lawyers begin their acquisition of these professional skills.

Fundamental Lawyering Skills

Skill 1: *Problem Solving*

In order to develop and evaluate strategies for solving a problem or accomplishing an objective, a lawyer should be familiar with the skills and concepts involved in:

  1.1   Identifying and Diagnosing the Problem;
  1.2   Generating Alternative Solutions and Strategies;
  1.3   Developing a Plan of Action;
  1.4   Implementing the Plan;
  1.5   Keeping the Planning Process Open to New Information and New Ideas.

Skill 2: *Legal Analysis and Reasoning*

In order to analyze and apply legal rules and principles, a lawyer should be familiar with the skills and concepts involved in:

  2.1   Identifying and Formulating Legal Issues;
  2.2   Formulating Relevant Legal Theories;
  2.3   Elaborating Legal Theory;
  2.4   Evaluating Legal Theory;
  2.5   Criticizing and Synthesizing Legal Argumentation.

Skill 3: *Legal Research*

In order to identify legal issues and to research them thoroughly and efficiently, a lawyer should have:

  3.1   Knowledge of the Nature of Legal Rules and Institutions;
  3.2   Knowledge of and Ability to Use the Most Fundamental Tools of Legal Research;
  3.3   Understanding of the Process of Devising and Implementing a Coherent and Effective Research Design.

Skill 4: *Factual Investigation*

In order to plan, direct, and (where applicable) participate in factual investigation, a lawyer should be familiar with the skills and concepts involved in:

4.1 Determining the Need for Factual Investigation;

4.2 Planning a Factual Investigation;

4.3 Implementing the Investigative Strategy;

4.4 Memorializing and Organizing Information in an Accessible Form;

4.5 Deciding Whether to Conclude the Process of Fact-Gathering;

4.6 Evaluating the Information That Has Been Gathered.

Skill 5: *Communication*

In order to communicate effectively, whether orally or in writing, a lawyer should be familiar with the skills and concepts involved in:

5.1 Assessing the Perspective of the Recipient of the Communication;

5.2 Using Effective Methods of Communication.

Skill 6: *Counseling*

In order to counsel clients about decisions or courses of action, a lawyer should be familiar with the skills and concepts involved in:

6.1 Establishing a Counseling Relationship That Respects the Nature and Bounds of a Lawyer's Role;

6.2 Gathering Information Relevant to the Decision to Be Made;

6.3 Analyzing the Decision to Be Made;

6.4 Counseling the Client About the Decision to Be Made;

6.5 Ascertaining and Implementing the Client's Decision.

Skill 7: *Negotiation*

In order to negotiate in either a dispute-resolution or transaction context, a lawyer should be familiar with the skills and concepts involved in:

7.1 Preparing for Negotiation;

7.2 Conducting a Negotiation Session;

7.3   Counseling the Client About the Terms Obtained From the Other Side in the Negotiation and Implementing the Client's Decision.

Skill 8: *Litigation and Alternative Dispute-Resolution Procedures*

In order to employ—or to advise a client about—the options of litigation and alternative dispute resolution, a lawyer should understand the potential functions and consequences of these processes and should have a working knowledge of the fundamentals of:

8.1   Litigation at the Trial-Court Level;

8.2   Litigation at the Appellate Level;

8.3   Advocacy in Administrative and Executive Forums;

8.4   Proceedings in Other Dispute-Resolution Forums.

Skill 9: *Organization and Management of Legal Work*

In order to practice effectively, a lawyer should be familiar with the skills and concepts required for efficient management, including:

9.1   Formulating Goals and Principles for Effective Practice Management;

9.2   Developing Systems and Procedures to Ensure that Time, Effort, and Resources Are Allocated Efficiently;

9.3   Developing Systems and Procedures to Ensure that Work is Performed and Completed at the Appropriate Time;

9.4   Developing Systems and Procedures for Effectively Working with Other People;

9.5   Developing Systems and Procedures for Efficiently Administering a Law Office.

Skill 10: *Recognizing and Resolving Ethical Dilemmas*

In order to represent a client consistently with applicable ethical standards, a lawyer should be familiar with:

10.1   The Nature and Sources of Ethical Standards;

10.2   The Means by Which Ethical Standards are Enforced;

10.3   The Processes for Recognizing and Resolving Ethical Dilemmas.

Fundamental Values of the Profession

Value 1: *Provision of Competent Representation*

As a member of a profession dedicated to the service of clients, a lawyer should be committed to the values of:

1.1 Attaining a Level of Competence in One's Own Field of Practice;

1.2 Maintaining a Level of Competence in One's Own Field of Practice;

1.3 Representing Clients in a Competent Manner.

Value 2: *Striving to Promote Justice, Fairness, and Morality*

As a member of a profession that bears special responsibilities for the quality of justice, a lawyer should be committed to the values of:

2.1 Promoting Justice, Fairness, and Morality in One's Own Daily Practice;

2.2 Contributing to the Profession's Fulfillment of its Responsibility to Ensure that Adequate Legal Services Are Provided to Those Who Cannot Afford to Pay for Them.

2.3 Contributing to the Profession's Fulfillment of its Responsibility to Enhance the Capacity of Law and Legal Institutions to Do Justice.

Value 3: *Striving to Improve the Profession*

As a member of a self-governing profession, a lawyer should be committed to the values of:

3.1 Participation in Activities Designed to Improve the Profession;

3.2 Assisting in the Training and Preparation of New Lawyers;

3.3 Striving to Rid the Profession of Bias Based on Race, Religion, Ethnic Origin, Gender, Sexual Orientation, or Disability, and to Rectify the Effects of These Biases.

Value 4: *Professional Self-Development*

As a member of a learned profession, a lawyer should be committed to the values of:

4.1   Seeking Out and Taking Advantage of Opportunities to Increase His or Her Knowledge and Improve His or Her Skills;

4.2   Selecting and Maintaining Employment That will Allow the Lawyer to Develop As a Professional and to Pursue His or Her Professional and Personal Goals.

This book explores and analyzes many of these skills and values so that students of the law can learn to be competent, confident, ethical, and responsible practitioners.

Learning how to be a lawyer also requires observing and experiencing how attorneys practice. This can be accomplished by studying videos of lawyers conducting skills, by observing professionals in practice through internships, by participating in lawyering skills courses, and by taking clinical courses that bring to life these experiences. We hope you involve yourselves in these types of courses during law school.

Learning about lawyering requires reading about how lawyers represent clients. We encourage you to read and re-read this text and other books and literature about lawyers, clients, and cases to obtain a broad view of practice. Lawyering is portrayed, sometimes realistically, in movies, on television, and in the theater. You can further explore lawyer relationships and experiences through these mediums.

The conceptual and pragmatic considerations addressed in this book provide an overview of the dynamics of practice. This text is based upon the authors' experiences as practitioners and professors, the contributions of colleagues and commentators, common sense, and the law. We offer our view of what practice is and should be with the hope that you will develop your own view.

The representation of clients involves a sequence of events that typically occur in a reasonably patterned order. The table of contents of this book outlines that pattern, although this outline is certainly no guarantee that every case will unfold in this order. You should not presume that the real world reflects this precise sequence.

Our occasional attempts at humor that appear throughout the text may, with the right timing, even be funny. We often take ourselves and the practice of law too seriously, and an occasional chuckle or groan may help put things in proper perspective.

We now begin this book with the hope that you will discover the excitement and adventure that accompany the practice of law. We encourage you to send us comments, suggestions, stories, anecdotes, and examples that we can include in our next edition.

ROGER S. HAYDOCK
PETER B. KNAPP

January, 2011

Companion Materials

Videos and transcripts of videos provide demonstrations and examples of lawyering skills. Some of these videos include:

Lawyering Skills Video Series by Professors Peter Knapp, Ann Juergens, and Roger Haydock

Interviewing, Counseling and Negotiation illustrates effective client interviewing and counseling and successful negotiation strategies, tactics, and techniques.

Mediation and Arbitration demonstrates essential stages of a mediation and the presentation of an arbitration.

Depositions and Trial presents effective deposition questioning and the trial of a case before a judge.

Additional educational titles for law students include:

Fundamentals of Pretrial Litigation, 8th Edition by Roger S. Haydock, David F. Herr, and Jeffrey W. Stempel (West) extensively covers pleadings, discovery, motions, and litigation practice.

Trial: Advocacy Before Judges, Jurors and Arbitrators, 4th Edition by Roger S. Haydock and John O. Sonsteng (West) contains explanations and examples of effective trial, arbitration, and hearing practice.

Trialbook, 3rd Edition by John O. Sonsteng and Roger S. Haydock (National Institute for Trial Advocacy) presents a systematic way to prepare and present a case for trial.

Additional informative titles for lawyers include:

Fundamentals of Litigation Practice by David F. Herr, Roger S. Haydock, and Jeffrey W. Stempel (West).

Discovery Practice, 5th Edition by Roger S. Haydock and David F. Herr (Aspen).

Motion Practice, 5th Edition by David F. Herr, Roger S. Haydock, and Jeffrey W. Stempel (Aspen).

These texts explain and describe pleading, discovery, and motion practice in litigation, arbitration, and administrative hearings and effective strategies, efficient tactics, and economical techniques.

Summary of Contents

Table of Contents

TABLE OF CONTENTS

LAWYERING

PRACTICE AND PLANNING

Third Edition

Chapter One
WORK OF THE LAWYER

"Oh, do not ask, 'What is it?'
Let us go and make our visit."

—*T.S. Eliot*
The Love Song of J. Alfred Prufrock

A. INTRODUCTION

1.1 WELCOME TO THE PRACTICE OF LAW

There is a continuing need for lawyers in America and throughout the world. In the distant and recent past as communities evolved, people formed relationships, created transactions, caused problems, and became involved in disputes. Parties needed someone to help them create legally recognized relationships and craft legally enforceable transactions. And parties needed professional help with resolving legal disputes that arose in their communities. They still do. That is why you're in law school today: to join our helping profession.

Lawyers have both the privilege and responsibility to help clients. Clients will expect you to complete their business deals or end their legal disputes. A humanistic view of lawyering shapes and influences our work. The situations presented in this book, discussed in class, explored in a clinic, or demonstrated in a video involve and affect the lives of real people with dreams or who face tragedies. You need to bring to life what you read, see, and discuss so you can experience this human dimension of practice.

The decisions lawyers make—from the initial client interview to the conclusion of a case—are based on the reasoned analysis of the law, but are also based on incisive judgments about people and events. We hope that these materials will help you develop and refine the judgment you'll need as a practicing lawyer.

Ethical issues permeate the practice of law. A major premise of this book is that lawyers must hold themselves to high ethical standards. An understanding of your responsibilities and duties as explained in this text will help you identify and resolve ethical concerns.

There is no one way to "practice" law. Lawyering involves judgments about which road to take: to the right or to the left or on the road less traveled. Yes, there are some established rules and there are some commonly accepted approaches, but much in the practice requires you to exercise professional discretion. The choices may be many or few, but the decision of what to say and do will be up to you and your client.

The practice of law is difficult. Problems occur routinely and sometimes lawyers make mistakes. One of the keys to being an effective lawyer is not to let the mistakes and problems overwhelm you. Thorough preparation and an understanding of available solutions explained in these materials will help you anticipate and avoid mistakes and problems.

Civil practice resembles most life and law school experiences. There will be times of success, failure, happiness, frustration, excitement, anxiety, and satisfaction. You may experience these psychological and emotional dimensions as you study these materials, participate in class, perform skills exercises, or represent clients in a clinic. For sure, you'll experience all this in your future work as a lawyer.

1.2 THE FOCUS OF LAWYERING

This book explains and explores fundamental professional skills involved in practicing law. You will learn how to interview and counsel a client, investigate cases, negotiate with other attorneys, participate in mediations, plan for transactions and dispute resolution, initiate and defend claims, gather and discover information, take depositions, and prepare a case for resolution. You will learn what to do, when to do it, where to do it, and why to do it.

These materials focus primarily on the civil practice of law, although much will apply to whatever you do in your professional life after law school. Law graduates employ basic interviewing, counseling, negotiating, and planning skills in whatever they do, including those who do not represent clients in practice. The materials analyze and present approaches used by successful lawyers. Each chapter describes alternative strategies, tactics, and techniques.

Companion videos supplement this book. You can and will learn much by observing and critiquing lawyers practice law. The videos present client interviews, counseling sessions, negotiation conferences, mediation sessions, and depositions. Observing what these lawyers do and don't do, evaluating their efforts, and suggesting alternative approaches will help you further understand how to think, be, feel, and act like a lawyer.

The ultimate goal of this book is to help you become a competent, professional, and confident lawyer. We learn from how things have been done in the past, from each other, and from thinking about how things should be in the future. As you read and digest these materials you will become knowledgeable, informed, surprised, curious, and shocked. Not everything in the practical and theoretical world of lawyering will conform to your experience, your expectations, and your notions of what it means to be a lawyer. We present both the way things are and the way things could or should be. Your task, in part, is to make all these things coalesce.

1.3 THE TAPESTRY OF LAW PRACTICE

The notion of a tapestry provides a helpful metaphor in explaining lawyering. A lawyer has to weave threads together when practicing law. These threads include:

- Interviewing clients
- Gathering information
- Counseling clients
- Planning transactions
- Preparing to resolve disputes
- Investigating matters

- Interviewing witnesses
- Creating agreements and relationships
- Negotiating with opposing counsel and parties
- Mediating cases
- Resolving problems
- Drafting pleadings
- Bringing and defending claims
- Selecting dispute resolution forums
- Discovering information from opposing parties
- Planning cases before dispute resolution forums
- Leading a balanced life and enjoying it all

These are the threads you will need to weave together with the other threads you learn in law school and life to create a pattern of effective practice.

1.3.1   The Tapestry Practice Pattern

A number of basic elements compose this tapestry of the law:

Facts. The gathering and selection of facts occurs throughout client representation. For example, a lawyer drafting a will needs (at a minimum) to know the testator's identity, family relations, financial life, and desired disposition of wealth. Only then can a lawyer draft a will that both fulfills the client's objectives and complies with legal requirements. For another example, a lawyer representing a client in a dispute must (at a minimum) know the client's story, the other side's version of that story, the issues that need to be resolved, and the applicable law. It is critical, obviously, for lawyers in all types of cases to gain a mastery of all relevant facts connected with the transaction, project, or dispute before moving forward to draft a contract, propose a solution, or file a complaint. But the fact-finding lawyer is constrained by limited client resources, time pressures, and deadlines.

Law. You are learning and will continue to learn substantive and procedural law in your other law school courses. You will also learn in this book some of the procedural laws, rules, and regulations involved in civil practice. After law school, you will need to continue to learn much more about the law to adequately represent a client. You will need to become an expert in the area of law affecting your client's interests. Law school is only the start of that process.

Application of law to facts. All the most brilliant legal learning and sophisticated fact gathering will amount to nothing if the lawyer cannot effectively apply the right law to the right facts. The right choices, decisions, and judgments made forms the art of being an effective lawyer.

Weaving theory and skills. If you know what to do but not how to do it, you'll create a mess. And if you know how to do it but not what to do, you'll be a menace. Effective lawyering requires you to weave together the theories and professional skills of lawyering into a whole tapestry.

1.3.2 The Tapestry

People tend to act in certain ways, whether they are a client, an opposing lawyer, or a decision maker. While we have divided the lawyer's work into discrete segments, there are similar approaches to lawyering whether an attorney is working with the client, an opposing attorney, or a decision maker. For example, questioning tactics that make a good client interview also make an effective witness interview, enhance information needed during negotiations, develop successful deposition questions, and may later make for a good direct examination.

These common threads and patterns of lawyering apply across the whole height and width of the tapestry of client representation. You will need to study each thread separately, step back and view the pattern, step further back to see the entire design, and then step forward to touch and feel the tapestry of legal practice.

Think Twice

Throughout this book, we have created Think Twice to provide additional commentary about a topic. We trust you will find these comments insightful. Well, that's our hope. Their purpose is to provide a viewpoint from a different perspective, highlight an important point, refer-ence a previous or subsequent section, or permit us to spout off.

We begin with the tapestry metaphor because we believe it's helpful to try and picture the law while reading this book. The challenge for us is to recreate how successful lawyers think and feel and what they do and accomplish restricted to this two dimensional plane of words. But the practice occurs in 3D, so we hope you reconstruct the second and third dimensions as you explore this text.

B. RELATIONSHIPS

1.4 LAWYER RELATIONSHIPS

The practice of law involves an appreciation and understanding of a number of relationships. Lawyers spend their time:

- Working with clients
- Dealing with other attorneys and parties
- Seeking information or help from others
- Appearing before decision makers
- Working within the legal system
- Working as a practitioner
- Working with colleagues
- Working with oneself

1.4.1 Working With Clients

How does one become a practicing lawyer? The right answer is: Get a client.

What our clients expect from us, at a minimum, is this: during our representation of them, they expect that nothing in our professional life will be more important. They expect the full measure of our energy and efforts to fulfill their needs. They expect our best commitment whether it takes five minutes or five years of representation.

This is not easy to do. We have other clients (hopefully). We have other responsibilities in our professional and personal lives.

We have our own needs. As a professional we have a genuine obligation to meet our clients' minimal expectations. They would not retain an attorney—would you?—who would say to them: "I'll devote less than my full attention to your case. I'll make half-hearted attempts to get what you want. I'll make mediocre efforts to represent you." They have a right to expect our very best.

One of the dilemmas of practice is that we are often asked to help people who are in need or in trouble and expect you to make it right or to go away—now. They may want you to draft an agreement that doesn't seem in their best interests. They will come to you having made stupid mistakes or suffering through a personal or business tragedy. And some will expect more from you than you can ever deliver.

Lawyers have to understand these human dimensions. Across the course of your career, you'll need to remind yourself that your clients are *people with problems* and not just problems who cause you more problems. A major dissatisfaction with practice comes from focusing on failed efforts and solving problems instead of on *helping people* fulfill their dreams and dissolve their problems. As a lawyer, you'll need to welcome the challenge of difficult cases, feel the excitement of helping others, and enjoy resolving seemingly irresolvable situations.

1.4.2   Dealing With Other Attorneys and Parties

Dealing effectively with other attorneys and parties is primarily a matter of how we treat them. We know we ought to be professional and civil. But how best to do so? Many judges, professors, and lawyers have written and spoken about "professional civility" in journal articles, at bar association lunches, and at CLE conferences. An underlying principle common to all these views is the golden rule: do unto others as you would have them do unto you. Lawyers who exhibit the right attitude and approach and treat others as they would expect to be treated are true professionals.

This approach helps eliminate or reduce the debate about whether we can or should be disrespectful, engage in personal attacks, dishonestly withhold information, but not entirely. Some lawyers believe it's okay to be mean and nasty toward certain attorneys and opposing parties. It may be done in retaliation or as a strategy.

One problem with uncivil behavior is recognizing it in ourselves. It is usually easy to perceive the conduct of others that is unprofessional, but it's not uncommon for us to excuse our own similar conduct as appropriate in the moment. Imagine yourself being video recorded dealing with them. Would you or others reviewing what you said or did believe it to be a professional and civil way to treat others? If so, do it. If not, become a mud wrestler. You can be effective and successful while being decent and true to yourself.

1.4.3   Seeking Help or Information From Others

In addition to relationships with clients and other attorneys and parties, lawyers frequently contact individuals for information or assistance. An attorney may contact someone for assistance or an expert for advice. How should a lawyer treat these individuals? Reasonably and respectfully, of course. These approaches are not only the right thing to do, they usually will get you what you want quickly and affordably. Some situations will require you to be persistent, firm, and even aggressive. But no situation justifies you being unprofessional and uncivil. This approach is not only a poor tactic but is also a slur on you and our profession.

Think Twice

So why doesn't this common sense approach to relationships work in legal practice? Why are there so many complaints about lawyers?

One reason is that we are all imperfect humans. Another reason is that representing clients can be very hard and strenuous work and it takes its toll on niceness and politeness. Practice can be hectic and exhausting and tired professionals do and say things they later regret. What's clear to one lawyer is a mystery to another, and what one considers good conduct another chafes at.

Still another reason is that the other side or opposing lawyer may dislike or disrespect what you say or do. In a dispute situation, the adversaries may truly be adversarial to a fault. Even in transactional work, one side may perceive the other as being greedy or disingenuous. These viewpoints may lead to inappropriate treatment. You'll need to remind yourself to continue to take the high road even in unpleasant journeys.

Of course, it's easy for us to preach about these relationships and how you ought to be a good natured person no matter what. At the same time, it's vital you understand the importance of being professional and civil. And you can begin now to critique yourself on whether you act that way with others. Who you are now is going to be, pretty much, who you are as a lawyer unless you decide and are willing to enhance your interpersonal skills and talents.

1.4.4   Dealing With Decision Makers

Much of lawyering involves lawyers in decision making processes. Clients make choices, opposing lawyers take positions, and decision makers decide cases. The person or persons who will decide your client's fate need to be treated in a way that will increase the chance of your client winning. You want to be perceived by the decision maker as being honest, well prepared, and right. You don't want to be perceived as acting inappropriately.

What is appropriate may be a matter of perception and disagreement. Lawyers may believe they need to be liked by the decision maker to be influential. The risk of wanting to be liked is that you may become too reverential toward the decision maker and consequently ineffective. The risk of not being liked is that you may be perceived as being unprofessional and ineffective.

The initial critical question to ask of your dealings with decision makers is this: How will this decision maker decide this case? Judges, juries, and arbitrators are expected to decide based upon the facts and law. But they will also be influenced by other factors that may determine whether your client wins or loses.

Beyond the law and facts, common factors that influence all people who have to make a choice, take a position, or decide are:

Values. Values reflect a person's beliefs, morals, norms, or goals. Values may be based on a sense of individual needs (me), the collective good (family, friends, society), or spirituality (an ultimate source). It is more likely that people will make a choice that reflects their values than agree to something that contradicts their values.

Needs and Interests. Everyone has some needs or interests that they will be inclined to promote or enhance when they say or do something. These personal and professional needs and interests may be as varied as individuals. Common needs are security, safety, comfort, love, self-esteem, and a sense of belonging.

Financial Considerations. Much of what a lawyer does affects personal and professional financial matters. It may involve the completion of a financial transaction or seeking or defending claims for money damages. Economics will sharply affect what clients decide to do, or not to do, and how wealth should be distributed may affect decision makers.

Feeling good. Psychological and emotional demands and expectations influence people's statements and actions. Healthy people prefer to say or do things that make them feel good. Feeling good may be based upon a spectrum of sources and their own interests, from getting what they want to altruism.

And so it's quite helpful to consider the following four questions in dealing with clients, parties, attorneys, and decision makers:

What values does this person consider important?

What are the needs and interests of this person?

What economic considerations affect this person?

What will make this person feel good?

You likely knew all this before you decided to become a lawyer. It bears repeating, however, because working in the midst of statutes, rules, and appellate court decisions, it is easy to lose sight of the fact that people make choices that are based on factors other than the law alone.

Think Twice

Barring rare instances of outright corruption, judges, arbitrators, jurors, and hearing examiners all want to do the right thing. When a decision maker resolves a case, however, that means that at least one party will think the decision maker got it really wrong. Our system operates on the notion that decision makers are impartial and fair and base decisions on the facts and law. But decision makers are not robots or computers. They have feelings, emotions, biases, and prejudices, and they need to take these into account when they make a decision. And so do advocates.

We have to predict what decision makers will decide and what will influence them. We have to craft a theory of the case that will cause them to shout: "Alright, alright, you win. Enough." That's our challenge.

1.4.5 Working Within the Legal Profession

Take a moment to consider why you chose the law as your career.

Whether it's clear or unclear why you selected the legal profession, you have. Your decision (along with passing the bar exam) will permit you to practice law. Your attitude towards practice will help make you an effective or ineffective lawyer.

The legal profession allows you to practice in various areas that match your interests and values. You can work with and for others or you can work for yourself. You can represent individuals who seek to recover for wrongs done to them. You can represent businesses that produce jobs. You can be a legal services lawyer, or devote a significant part of your private practice to pro bono work. You can represent the government and pursue public policies.

What you end up doing should be based on your preference and on the market. You should accept a job that matches your interests and values and provides you with the standard of living you want. You should select areas of the law that will satisfy you philosophically, economically, psychologically, and emotionally.

The responsibilities of being a lawyer create conflicts. What is best for your client may not be best for you. Resolving a dispute quickly may meet your client's needs but deny you an opportunity to gain experience or deprive you of a significant source of income. What is best for your client may not be best for the community. Your client may benefit tremendously from a deal, but the transaction may have some adverse effects on your community. What is best for the client and community may not be good for your family. The time it takes to help your client and others takes away precious time from the ones you love.

How much of your time are you willing to devote to your being a lawyer? What are you willing to do to maintain this role? Accept fewer clients? Work harder? Reduce your income? Take on that big case? What are your goals as a person? How do you want to live your life? You get to decide.

1.4.6   Working as a Practitioner

Working as a practitioner involves an understanding of types of lawyers, their various roles, and client expectations. There are two broad categories of attorney types: lawyers who represent clients and all other lawyers doing whatever they do. The focus of this book is the representation of clients. These clients include individuals, corporations, organizations, government agencies, fee-paying clients, indigent clients, and others. This book focuses on practicing law as a private practitioner or as a business or public lawyer and explains professional skills covering this type of lawyering work. These skills also parallel much of the work law graduates do who do not practice law.

What is it that these other lawyers do? They can be:

Business executives. There are many business people with law degrees who are not involved in traditional law practice. They may do many things lawyers do, but they do not hold themselves out nor consider themselves to be acting as lawyers. For example, a corporate executive who holds a law degree but who does not work for the legal department of the corporation may act as both a lawyer and an executive for the company.

Lobbyists. Lawyers may be retained by clients (individuals, associations, businesses) to work on legislative matters. Many lobbyists are lawyers, although many are not.

Public employees. Government work finds many lawyers working as legislators, administrators, staff members, politicians, regulators, and in myriad other positions. For more information, move to Washington or your local seat of government, depending upon your preference.

Public service workers. Lawyers may work in a variety of positions for non-profit organizations. Their work may involve some of the skills discussed in this book as well as work similar to what occurs in the business and governmental world. Many practitioners contribute substantial amounts of time to these organizations on a pro bono basis.

Think Twice

You may already have a notion or perhaps even a clear idea about what you want to do after law school. About two-thirds of law graduates practice law, but the remainder use their law degree for other purposes. We understand that and we also understand that the market for legal services on graduation day may determine or influence what you decide to do. The thrust of this book is to prepare you for whatever work you do using lawyering skills.

1.4.7 Working With Colleagues

Colleagues include all employees, partners, associates, attorneys, paralegals, secretaries, law clerks, and other co-workers. Working effectively with all of them is usually a reflection of how well you treat them. All these individuals deserve to be treated the way you would want to be treated—with respect, understanding, and caring. You may decide to treat them this way because it is pragmatic and you realize without them you cannot be an effective practitioner. Or you may decide to treat them this way because it is the right thing to do. Whatever your reason, your success depends upon their success.

Your effectiveness as a professional also depends upon how good a businessperson you are. You need to understand how to succeed in business and you also need to know how to manage your law practice efficiently and economically. Many of you will actively manage your law firm, including small, large, and government firms. Knowing how to work with your colleagues and administer your firm will be essential to your being an effective lawyer.

1.4.8 Working With Yourself

You spend a lot of time with yourself now. You will spend a lot of time with yourself as a practitioner. You'll be most effective if you like yourself, your life, your work, and your profession. How to like yourself and others is well beyond the scope of this book. You need to assess that on your own and with others you know.

How to like your work and your profession is both within and without the scope of this book. We can describe how the practice of law can be enjoyable, rewarding, and fulfilling. We can tell you that this reflects our experience with practice. We can also suggest that we believe lawyers who like their work and profession are more effective lawyers and happier people. We cannot tell you how you can best enjoy your work and profession. But you can and will need to do that.

The law can be a wonderful profession. As we describe throughout this book, the law is a helping profession in which you can do great good. You can achieve success, a sense of purpose, and financial security. But at times, the practice of law can also be unsatisfying, boring, mundane, frustrating, and difficult.

You had a life before law school and you bring it with you to your life as a lawyer. You came to law school with experience about the skills discussed in this book. Some of you have a lot of experience. All of you in your life have asked questions, obtained information from others, provided advice, negotiated, and tried to convince a variety of decision makers they should give you what you want. Some of you have experienced these skills in other areas, such as employment, business, volunteer work, and just being around.

As you read our analysis of lawyering, you need to analyze yourself to understand your own level of experience and how you already understand and do some of the things lawyers do. How you do them now will affect how you will do them in the future for your clients. After analyzing yourself, you want to continue to use those skills that are effective and discontinue those that are ineffective. As you develop as a lawyer, you want to continually analyze what you do, how you do it, why you do it, and how you can improve.

Think Twice

As we interview senior lawyers and work with them, we frequently ask them why they continue to enjoy and even relish being a lawyer. Almost uniformly, they tell us that they both are proud and humbled to be a lawyer. They understand what an honor and privilege it is to help clients. They appreciate how fortunate they are to have selected the profession. They love the law. And it's that recognition, attitude, and belief that can sustain you through law school and beyond.

1.5   THE BALANCED LIFE

You have a life inside law school. What you learn in other courses during law school will help you be a better lawyer. But some of what you learn in law school may hinder your development as a practicing lawyer. Law school encourages and rewards students to reach decisions quickly, conform the facts and law to their positions, use legal jargon, and state opinions without hesitation. These approaches can be useful in practice, or can interfere with being an effective lawyer. Novice lawyers need to adapt approaches they developed in law school to the requirements of the real world.

You also have a life outside of law school. You need to nurture and develop a balanced life that will continue during after you matriculate. A lawyer's personality and temperament are often as important as knowledge and intellectual ability. Lawyers (and law students) are more effective if they balance their practice (and their studies) with a reasonably healthy dose of other adventures of life. These experiences will make you a more relaxed and effective attorney. You'll also be better able to understand the forces that drive client's interests and needs, better able to appreciate the pressures felt and reacted to by opposing counsel, and better able to handle losses and celebrate wins.

You need to lead a life balanced with family, friends, hobbies, leisure time, and vacations. This balance is critical to your being a well rounded lawyer. Admit it, wouldn't you rather be painting an oil canvas, shooting hoops, singing in harmony, working out, reading best sellers, visiting the Inns of Court in London, touring the Black Hills, taking a nap, tending your garden, motorcycling the Alps, or _____ (fill it in). Do it now, and do it while you are a lawyer.

There will also be a life for you after law school. There is hope. This life can be a rich life, with many opportunities to help others and to help yourself. Lawyers help people in ways no other professionals can. Clients may seldom host a celebratory thank you party after you represent them, but you will be blessed with gifts of internal satisfaction and accomplishment.

Not everyone will think you are great. Our legal profession is not viewed as the most cherished profession by many in our society and the world. The perception of many is that lawyers are nit-picking deal killers, or combative gladiators, or greedy money-grabbers, or all three. You will need to understand this perception, and you will need to be as good a lawyer as you can be to reduce this perception. For every person who thinks there are too many lawyers doing useless work, there is a client wanting to retain *you* to help them.

Think Twice

It's easy for us to tell you to take time for yourself, but is that really possible? During law school? We strongly suggest you do and we also understand how difficult it can be. We remember. But we know that successful lawyers take time for themselves, and we know that habit began in law school.

1.6   ENOUGH, ALREADY

As you read this chapter, you may well be thinking: "I know this already." As you read some of the subsequent sections, you may have the same reactions. For example, we'll suggest that during the client interview you should listen to your client. And it would be appropriate for you to wonder why you had to buy this book to read that. And, we'll encourage you to "prepare diligently" before negotiating. And you may conclude that you could have written that bromide.

The practice of law is based on the obvious and on common sense—but it also based on a whole new set of skills, techniques, tactics, and strategies. Interviewing a client has much in common with interviewing other types of individuals, and you have already done some or much of that. Negotiating for a client can resemble the negotiation approaches you already know and perform. But there are significant differences that you need to learn about client interviews and legal negotiations, and other events, which this book explains in detail.

During a client interview there are a variety of legal skills you must exercise—some of them simultaneously. During a negotiation with another lawyer, you will be engaged in numerous strategic and tactical decisions while pursuing the best interests of your client. You need to carefully study and thoroughly understand these and other skills so you can perform them effectively.

Some of these lawyering skills will be intuitive, others obvious, and many others new and challenging. The basic difference is that you will be thinking and acting like an ethical professional helping someone else to get something they want or need, and that is not something you have experienced before. Your own common sense is a result of your lifetime of experiences and your approach to dealing with other people. In your development as a professional, part of your task is to learn what portion of your own common sense will best serve you and your clients in your role as a lawyer.

Our challenge as authors is to explain alternative legal strategies, tactics, and skills in an understandable and useful format. We break down complex lawyering skills into simple steps. We take complicated professional strategies and present them as common sense tactics and techniques, which we hope, make them more useful and memorable.

This book distills in a compact format the basic information you need to know about essential lawyering skills. Based on what you already know, what is reinforced in this text, and a lot of what will be new, you should be able to build and develop your own lawyering skills.

Think Twice

We understand that while you read sections of this book you may think we restate what everyone knows or ought to know. So why should you spend your valuable time digesting this book? After all, we just suggested you preserve some time for yourself.

As we have already written and will emphasize in later sections, we acknowledge that life experiences have already taught you some of what you'll be reading. Here's a big difference: now you are on your way to becoming a lawyer and you need to see things through the perspective of a lawyer.

Some of these things will be the same, many others will be different and new. You'll have to apply what you know and what you learn to your developing professional life. What you know, or think you know, needs to be placed in perspective. You have to adapt to your role as a lawyer helping people.

You are becoming a professional who has to acquire and implement a considerable array of lawyering *skills. Right now, you don't have all or many of those skills. And even if you did or think you do, you can always enhance your talents and abilities and get better.*

C. REPRESENTING CLIENTS

1.7 THE HALLMARK OF LAWYERING

Representation of clients is the hallmark of lawyering. A lawyer in private practice may serve many; a government lawyer or in-house counsel may serve only one. The lawyer's primary duty, regardless of the number of clients, is responsible and effective representation.

The link between the lawyer and the client can be simple or complex, distant or close. A lawyer working on behalf of a client may become involved in much more than legal representation.

Working on transactions or resolving disputes may have as much to do with personal issues, economic interests, psychological matters, family conflicts, business difficulties, or moral dilemmas as with legal issues. Through it all, the client's needs and interests remain the primary goal.

Every person, business, and government agency needs legal advice at some point. These different clients have vastly different kinds of legal needs and vastly different levels of experience dealing with the legal system. There are, however, two common rules relating to clients: first, the client isn't necessarily that person sitting on the other side of the desk; second, no two clients are alike.

With regard to the first point, lawyers have as clients individuals, corporations, partnerships, associations, and a host of other legal entities. The lawyer owes a professional allegiance to the corporation or agency, and not the individual representing the entity. A corollary to this rule is that the client isn't necessarily the person paying the bill. For example, insurance companies frequently hire and pay lawyers to represent policyholders. The insurance company may sign the check, the lawyer may report regularly to the claims supervisor, but the policyholder is usually still the lawyer's client and entitled to have the lawyer place the client's interests above those of the insurance company.

Second, no two clients are alike. It is easy to make assumptions about clients based on jobs, income, or status, but these assumptions are often inaccurate. The corporate executive who has virtually no experience in litigation may need a lengthy explanation of an upcoming deposition instead of only a cursory description. The government benefits recipient who understands administrative procedures does not need a detailed and condescending explanation of the law. Categorizing clients is difficult as well as dangerous. What each client needs should be based upon their individual identity, experience, knowledge, and background.

For the most part, the relationship between lawyer and client is not defined by rules or laws. There are, however, three important areas of regulation: the attorney-client privilege, professional responsibility rules, and legal malpractice.

1.7.1   The Attorney–Client Privilege

The attorney-client privilege provides communications between a lawyer and a client with a unique sort of protection. While the law differs somewhat among jurisdictions, in general the attorney-client privilege protects communications:

- Between a lawyer and that lawyer's client

- Meant to be kept confidential

- Concerning the work the lawyer does for the client.

The attorney-client privilege can be powerful because it prevents the attorney or the client from being compelled to testify about protected communications. It can also be fragile because its protections can be easily lost. If confidential client communications are disclosed to a party outside the attorney-client relationship, then the privilege may be waived to the extent of the subject matter of the disclosure. For example, a client may tell friends or co-workers about what the lawyer said. Or, a lawyer could destroy the privilege through the accidental disclosure of client communications, such as the inadvertent production of a privileged email during discovery. It is the lawyer's responsibility to safeguard the privilege, and because it is a privilege that can be lost, it is a responsibility that must be exercised vigilantly.

1.7.2   Professional Responsibility Rules

In all jurisdictions, rules or codes of professional responsibility govern lawyers' ethical behavior and conduct. Many states have adopted some form of the "Rules of Professional Conduct." The professional rules are a mix of aspirations, common sense, and taboos. They guide us to be good lawyers; they remind us about what we already know; and they tell us what we cannot do. You will or have learned more about these rules in another course entitled Professional Responsibility. These rules require a lawyer to be competent, diligent, and communicative while representing clients, and also forbid a lawyer from divulging client confidences and from representing clients with conflicting interests. Section 1.13 highlights these provisions.

1.7.3   The Law of Malpractice

Each jurisdiction has its own law about what constitutes attorney malpractice. Knowledge of this law is important, and lawyers need to be aware of the relevant case law defining legal malpractice in their jurisdiction. But reading these cases to learn how to practice law is a little like watching car wrecks to learn how to drive. You really don't need to be told *not* to drive drunk or recklessly. Likewise, you don't need to be told *not* to lie, cheat, or steal.

Think Twice

The practice of law is really self-regulating. There aren't that many rules or standards considering the vast amount of work lawyers do. And it's usually a group of peers or judges who review our work. So the real impetus for being a good lawyer comes from within us. If you recall you are proud and humbled to be a lawyer, you'll be a good one. If you stray from norms established by the community you are a part of, you'll run into trouble. Malpractice starts with you. Stop it by not starting it. Be good, be well, and you'll be successful.

1.8   THE ROLE(S) OF A PRACTICING LAWYER

The literature of the law is filled with attempts to define our profession and to explain just what it is that makes us different or special. Some of this writing is self-absorbed and jargon-laden, but much is the product of honest attempts to survey the occupational, ethical, and moral boundaries of the practice of law. The writings on these issues are sufficiently complex and voluminous to defy either easy summary or even easy characterization. The subject is important, though, because the literature is really just the theoretical tip of a practical iceberg of different views of what it means to be a lawyer—views that are played out and applied every day by hundreds of thousands of practicing lawyers representing clients.

Boiled down to its essence, most of the discussion of what it means to be a practicing lawyer consists of two questions:

What amount of responsibility do we have **for** our clients?

What amount of responsibility do we have **to** our clients?

The answers to these questions are scattered across a wide spectrum of views of what it means to be a lawyer.

1.8.1   The Lawyer as Technician

Near one end of the spectrum is the vision of the lawyer as technician. Some lawyers see themselves as professionals who do little more than find the law for clients and then help clients reach immediate goals as efficiently as possible. These lawyers conceive of the profession as a craft, and believe that the good lawyer is the lawyer who effectively plies this craft.

These lawyers see their responsibility **to** a client as a limited one: once the lawyer has finished with the promised legal work, the responsibility to the client ends. In the same way, these lawyers also view themselves as having limited responsibility **for** a client: the lawyer is only responsible for completing legal tasks competently, the client (and perhaps the justice system) are responsible for the results. Under this view, the lawyer is accountable for the means and the client is accountable for the ends.

This view of the profession is sometimes condemned as a "hired gun" perspective, but this is somewhat unfair. Much of any lawyer's work does involve the capable performance of particular legal tasks, and some lawyers find that competence is the surest touchstone of professional satisfaction. Many lawyers, however, rebel at the notion that their responsibility to and for clients is limited to the competent performance of legal tasks.

1.8.2   The Lawyer as Wise Counselor

Near the other end of the spectrum is the view that the lawyer serves the client best when the lawyer takes on the role of wise and trusted counselor. Lawyers who see themselves in this role believe that they have a responsibility to clients that extends far beyond competent performance of particular legal tasks. In a sense, these lawyers view themselves as "legal healers" charged with the duty of treating all their clients holistically.

Not surprisingly, these lawyers also see themselves as having a much greater responsibility **for** and **to** their clients. Wise counselors are, in some sense, responsible for both the ends and means of their clients. Lawyers acting as wise counselors should be accountable for what they help clients do and should not, it is contended, be permitted to excuse themselves or their clients with the explanation that they were simply doing what the law allowed.

Critics complain that this view of lawyering is too hard on lawyers and too hard on clients. It is too hard on lawyers because no practicing lawyer ought to be expected to solve all of a client's problems, nor should any practicing lawyer be held morally accountable for what a client chooses to do. It makes little sense, for example, to say that a lawyer who properly advises a client regarding environmental laws is somehow personally responsible for later environmental damage intentionally committed by the client.

Critics also charge that this view of the profession is too hard on clients. Clients should be permitted to make their own decisions and should be expected to bear the legal, social, and moral consequences of those decisions. Anything less suggests that clients are somehow less human than lawyers. A wise counselor is, these critics charge, little more than an unwelcome meddler for many clients—a meddler trying to foist an unwanted moral agenda on an unsuspecting client.

Even in the face of these complaints, the vision of the lawyer as wise counselor still has much to recommend it. It is important, for example, to see clients as something more than customers at a "legal pharmacy," with prescriptions in hand ready to be filled. Lawyers should be attuned to clients' immediate goals, but should also be aware of the clients' long-term goals (overarching goals) and the clients' preferences about how to do things (process preferences). It is also important for a lawyer to feel a responsibility to society that is independent of the lawyer's responsibility to a client. There is something unpersuasive and morally chilling about a lawyer who says: "I helped my client do something evil but that's not a problem for me because it's not my fault that my client is evil.''

1.8.3   The Lawyer as Creator or Problem Solver

Somewhere in the middle of the spectrum is the view of the lawyer as a creator or problem solver. According to this view, the lawyer is responsible for more than the competent performance of particular legal tasks. The lawyer is responsible for learning about concerns and problems that motivate the client to seek legal advice, and is then responsible for offering the client potential solutions.

This view suggests that lawyers also bear a greater responsibility **for** clients. Lawyers should advise clients of the legal—and perhaps ethical—risks of seeking unjust ends. In extreme cases, if the lawyer feels strongly that the client is seeking something that is truly unjust, then the lawyer should refuse to represent the client. Of course, lawyers should also recognize that they are asked to solve client problems within the context of a legal system that is basically good, though sometimes flawed. For proponents, the view of lawyer as a creator and problem solver makes our legal system primarily accountable for the unjust ends that lawyers sometimes achieve.

Like any moderate position, there is much appeal to the vision of lawyers as creators or problem solvers. Like any moderate position, however, this view also suffers from some significant "So What?/Now What?" problems. For instance, if this view says nothing more than lawyers should make sure that the legal tasks they undertake might actually help the client now or solve the client's immediate problem, then "So What?" That is not a particularly deep or helpful insight. On the other hand, perhaps the view means to go further and advise a lawyer to make sure that the legal tasks will serve the client's interests but also prevent problems from recurring. If that is the case, then where are we to draw the line between this moderate view and the view of lawyers as wise counselors—in short, "Now What?"

We offer no neat theoretical solutions to these quandaries. Our point is not to advocate a single vision of the lawyer's role in society. Indeed, most lawyers find that there are times that they are called upon to act as wise counselors, as well as times they are called upon to act as technicians. Rather than proclaiming one of these views as correct, we invite you to use all three of these visions of lawyering as tools to help understand some of the problems involved in day-to-day practice.

1.9　CLIENT VIEWS OF OUR ROLES

Though clients do not usually write about their own views of the lawyers' roles (at least not at the length lawyers, judges, and professors do), clients certainly do have expectations about what it is their lawyers should do. These views and expectations can, of course, vary enormously. Some clients come to lawyers looking for wise counselors; some come looking for legal technicians. Some clients come to lawyers looking for little more than competent performance of a specific legal task. For example, a defendant in a fraud case may want nothing more from a lawyer than victory; a corporate client may only want a lawyer to negotiate and draft documents implementing a particular transaction. On the other hand, the defendant may want the lawyer to help restore his reputation in the community; and the corporate client may need the lawyer to offer guidance about alternative means of accomplishing the strategic goals of the transaction.

Do the clients' choices about what they want or need from a lawyer make a difference? Certainly, a client may have very definite expectations about what the lawyer is paid to do, and these expectations will shape the business agreement between the lawyer and the client. Well then, does a lawyer's choice about the proper role make any difference? Absolutely, but lawyers need to be aware that their own expectations about their role may, at times, be dramatically out of sync with their clients' expectations. If expectations do differ, these differences need to be sorted out near the beginning of the relationship with the client. A client who wants a legal technician may have a great deal of difficulty working with a lawyer who means to serve as a wise counselor. A client who is looking for a wise counselor may feel ill-served by a lawyer who intends to be only a legal technician.

Lawyers who feel that clients routinely have different role expectations are receiving an important signal that they may be working in the wrong law job. The legal technician who is frequently called upon to serve as a wise counselor will feel incompetent and risks not only client dissatisfaction but also malpractice. The wise counselor who is asked to be a technician will chafe at this constraint, risking both professional and moral dissatisfaction. Both lawyers should think seriously about working with different type clients.

Think Twice

This section helps explain why clients complain about their lawyers. The most common complaint boils down to this: lack of communication. It may be that the lawyer fails to keep the client updated and informed by emails, text messages, phone calls, or letters. There is little excuse for that. More likely, it's because the client and lawyer had and have different expectations and never talked about those differences. They each had a differing vision and role for the lawyer and never got around to discussing it all. It's largely the role of the lawyer to engage the client in those discussions to avoid those communication complaints.

1.10   THE EXTENT OF CLIENT RELATIONSHIPS

My client is a young woman who doesn't have much money and has come to me to prevent her from being evicted. I can defend the eviction. Should I also advise her to look for a less expensive apartment or to look for a better job? Should I lend the client some money to buy groceries? Should I offer to take her apartment-hunting?

My client is a corporation that makes popcorn. The client has come to me and asked for trademark advice about a package design. There is no trademark problem with the design, but should I tell my client that the design is similar to packaging for an old brand of cat food? Should I advise the client to diversify their product line? Should I tell the client that I think their popcorn tastes bad?

At some point in practice, every lawyer—even those who see themselves as wise counselors—faces the question of where to draw the line between legal advice and unwanted meddling.

Clients come to lawyers with a wide variety of problems, and those problems have dimensions that raise issues well beyond the substance of our professional training. The line is not always easy to draw, but there are times when it must be drawn.

When it is time to draw the line, it is helpful to remember that there is a difference between a lawyer and a friend. Our friends usually have more freedom than our clients. We can decide to risk the friendship and say to a friend, "You need to change your life," or even, "What a stupid decision!" If they don't like us, our friends can choose new companions. Our clients do not always have this choice.

Clients come to the lawyer having made business or life choices that may seem to have been unwise or worse. As lawyers, we need to be reasonably accepting and non-judgmental about those past choices. We also need to remember that even clients seeking wise counselors come to a lawyer's office looking for **legal** advice.

D.   THINKING LIKE A PRACTICING LAWYER

1.11   SOURCES OF LAWS

Working within our legal system requires an understanding of the law itself, the sources of law, and factors that influence the development of law. Our society has developed and relies on the law for a variety of purposes. Our law regulates relationships and transactions, adjudicates disputes, articulates public values and behavioral norms, acts as a mechanism for organizing society, and establishes the parameters of rights or responsibilities for society. Our law is both autonomous and derivative, as are its sources.

The obvious sources are the common law, statutes, regulations, rules, constitutional provisions, and customs. Another primary source is you. Your clients come to you for legal advice and results. What you tell them and what you do for them will be the law that determines what they do and do not do. Your knowledge, understanding, and interpretation of the law form the basis of your legal advice.

More law is developed in the law offices of attorneys than in all the cases, statutes, and other legal sources you study during law school. Whether they are right or wrong, lawyers giving advice shape and influence the law for their clients. This law is as significant to these clients as the issuance of judicial opinions and the enactment of statutes. If you are going to be a primary source of law, you want to be as right as you can be.

The law today is a broad and demanding enterprise. Law has assumed, for better or worse, a much greater role in our society today than it has in prior generations or in other societies. Modern law is a multi-disciplinary enterprise, requiring lawyers to have a broad-based understanding of the many facets of law and other areas of learning. There are many factors that touch and influence the status and development of the law.

Economics. Macroeconomics examines how law distributes wealth and affects income; microeconomics studies how individual clients affect and are influenced by the law. The economics of practice also shape the law. Attorneys, as good business people, may only do or promote certain things they are compensated to do. Issues may be pursued and disputes resolved because economic forces encourage or allow resolution. Other important matters may be left untouched because of the lack of economic resources.

Sociological trends. Our society tends to view the law as a panacea for many issues and problems. Our citizens rely on lawyers for all sorts of assistance, while other cultures and societies look to other professions for this help. The number of lawyers in our society, and their individual and collective power, reflect society's reliance on your profession-to-be.

Psychological influences. We are, it seems, for better or worse, a society of individuals with varying psychological perspectives. We may not want to hold ourselves individually accountable, but want to insist that others are accountable to us. We may not want to take responsibility for events that happened to us, and prefer to blame others for problems that touch our lives. We may want to solve our own problems, while increasingly relying on attorneys and other professionals to help us. We may complain there are too many lawyers while retaining these lawyers to represent us in increasing numbers. We may complain about our civil justice system while continuing to pursue new and innovative legal theories and remedies. For whatever reasons our society reflects these influences, we lawyers provide these services.

Political trends. Partisan politics affects the kinds and numbers of laws enacted and the judicial philosophy which predominates on our federal and state benches. Less partisan political trends such as attitudes toward the government, views about government intervention, ethical norms, feelings about individual freedom, and confidence in private economic markets also significantly affect the law. Political attitudes have in the past spawned growth industries in the law, such as the growth of administrative agencies and regulation, the passage of consumer protection statutes, or the creation of transactions designed to use a provision of the tax code to shelter income.

Public policy. Whatever it is, however it is defined, whoever conceives it, public policy shapes the law. The grounding of this public policy reflects views of the American government. Should the federal government retain or expand its power and control, or share more of it? Should state and local government reclaim areas ceded to the federal government over the past few decades? Should there be greater or lesser legislative, administrative, and judicial interference with our public and private lives? Your view, your clients' views, and societal views of these public policy issues affect the law.

Jurisprudential thinking. The legal academy contains a chorus of different multi-disciplinary and theoretical voices. Legal realism, the law and society movement, critical legal studies, feminist jurisprudence, critical race theory, and other schools of thought affect the development of law in courtrooms and offices. Although much of this debate may seem irrelevant to whether a Minnesota county court should grant a defense motion for summary judgment, much is not. The trend of jurisprudential thinking about the nature of law and adjudication can be harnessed by attorneys to better advise a client and advocate a client's case. Positions taken by a client or arguments advanced by an advocate can be clothed by some positive law such as precedent or legislation and can also be made persuasive when the defined issues include fairness, efficiency, due process or the enhancement of other widely accepted values.

Outstanding lawyers are both generalists and specialists. Your goal should be to become a well-rounded student of the law, both because of the theoretical reasons described in this section and because well-rounded persons are usually more effective attorneys. They better understand the role of the multi-disciplinary factors, they possess a better sense of appropriate and inappropriate behavior, and they are able to be more creative and adaptable.

Knowing everything can be quite exhausting. Keeping current can be very tiring. You need to rely upon others to help you understand the major influences on the law. Experts, colleagues, authors, friends, family, scholars, directors, artists, and poets can tell us much about the law. It should now be apparent to you that you can learn a lot about the law from sources outside of law school. But you should still hang around.

We suggest as part of the course requirements for this course and other law school classes that you learn as much as you can about the various factors that comprise the multi-disciplinary facets of the law. Books, newspapers, blogs, magazines, television, movies, theater, software, DVDs, CDs, and the Internet provide sources of the law and life that will make you a better lawyer.

Think Twice

It does help to be a renaissance professional, even if you end up specializing as a lawyer. The danger of focusing your attention primarily on the law is that you may limit your ability to be creative and broad minded. Helping clients craft deals often requires a good grasp of business. Trying to resolve disputes may require an understanding of cultural differences. Developing these insights requires an exploration of areas beyond the law.

1.12 THE ROLE OF THE THINKING LAWYER

What does it mean to think like a lawyer? Lawyers think similarly and differently than other professionals. Law school initially, and some may say primarily, teaches you legal reasoning and critical analysis, along with how to read footnotes with understanding, and how to write clearly or ambiguously. This book broadens this scope of thinking to include the professional skills appearing in the table of contents.

When professors tell you to "think like a lawyer," they are usually advising you to be analytical, to reason with "rigor." Critical analysis is an important skill for a lawyer, but you will need more than analytical thinking to succeed in practice. You will also need to think *creatively* and *productively*.

1.12.1   Thinking Creatively

Telling someone "Be creative!" is a lot like telling someone "Be smart!" or "Be really persuasive!" No one can disagree with the advice because, after all, no one would tell a lawyer: "Be really dull and unimaginative." The advice isn't very helpful, however, because it simply points to a destination when what is really needed is a pathway to that destination. It's not easy to explain how to be creative, but there are some steps that will help develop creative thinking:

- Move beyond the first thought
- Move beyond the traditional
- Move beyond "lawyer" approaches

Move Beyond the First Thought. When a client brings a legal problem or concern to a lawyer and asks for advice, one approach to dealing with the problem will usually occur to the lawyer fairly quickly. This "first thought" approach may be obvious or it may be subtle. It may be the standard approach; it may be the approach the lawyer has used before; it may be the least costly approach; it may be the easiest approach. Whatever its merits, this "first thought" approach has one significant drawback. This first thought may stifle any second thought or third thought. Rather than attempting to think of alternatives, the lawyer may focus efforts on perfecting and implementing the first thought.

Novice lawyers in particular need to resist this impulse. The first thought may possibly be the best, but there is no way of knowing that unless the lawyer has second and third thoughts as well. One of the best ways to move beyond the first thought approach is to imagine that it is not an alternative for this client: "If this approach weren't available, what would the alternatives be?" Finding the answer to that question—through research, investigation, or cogitation—is the first step to thinking creatively. The assumption that the first thought approach isn't available is important, because it forces the lawyer to **think seriously** about other alternatives. Without the assumption, it is too easy to dismiss alternative approaches as inferior to the first thought.

Move Beyond the Traditional. The second step toward creative thinking is moving beyond traditional legal approaches to a problem. Moving beyond the traditional means thinking imaginatively about the range of legal remedies available to the client, and considering new or different ways of solving familiar problems. Is there a new statute or new case that creates an alternative remedy? Is there a different way of structuring the transaction? Different and new certainly do not mean better—in fact, approaches to problems often become the "traditional" way of doing things because they work well. But a willingness to at least **consider** the different or new is another step toward creative thinking.

Move Beyond "Lawyer" Approaches. An important part of creative thinking is **not** thinking like a lawyer. Solutions involving the justice system, lawyers, litigation, and deal making are all well and good—but they tend to be expensive and time-consuming. Not all client concerns and problems will bear this time and expense. Sometimes solutions involving quick telephone calls, responsive emails and text messages, client-conducted negotiations or other lawful forms of self-help better meet clients' overarching and immediate goals. The lawyer who fails to consider these solutions is failing the client and failing to think creatively.

1.12.2   Thinking Productively

The realities of practice make productive thinking as important as creative thinking. Imaginative lawyers also need to be practical lawyers. The options and choices lawyers present to clients need to be workable, plausible solutions. Lawyers are well-attuned to the practical limitations they deal with on a daily basis, and lawyers tend to take these limitations into account when presenting options to clients. Most lawyers would recognize, for example, that time spent crafting a legally implausible option for a client is time spent unproductively.

Productive thinking requires more than attention to the limitations of the law and legal process. It also requires lawyers to be attuned to the practical limitations their clients face. Too often, lawyers (and law professors) create options that work in the law office or courtroom, but not in the "real world." The best remedy for this problem is a thorough understanding of a client's immediate and long term goals and of a client's process preferences. For example, a lawyer who loses sight of these goals may suggest a "scorched earth" litigation strategy to resolve a dispute with one of the client's long-time customers. Taking the time to understand the client's goals will help prevent this. Taking the time to match legal strategies with client goals will insure that thinking is productive, as well as creative.

E. PRACTICING LIKE AN ETHICAL LAWYER

1.13 ETHICAL RULES

Every jurisdiction has adopted rules of professional conduct that regulate and guide lawyer conduct. Individual lawyers have also developed their own set of ethical guidelines and rules. This section highlights some of rules reflected in the Model Rules of Professional Conduct applicable to lawyering relationships.

1.13.1 Competent Representation

Model Rule 1.1 requires a lawyer rightfully to provide competent representation to a client, which is defined as "... the legal knowledge, skill, thoroughness, and preparation reasonably necessary for the representation." In other words, you need to know what you are thinking and doing. And you will know by your level of experience or knowledge, the degree of your appropriate confidence, and the feeling in the pit of your stomach that you do know what to say or do.

1.13.2 Obligation of Diligence

Model Rule 1.3 requires lawyers to act with "reasonable diligence and promptness." This requires a lawyer to act on behalf of a client: (1) with dedication and commitment and without regard to personal inconvenience, (2) with prompt responses and without procrastination, and (3) by completing the representation and not refusing or failing to complete the work undertaken. Lawyers need to stay committed to their clients and take the time to do what is necessary to represent them. This can be difficult for lawyers who have busy professional and personal lives but it is an ongoing duty.

1.13.3　Effective Communication

Model Rule 1.4(a) requires a lawyer to keep a client "reasonably informed" and promptly reply to "reasonable requests for information." As with any relationship, its success often depends upon the quality and frequency of communications. A major complaint clients have with lawyers, and a frequent basis for pursuing a complaint with the state board of professional responsibility, is the failure of the lawyer to regularly inform the client of what is happening. Periodic, confidential emails, telephone calls, or letters to a client are essential to fulfill this responsibility.

1.13.4　Scope of Representation

Clients determine what it is they want or need from an attorney. Model Rule 1.2 provides that the client decides the objectives of the representation, that the lawyer is to consult with the client regarding the means to be pursued to achieve the objectives, and that the lawyer is not to assist a client with criminal or fraudulent conduct. This rule has clients determine their goals, interests, and needs and has lawyers implement the strategies, tactics, and techniques to achieve those objectives, in consultation with the client. The client and lawyer may reasonably agree to limit or expand the objectives of a relationship.

The distinction between objectives and strategies in specific cases may not always be obvious. A general distinction is the ends/means division, with the client establishing the ends and the lawyer carrying out the means. Another difference is the substance/procedural distinction, with clients deciding their substantive rights and interests and the lawyer determining procedural matters. These guidelines help, but cannot resolve all dilemmas. A lawyer can resolve differences and prevent misunderstanding by consulting with the client and determining the applicable boundaries.

1.13.5 Preserving Confidentiality

Confidentiality is a touchstone of the lawyer/client relationship. Lawyers must maintain the confidences of their client because it is essential to the establishment of trust and because it is mandated by the attorney/client privilege, evidence law, work product doctrines, and rules of professional conduct. Model Rule 1.6 provides that a "lawyer shall not reveal information relating to representation of a client." This broad prescription covers virtually everything a client tells a lawyer.

Obviously, a lawyer in representing a client has to reveal some information. And so the rule allows a lawyer to reveal information impliedly authorized in order to carry out the representation or agreed to by the client after consultation. And the rule recognizes that there are extraordinary situations that may require disclosure: if a lawyer believes a client is likely to commit a criminal act that is "likely to result in imminent death or substantial bodily harm."

Otherwise, this duty of confidentiality is all encompassing and vital to the creation, development, and maintenance of the attorney/client relationship.

1.13.6 Professional Judgment

Clients retain lawyers because of their professional judgment. Model Rule 2.1 requires a lawyer to "exercise independent professional judgment and render candid advice." Whether a lawyer acts as a legal technician, a wise counselor, or in another role, the client is entitled to honest, straightforward, and understandable information from the lawyer. Some clients and lawyers regularly see each other while others may develop social and friendship relationships. A lawyer is to represent a client with emotional detachment. This does not mean that a lawyer is to be unmoved by the human dimensions of a case, but this does require a lawyer to remain balanced. Clients may rightfully be in pain or very angry or exhibit emotional reactions. Lawyers need to empathize with the client but not base professional judgments on overly emotional influences.

1.13.7   Conflicts of Interest

Lawyers owe clients loyalty. A conflict of interest would interfere with this duty. Model Rule 1.7 generally prohibits a lawyer from representing one client if that representation would directly and adversely affect the representation of another client. A lawyer is prohibited from representing a new client whose interests are directly adverse to a current client.

Lawyers who represent adverse interests would be unable to remain loyal to clients and to vigorously represent conflicting positions. Clients, after consultation, can permit lawyers to represent them even if there may be adverse interests. Clients can knowingly agree to allow their lawyer to represent adverse interests and waive the protections afforded them under the rules.

These rules prohibit a lawyer from representing the plaintiff and defendant in the same personal injury case, as would common sense. Similarly, lawyers are usually prohibited from representing buyers and sellers in the same transaction. Model Rule 1.7 prohibits a lawyer from representing a client when that representation would be materially limited by the representation of another client.

The rules do generally permit a lawyer to represent unrelated clients who have broad adverse interests. "Directly adverse" does not include generally adverse or competing economic interests among clients. This means that a litigator can maintain a practice and represent both plaintiffs and defendants in tort cases; and a lawyer can represent different parties in the same types of transactions (real estate, for example). This also means that a lawyer who advocates a specific legal position in a jurisdiction on behalf of one client cannot represent a client with an adverse interest in that same jurisdiction. Conflict cases, as you can imagine, have created their own conflicts about what is permissible.

Conflict rules apply to both the individual lawyer and the law firm of that lawyer. Law firms may create "walls" to separate conflict proceedings, if the clients agree. Additional conflict rules establish restrictions arising when former government lawyers seek to practice privately and occurring in judicial and arbitration representation.

1.13.8 Declining Representation

A client can decide to retain a lawyer; and a lawyer can decide to accept or reject a client. Model Rule 1.16 specifies situations where a lawyer *shall* decline to represent a client or *must* withdraw from representation:

- If the representation results in a violation of rules of professional conduct or the law.

- The lawyer's physical or mental condition materially impairs the representation.

Model Rule 1.16 also details situations where a lawyer *may* decline to represent a client or *may* withdraw from representation:

- A client persists in actions that the lawyer believes are criminal or fraudulent or perpetuate a crime or fraud.

- The client pursues an objective the lawyer considers repugnant or imprudent.

- The client fails to fulfill an obligation to the lawyer and has been warned that the lawyer will withdraw if the failure continues.

- The representation will result in an unreasonable burden on the lawyer.

- For other good cause, including a refusal of a client to pay for the services of the lawyer.

Think Twice

A wise colleague once told us that you begin to develop your values when you are a toddler and you spend your formative years developing your sense of morality and ethics. While there are specific regulations that guide our conduct as lawyers, much of what we end up doing and deciding reflects our sense of what is right and what is wrong. Being consistently principled will almost always serve you well.

F. THE WORK AHEAD

1.14 SMART PREPARATION

Some things in life go better if spontaneous and unplanned, such as improvisation. Good lawyering is not an extemporaneous comedy routine, although it may seem that way on a particularly hectic day. Lawyering activities generally work best for all concerned when they occur within a matrix of planning. This is a maxim for all lawyering including transactional work and dispute resolution.

In all phases of practice, the concept of planned lawyering starts well before the lawyer's specific preparation for a particular client in a specific situation or case. Most lawyers today are specialists. They do not attempt to represent every client in every situation. Good lawyers recognize that they may lack adequate competence in an area, or that it is not cost effective for the client to subsidize the lawyer's obtaining adequate competence. Part of good planning is knowing what you can and should do and what others can and should do, and keeping current with CLE courses.

Once a lawyer has a defined practice, planning usually means assessing the client's situation and organizing the strategy for achieving the client's objectives. The objective sought may be positive, affirmative, and even grandiose ("acquire the Omega corporation" or "file a class action lawsuit against the federal government") or may consist largely of damage control (protect the business or consumer client from bankruptcy). The client's needs and interests require an attorney to develop a strategy (a general policy for dealing with the situation) and tactics (particular steps for implementing the strategy).

Subsequent chapters will discuss what clients need from us and how we can effectively plan for specific situations and cases. Part of that process involves initial planning and preparation such as:

Exploring applicable law. The lawyer needs to both review the current law and consider proposing new law. The substantive law of the jurisdiction determines what law applies. Other courses you take in law school help prepare you for this planning. The lawyer may also need to create a legal theory or remedy by developing a good faith argument expanding existing law. Usually this process occurs in small increments in an evolutionary way. Occasionally, it occurs in a revolutionary way with a big bang.

Finding facts. The lawyer must also gather and create facts. Fact gathering includes learning about all sorts of information about a client's situation or case. The lawyer may also need to "create" information by shaping and molding the information that is gathered. Additional sources of information must also be used to gather facts, such as the Internet, documents, and witnesses.

Selecting the right approach. Whether it is transactional or dispute resolution work, the lawyer must select the most effective approach to satisfy the client's needs and interests. There are almost always alternative approaches to situations and cases lawyers need to assess.

Developing a successful plan. The lawyer needs to develop details of the plan to do what the client has retained the lawyer to do. This plan consists of strategies, tactics, and techniques to get what the client wants or needs.

Predicting the future. Various aspects of planning require the lawyer to predict the future. Effective planning means anticipating problems and setbacks. Dealing with other lawyers and decision makers requires the attorney to predict how they may react and what they might do. It helps to be naturally clairvoyant but extra sensory legal abilities can be developed through experience.

Helping the Client. The lawyer throughout planning needs to continually review how the client is doing. Circumstances of a situation determine the scope of this concern. Two important areas of concern are cost and time. An attorney needs to develop and implement a plan that is cost effective and time efficient. Other areas of concern may include business and personal matters. Does the plan advance or hinder the business of the client?

How may the plan affect the psychological and emotional state of a client? A lawyer needs to remember that real people are involved and affected, most directly the client.

Implementing the plan. The remainder of this book focuses on implementing the plan.

Modifying the plan. The attorney will likely need to adjust elements of the plan as it is implemented. Change, as Euclid suggested, is constant.

Think Twice

Talent and capabilities will only get you so far. Hard work and more hard work will make you a much better lawyer. It takes time and effort, sometimes more than want, to do what is needed to achieve success for a client or for your job. But, that's what it means to be professional.

1.15   YOUR GOAL AS A LAWYER

Your goal is to be as good a lawyer as you can be. What is it that makes good lawyers? What is it that some lawyers have that make them better, sometimes much better, than other lawyers?

We know what it is not. It is not just law school class rank (although, you should still try to do your best). Nor is it pure knowledge of the law, nor is it an understanding of the skills it takes to be an excellent lawyer.

Several things combine to make a good lawyer. One is a yearning to be good. It could happen accidentally, but usually it takes a desire. Another is preparation. There is no substitute for concentrated work, most of the time. And another—and perhaps the most significant—is judgment.

Judgment is as judgment appears. It is difficult to define and categorize. When it happens, everyone knows it. When it happens occasionally, it may only be serendipity. When it happens more often, it is good lawyering. When it happens a lot, it is wisdom.

Your goal of being a good lawyer is to develop good judgment. It is the one elemental thing law schools attempt to develop. It is the primary thing law firms look for in new lawyers. It is why clients retain us again and again.

Part One
LAWYER AND CLIENT RELATIONSHIPS

Chapter Two
THE BUSINESS OF LAWYERING

Nice work if you can get it, and you can get it if you try.

—Ira Gershwin

A. INTRODUCTION

2.1 WORKING AS A BUSINESSPERSON

Are we professionals or businesspeople? Most of us enter the practice of law with at least some devotion to the ideal of being "a professional." Yet we need to earn a living and pay back all those loans from law school as well. So, are you entering a business or a profession? Well, of course, the right answer is both.

The original "professions" were law, medicine and theology. The term profession traditionally was associated with advanced study, service to humanity, and a special set of ethical standards. Being a member of a profession was distinguished from being "in trade," where goods or technical skills were exchanged in kind or for money and that exchange was an end in itself. When society was divided more explicitly into classes, professionals became elevated to a higher class status than those engaged in trade. The "Inns of Court" in London fostered a multi-tiered status, among the members of the legal profession, as English barristers tried cases and solicitors represented clients and collected and distributed fees in part to the barristers.

2.2 THE LOST, OR FOUND, PROFESSION

Lawyers have always sought to earn a living at their calling, and because of that, there has always been a business aspect to the practice of law. Several factors over the last decades have caused lawyers and their clients to pay more attention to the business side of law practice. These factors have resulted in some lamentation about lost "professionalism" and some dissatisfaction with the "business" side of practice.

First, the supply of lawyers has increased dramatically in recent years. The legal profession continues to be an attractive career choice for many university graduates and for many seeking a second career. Our society, courts, businesses, and legislatures continue to provide job opportunities for law graduates.

Second, clients have become increasingly savvy consumers of legal services. Large, institutional clients, such as corporations and insurance companies, routinely distribute their business to several different law firms. Lawyers and law firms are frequently called upon to bid competitively for legal work, with the client awarding the work to the firm with the best bid.

Third, lawyers' expectations for their earnings have increased as has the cost of a law degree. Unsurprisingly, the number of workable or billable hours required to achieve that degree and those earnings has gone up as well. Longer working hours and the resulting unpleasant lifestyle have increased dissatisfaction within the profession and led to criticism by some that the emphasis on marketing and billing has been detrimental to public service and personal satisfaction.

Fourth, the economy and market place affect the work of lawyers. Boom or bust financial cycles nationally, regionally, locally, and even internationally, influence the need for specific legal services and what clients are willing to pay for those services. Transactional lawyers may be incredibly busy, or bankruptcy lawyers may be in high demand. Disputes seem to continually arise in all economic climates, but parties facing lean times are more likely to be frugal with their dispute resolution funds and the use of litigators and arbitrators.

At their worst, these changes have combined to make lawyers feel their value as a lawyer is measured in hourly fees or annual incomes. On the other hand, the marketplace law of supply and demand has seen a renewed emphasis on client service as clients ask for more in a buyers' market. Law firms are learning that clients do not want to be treated primarily as profit centers. Client demand is causing the pendulum to swing back to an emphasis on good communication and efficient service.

New lawyers should not take any law office business norms for granted, because those standards change and are, right now, changing in response to the market. Rather, law practice business norms should be examined, understood, and adopted or revised in accord with lawyer and client needs. You as a lawyer can set high expectations for client satisfaction, establish more humane work patterns, or have more modest material expectations. You will have this choice to make before and during the practice you choose, or the practice that chooses you.

The following sections highlight some of the various business aspects of practice.

Think Twice

You may wonder why you're reading about this, now, while you're in law school, and not before, or during first year orientation. There are more areas of job opportunities open to lawyers now than ever before. While the traditional practice of law is undergoing evolutionary changes which affect job availability, businesses and organizations are looking to hire law graduates who have the training you are receiving in law school.

B. ORGANIZING THE PRACTICE

2.3 ORGANIZING THE PRACTICE ENTITY

All practicing lawyers work in some form of business entity. Some (notably in-house counsel) are true employees of another entity, and most practitioners are either employees (as associates) or owners or co-owners of a "law firm." Government lawyers are typically employees of some public entity, such as an administrative agency, or a city or district attorney's office. Lawyers doing full-time pro bono public service work are usually employees of a legal services office or a non-profit corporation.

2.4 LAW FIRM SHAPES AND SIZES

Law firms come in various sizes and shapes, though a few forms predominate.

Sole Proprietorships. This conventional form of small business is termed in lawyers' parlance the "solo practice." Many choose it because it is a remarkably simple organization, with a noted shortage of "bosses." The ability to "be on one's own" is one of the attractions of this form. A sole proprietorship is essentially the alter ego of the lawyer-proprietor, and often has a business name that is the proprietor's name following the phrase "Law Office of." Sole practitioners may also adopt some form of professional corporation, but there may be no good reason to do so.

Partnerships. The partnership is the traditional form for all law practices involving more than one lawyer. Partnerships are easy to establish (a written agreement isn't even legally required, but usually recommended) and a large body of partnership law defines the rights and obligations of partners. Many partnerships have been created between two or more lawyers who decided to join forces to practice together.

Limited Liability Partnerships or Companies and Professional corporations. Some decades ago most states allowed professionals, including doctors, accountants and other professions as well as lawyers, to incorporate as "professional corporations." Though similar to business corporations, professional corporations are generally covered by a different statute, and the nature of the limitations on liability are somewhat different. The statutes generally require the entity to include "P.C.," "S.C.," "Ltd.," or "Chartered" in the firm name to give notice of the limited liability. In the intervening years, an increasing number of states have passed laws that make it possible for lawyers to form other sorts of professional business entities such as Limited Liability Corporations ("L.L.C.'s") or Limited Liability Partnerships ("L.L.P.'s"). These business entities afford lawyers some attributes of a corporation or partnership, and some of the advantages, particularly tax treatment, of individual ownership.

Think Twice

The array of choices may seem somewhat confusing, but the key, if you have a choice, is to select the best organizational entity for your firm. To get the advice you need to make that choice, you should probably ... call a lawyer, preferably a transaction lawyer who specializes in forming law organizations.

C. FINDING CLIENTS

2.5 ATTRACTING AND RETAINING CLIENTS

By some means, every practitioner needs to develop and cultivate clients, and the more the merrier (within reason). As the practice of law has become more bottom-line oriented, this need is becoming more apparent and more pressing. In larger firms a lawyer may not need to cultivate clients immediately upon embarking on practice, but eventually all practitioners want or need to develop clients of their own.

Marketing 101 students learn that an important part of attracting business is developing a product (or service) to sell that customers (or "clients" as we call them) want or need. Honing your legal ability and becoming a competent or even excellent professional is a great way to start developing a practice. Many lawyers choose to focus their practice on a narrow area of law; but across the nation, there are still thousands and thousands of lawyers who make a good living in general practice, doing work in a number of broad areas. Eventually lawyers are rewarded for handling cases competently and professionally. Clients call with a new matter to handle, and former adversaries may call to hire you or refer a matter to you.

In addition to having the ability or expertise to handle legal matters, somehow that ability has to be known to clients. In some cases, you will have developed that expertise on behalf of a client with repeat legal business, and the client will call again. More often, legal business comes from getting the word out to other prospective clients and referral sources. In practice, many lawyers get a majority of their work from other lawyers.

2.5.1 Referrals

A significant portion of most lawyers' new business comes from referrals—from clients, other lawyers, even from former opposing parties. Referrals can be encouraged by letting referral sources know of your availability and interest in handling additional matters. Lawyers also encourage referrals by letting the potential referral sources know they will competently handle matters and will bill fairly.

A referring lawyer should want, more than anything, to know that the client will be satisfied with the referral recommendation. Some referring lawyers want to know that by referring a single matter to the new lawyer, especially where the referral is prompted by a conflict of interest relating to the single referred matter, the new lawyer will not take all of the client's business. Some lawyers want to be assured that if they make a referral it will be reciprocated. Such an understanding, though not uncommon, raises ethical issues relating to the motivation for and independence of the referral advice.

Depending in part on the referring lawyer's continuing involvement in work on the matter, an agreement to pay a referral fee may be appropriate or may be unethical. The referring attorney may properly earn a fee that reflects the work the lawyer has performed in obtaining and interviewing the client or for additional work on the case. It is unethical, in most jurisdictions, to split fees with a lawyer who does no work on a case.

Referrals come for all sorts of reasons. Actual expertise and personal experience with the lawyer may prompt a referral. In many cases, the referring lawyer will make a referral based on reputation, knowing of a lawyer's writings, CLE speeches, the handling of a well-known case, or any number of other factors. A lawyer setting up a private practice probably wants to maximize all these potential reasons for referrals.

2.5.2 Advertising

There was a time when lawyers simply didn't advertise, or at least when they only advertised in "dignified" ways. Simple yellow-page listings of name and phone number were allowed, as were "tombstone" announcements of new firms in the newspaper. These forms of advertising continue to be what some firms with established practices want. Federal and state court decisions and professional rules, however, permit expanded advertising. Many lawyers use a wide variety of more extensive (and more expensive) advertising, including print, web based, radio, and television ads; public service sponsorships; direct mailings of letters, brochures, or videos; emailings, blogs, websites, and almost everything imaginable short of going door to door.

The nature of a lawyer's practice may determine the wisdom of advertising and the type of advertising, if any, likely to bear fruit or clients. Blanketing the airwaves with cable TV ads every half-hour is an expensive way to troll for prospective clients. If a lawyer entering practice plans to advertise for clients, the advertising program should probably be targeted to a specific type of client and type of legal matter. The use of internet and social network communications provide another opportunity for lawyers to spread their name and fame.

Think Twice

Where you practice often influences how and to what extent you market yourself. If you join an existing, successful law firm, there may not be much to do after an initial notice is sent worldwide rejoicing in the fact you joined the firm. In years past, novice lawyers in law firms did not usually have to focus or worry about new business. Today, it's more common for all lawyers in a firm to work on developing new business. If you move to a small town and set up your practice, you may be the best, or only, legal services available, and the clients will come to you as they come to know and trust you. Wherever you practice, you want to make sure you establish for yourself an excellent reputation, because that is usually the best way to achieve success.

D.   MAKING MONEY

2.6   CHARGING FEES

The essence of the private practice of law, as opposed to public interest or government practice, is the hiring of the lawyer by a client. Payment for services rendered is a fundamental part of this relationship. Some lawyers enjoy sending bills. More enjoy getting paid.

The overall fee a lawyer charges a client must be reasonable regardless of how it is calculated. Fees may be charged in a variety of ways, or by a hybrid of the following ways.

2.6.1 Hourly Billing

Abraham Lincoln said that a lawyer's time is a lawyer's stock in trade. For many, many years, the principal way lawyers in the United States have charged for their services is by billing clients an hourly fee for the time the lawyer spends working on the client's matter. This method of billing is particularly common when the lawyer is defending the client in civil litigation or providing services to the client on a business matter.

Most lawyers billing by the hour charge clients their normal hourly rate for all their time spent working for the client, including time for legal research, fact investigation, and discussions with the client. Some lawyers charge less than their hourly rate for travel time or other "non-productive" time; some lawyers do not charge their clients at all for this time; others charge their full hourly rate. Lawyers billing by the hour should charge their clients on the basis of the number of minutes worked, including all preparation, thinking, and event work. Many lawyers record their time on the basis of tenths or quarter hours for the time charged.

2.6.2 Contingent Fees

In the United States, lawyers representing plaintiffs in civil litigation typically charge their clients "contingent fees." This means that the client will pay the lawyer a portion of the total recovery as a fee. If the lawyer fails to recover on behalf of the client, then the lawyer will receive no fee. The percentage of recovery lawyers request as a contingent fee varies according to the lawyer's experience and reputation, as well as the type of the case. Typical contingent fees in a plaintiff's personal injury range from thirty to forty percent. Most jurisdictions forbid a lawyer from charging contingent fees when representing divorce clients or criminal defendants.

2.6.3 Flat Fees

A third common fee structure is the flat or set fee. A lawyer charging this fee will agree to handle the client's legal transaction or litigation event for a fixed sum. The client pays this sum regardless of the outcome of the matter or whether the lawyer has to work excessive, or fewer, hours. Or a client may agree to pay a base sum plus some additional set amount if, for example, an appeal is filed in litigation.

Set fees are a common way transaction lawyers may charge for their services. It can be easier to determine the time involved in drafting some common agreements, and the fee is based on the estimated time to be spent. Flat fees paid in advance have been the traditional way lawyers have charged clients when defending them in criminal matters. Set fees are becoming more common in other kinds of civil work, in part because large business clients have found them an effective way to control legal costs.

2.6.4   Hybrid Fees

A variation or combination of these three fee structures may comprise value billing. Factors that affect the amount of a fee include the case's complexity, novelty, and value to the client. A portion of the fee may be figured on an hourly or flat fee rate, and another portion may be based on a contingency fee. Some business clients are negotiating fee arrangements that provide for hourly billing on some types of work on a matter, but specify a flat fee for tasks such as legal research.

A growing number of clients, especially business clients, may have different lawyers bid for their services, or estimate the prospective fees and hold the lawyers to a final bill closely tied to that estimate. Lawyers with a national or statewide practice may find clients in different locals have a need for basically the same legal research and advice. They may be able to provide these same or similar services at lower costs to these clients.

2.6.5   Costs

Clients are responsible for paying costs associated with their legal matters, and lawyers typically require their clients to reimburse them for advancing the costs. The Rules of Professional Responsibility require clients to pay litigation costs, though lawyers may advance clients these costs until the completion of litigation. Lawyers charge clients for filing fees and process serving, and many also charge for the costs of services such as computer services, copying, printing, or telephone calls. In addition, lawyers also require clients to reimburse costs associated with taking depositions, hiring expert witnesses, and travel related to the client's matter. Some lawyers charge clients amounts for services such as reproducing documents that exceed the lawyer's actual costs for those services. A lawyer charging for "costs" in this fashion should discuss this practice with clients at the outset of the attorney-client relationship.

2.6.6 Retainers

Quite often, a lawyer will require a client to make an initial, up-front payment before beginning work. This payment is usually called a retainer. If the lawyer is billing the client on an hourly basis, the lawyer's time may be charged against the retainer. The lawyer may also draw on the retainer to pay costs and expenses associated with work on behalf of the client. Lawyers are required to return, at the end of their work for a client, any advanced payment of unearned fees.

2.6.7 Billing Mechanics

In the past, many lawyers sent clients bills that contained precious little information other than the total amount the client owed the lawyer. Quite often, lawyers would not bill a client until completion of work. Times have changed. For many years now, it is a common practice for lawyers to send clients bills that contain a detailed day-by-day, hour-by-hour description of the different tasks done for the client and an indication of how long each individual task took. Many lawyers now bill clients on a regular monthly basis. Contingent or flat fees are exceptions to this practice, of course. Contingent fees are collected at the time the settlement or judgment is paid. Set fees may be paid when the work is completed, or as it progresses, or even in advance.

2.6.8 Business Agreements

Depending on the state in which you practice, the applicable ethical or disciplinary rules may require a fee agreement to be in writing, especially if it is a contingent fee agreement. Regardless of whether this is required by the rules, however, prudent lawyers put all fee agreements in print by email, a letter, or a formal agreement. This practice avoids disputes later in the relationship, helps preserve the attorney-client relationship, and facilitates collection of fees if a dispute later arises.

Furthermore, the written business agreement provides the lawyer with an excellent framework and checklist for discussions with the client. At some point before beginning work for the client, the lawyer can walk the client through the business agreement step-by-step. This will provide the client ample opportunity to ask questions about billing and about the work the lawyer will do.

The fee agreement need not be cumbersome or arcane. An engagement email or letter can simply welcome the opportunity to assist the client, confirm the terms of the representation, the fee to be charged, the basis for reimbursement of expenses, the right to withdraw, and any other matters that warrant preservation. The document should be composed in a way so that the client can readily understand the terms.

Think Twice

A lawyer needs to be a smart businessperson. This includes knowing how to bill so that fees are reasonable and also sufficient to cover costs and expenses. Being a good businessperson also means knowing how to collect bills. Billing clients can be an unpleasant part of practice. Some lawyers find it difficult to determine what fee is reasonable for a transaction or a dispute. Some lawyers worry that they will lose a client to someone charging less. Other lawyers find it uncomfortable to try and collect unpaid fees and don't do so. A good business head is as important as a good legal mind, and recognizing you deserve to be paid reasonably well for your expertise is as important as knowing the law. If you don't have the interest, time, or enthusiasm to run the business side of your practice, you can hire an office manager.

E. PROTECTING AGAINST MALPRACTICE

2.7 INSURING AGAINST MALPRACTICE

Lawyers, like doctors, are subject to malpractice claims, and lawyers, like doctors, make provisions to protect their practices from those claims. Malpractice insurance is an important consideration for any lawyer in private practice. The premium may be one of the more significant expenses the lawyer incurs. Insurance is only part of the way lawyers safeguard themselves from malpractice claims.

2.7.1 Risk Management

Risk management in a law firm includes a number of important components. The most important part of the program ought to be prevention of mistakes or misdeeds that could give rise to a malpractice claim. This is essentially "quality control," and is intended to assure that the legal work performed by the lawyer or the firm is of the quality the firm expects and of the quality the client expects.

Another important part of risk management is establishing practice norms that help insure client satisfaction, and in so doing, also help prevent malpractice claims. Many malpractice claims occur not because the lawyer has deviated in any way from the standard of care for lawyers. Rather, lawyers get sued because clients are dissatisfied with the services rendered, without particular regard to the quality of the legal work.

Think Twice

It is not uncommon for new lawyers to believe that clients will be satisfied with the work the lawyer has done, as long as the outcome is favorable for the client or, at least, the work has been done competently. In fact, this is not true. Why would a client be dissatisfied with legal work that meets professional standards? One good example of how lawyers doing good work still get challenged is a failure to adequately communicate. A client whose calls and questions go unanswered or a client who is kept waiting for an update builds up a dangerous level of dissatisfaction with the lawyer. This is true regardless of whether the lawyer has won discovery battles increasing the value of the client's case, has done brilliant research to clinch a deal, or has done other wonderful things. Clients have a right to know promptly what you are doing and why, and how you are spending their money. Future sections highlight the importance of ongoing communication with clients.

2.7.2 Insurance

Insurance against professional liabilities (e.g., malpractice) is the last line of protection against malpractice claims. Although not required in most states, malpractice insurance offers important protection to the lawyer against a wide variety of potential liabilities. Purchasing a malpractice policy gives the lawyer two forms of protection: first, the policy will pay for any legal judgment or settlement due to the malpractice claim (the indemnity provision of the policy); second, the policy will pay for the cost of hiring a lawyer to defend against any claims that are made (the defense provision).

This protection can be very comforting, especially so if it unfortunately has to be used. In many malpractice claims, the defense provision of the policy may be more valuable since a large number of claims are ultimately dismissed without any judgment or settlement. There is great value to most lawyers in being able to turn the claim over to the insurer and letting assigned defense counsel take care of it. After all, you don't want to have to represent yourself, and run the risk of having a fool for a client.

Professional liability insurance is usually available from a number of different insurance carriers. Many state bar associations have "captive" insurers for this coverage; more have arrangements with an "endorsed" insurer that offers a standard policy with a standard schedule of terms. Other domestic professional liability insurance carriers operate in most states, and larger captive insurers may be available, such as for large law firms. These insurers offer policies either tailored to the particular type of firm or law practice. Larger firms or firms needing either tailor-made coverage or special considerations in insurance may find custom insurance written through large carriers.

F. OPERATING A PRACTICE

2.8 SETTING UP A LAW PRACTICE

Set up a firm, hang out the shingle, complete some big deals, win a few cases, send some bills, buy a tropical island and retire. What could be easier?

In reality, running a law practice is often an arduous and time-consuming task that causes many lawyers stress and distress. The ability to practice law without the concerns of running a practice is one thing that draws many lawyers to large firms or law departments, though many lawyers in those types of practice spend substantial amounts of time and energy on the operation and administration of their law firm, as well. Operating any law practice involves a plethora of minute details. Arrangements for an office, access to a conference room, provision for computer and telecommunications support, all require attention. Colleagues and other staff require ongoing management time and attention.

Despite the challenges, it is possible to run a law practice for fun and profit. Equipment to assist in the practice is widely available. Computers, printers, telephones, voicemail, filing and time-management software systems, and the like help lawyers create an effective legal practice. Many state and specialty bar associations have resources meant to help lawyers in sole or small practices run their offices efficiently. Staff and personnel are also readily available. Office sharing arrangements, trained paralegals, and employee leasing arrangements provide experienced support staff. A law office can be set up with a minimum of effort (and at much lower cost than years ago). Some lawyers have found that, with the widespread availability of computer and communication systems, they have little need of dedicated physical space for a law office, and conduct their practices from their homes.

A variety of essential legal tasks can be accomplished online. Access to legal research databases, such as Westlaw and Lexis, as well as other web-based databases, is now a nearly indispensable part of legal research. Communication over internet or intranet networks is also very important and helpful to lawyers. Many courts, and more all the time, provide access to court records electronically. Electronic document management systems, once exclusively the province of high stakes litigation involving large law firms, are now available and useful in small cases.

2.9   EMPLOYING AND MANAGING STAFF

Lawyers in private practice quickly become employers, or at least supervisors, of others shortly after they begin practice. And even if you work by yourself, you still have to tell yourself what needs to be done. Supervising others is not a skill everyone has, and certainly is not one deeply cultivated in law school.

Nonetheless, lawyers generally find themselves employing, either directly or indirectly, receptionists, messengers, legal assistants, law clerks, paralegals, and other personnel. In addition to hiring these people, the lawyer must supervise them. This is an express ethical responsibility under the Model Rules of Professional Conduct. It's also common sense.

The lawyer's role as employer also carries with it the duty to comply with broad and increasingly complex employment law requirements. These may include enforcing discrimination laws, providing a safe workplace, accommodating workers' disabilities, and complying with wage and hour laws. Whether you want to or not, you or someone else in your firm will need to know all about employment laws, rights, and obligations.

A premise of this book is that the work of lawyer is about relationships. And that begins with the people you work with in your law firm or office. Treating all of them the way you would expect to be treated is the right way to begin and continue these relationships.

2.10   PAYING TAXES

Another important detail of practicing law is paying taxes. Lawyers obviously have to pay their own income taxes, at least if they generate income, which is always a better option. Failure to do so may subject the lawyer to professional discipline as well as tax law penalties. Lawyers also may be required to collect and pay sales or service tax on the services they render, though most states have avoided imposing this particularly burdensome form of misery tax. As employers, lawyers or law firms must withhold and pay various taxes on behalf of their employees. Yes, the practice of law can be taxing, but it can also be a deeply rewarding adventure, which begins when the client seeks help from you.

Think Twice

Okay, lawyers should be respectful to those they work with. And, well, of course, lawyers have to pay taxes. So why would anyone, especially a lawyer, need to be reminded of all this? For starters, a major reason why the business side of lawyering goes awry is because the office or firm personnel do not work well together. And, oddly, a significant portion of professional disciplinary charges brought against lawyers arise from the failure to pay income taxes or—even more astonishingly—the failure to file income tax returns.

Why, you wonder: do smart professionals let this happen? Because these lawyers are poor managers of people and of their time and priorities. They become focused on other aspects of their work and life and initially lose sight of all of their responsibilities and obligations. And then, once they forget to do something like paying a quarterly tax estimate or two, or three, they forget to file a return. "Treat others respectfully" and "pay your taxes" may seem like simplistic bromides, but it's often the simple things in life that are the most important to remember.

Chapter Three
INTERVIEWING: WHAT WE NEED FROM OUR CLIENTS

Someone to tell it to is one of the fundamental needs of human beings.

—Miles Franklin

A. INTRODUCTION

3.1 THE FOUR BASIC ELEMENTS

In a nutshell, a lawyer in private practice beginning work with a client needs four things: trust, information, direction, and a business agreement. Lawyers who work with clients in house or in other practices need the first three things. This chapter explains these basic elements of a successful interview, and offers some suggestions about preparing for and conducting the first meeting with a client.

3.2 INTERVIEWING ELEMENTS: AN OVERVIEW

Without a doubt, a lot of interviewing is common sense. Establishing trust, obtaining information, gaining direction, and obtaining a business agreement are common sense elements of a successful attorney/client interview. While common sense may be a good starting point for understanding how to interview a client, there is much more to consider and study about interviewing and about these four basic elements.

One reason that we need more than common sense to interview a client is that our role as a lawyer has a professional dimension and a business dimension. Another part of the reason effective interviewing demands more than common sense is because lawyers need to develop a range of alternative ways to achieve these four basic elements. For example, you probably already have a good common sense approach for obtaining information about something that has happened, but as a lawyer you will to develop alternative approaches because no one way works for all clients. To conduct a successful interview, lawyer need to view the process from the perspectives of clients, who will have a variety of concerns, problems, and issues.

Consider the client who believes she has a brilliant idea for a business venture and who visits her lawyer acquaintance. The lawyer asks a series of probing, difficult questions relating to contract law, business organizations, intellectual property, and tax consequences the client never thought about and suggests a number of problems that may occur in the future in developing this business. The lawyer may understandably view these issues as the critical information needed to do legal work for the client. On the other hand, the client may rightfully wonder why the lawyer seems to be such a nay-sayer and prophet of gloom and doom and how this lawyer can really help.

Or consider the defense client in a civil lawsuit who comes to a complete stranger—the lawyer—and who is outraged at being sued. The advocate asks frank questions which may reveal how irresponsible the client was and how much the client may be liable for. The client may naturally wonder whether the lawyer disbelieves his story and why he should trust any advice from this lawyer.

All clients arrive at the law office with some kind of emotional stake in the matter that has prompted them to seek legal advice. A client may feel concern and anxiety, pain and outrage, happiness and joy, or sadness and depression. The challenge lawyers have is establishing the basic interviewing elements with clients who have these and other feelings. It is helpful to recognize that common sense may guide our work, but it is equally critical to explore and learn a variety of professional approaches and lawyering techniques to accomplish that work.

B. BUILDING TRUST

3.3 WHAT DOES TRUST MEAN?

When a client trusts a lawyer, that client has:

- Faith in the lawyer's fidelity.

- A belief in the lawyer's competence.

- Some degree of comfort when dealing with the lawyer.

Faith in a lawyer's fidelity means that the client understands that the lawyer will keep confidences, will put the client's interests ahead of the lawyer's own, and will continue to work on the client's behalf despite unforeseen problems and unexpected inconveniences. To be sure, a client cannot reasonably expect a lawyer's undying devotion forever. If a client believes that the lawyer will abandon the case when the going gets rough, however, that client will not trust the lawyer.

Likewise, a client need not believe that a lawyer can perform miracles in order to trust the lawyer, but trust cannot grow without client confidence in a lawyer's ability. Clients hire lawyers because they need help accomplishing tasks they cannot undertake themselves. Clients realize that they must rely on the special skills that lawyers have. If a client does not believe the lawyer is—at a minimum—competent, then that client will not trust the lawyer.

For many clients, dealing with lawyers may not be a particularly comfortable or pleasant experience. People typically visit lawyers either because they have a problem or because they are afraid they may have a problem sometime soon. And these problems may range from mild difficulties to horrific tragedies. Consequently, almost by definition, a client is a person under stress and, perhaps, enormous stress. So the goal of establishing some degree of comfort isn't to have the client rejoice at the prospect of meeting his or her lawyer. Instead, the goal is to have the client feel enough comfort to enable the client to reveal helpful information, including sensitive and even damaging information.

Faith in the lawyer's fidelity, belief in the lawyer's competence, and comfort when dealing with the lawyer all are part of the client's trust in the lawyer. These three elements work together to foster trust, each reinforcing the other two. For example, a client who has faith in the lawyer's fidelity will feel more comfortable telling the lawyer damaging information because the client will be less worried that the lawyer will sever the relationship due to the harmful information.

3.3.1 Why Is Trust Important?

Clients who trust their lawyers are clients who are willing to provide the lawyer with needed information and appropriate direction. Lawyers do not want clients who hide sensitive information or insist on watching over the lawyers' every step. In addition, clients who trust their lawyers are clients who bring their business back. Without sufficient trust, a client will neither talk nor listen to the lawyer.

3.3.2 Why Is Trust Elusive?

Trust between a lawyer and client may be elusive. Many people are somewhat distrustful of all lawyers. A client may be initially distrustful or suspicious of a lawyer, and may not feel any real trust for the lawyer until time and experience prove the lawyer trustworthy. Establishing trust with a client is similar to creating a bond in other types of relationships. There may be nothing that the lawyer can immediately do to establish a strong bond of trust, but along the way, there are steps that the lawyer can take to build and maintain a client's trust.

Think Twice

These challenges are especially likely when the lawyer initially is a stranger and the client is going through tough times. Consider a typical scenario: a client who is confused or fearful must tell a story that is painful or embarrassing, to a professional who is neither family nor friend. And exactly why should this client trust this professional with their inner most secrets and fears? It's up to the lawyer to create an atmosphere that permits this outpouring of facts mixed with irrational opinions and anxiety laced with rational apprehensions. That is quite a challenge even in the best of relationships. But that is your goal, and it requires the development of specialized skills.

3.4 COMPETENT COMMUNICATION

The first step in building a client's trust is competent communication. There is no substitute for regular communication with a client, and nothing can do more to prevent client dissatisfaction with the lawyer. A lawyer can build trust and goodwill simply by making regular progress reports to the client. The client who has to call the lawyer in order to find out what is going on is the client who begins to suspect that the lawyer cares less or is hiding something.

Competent communication begins with being clear and comprehensible. Unfortunately, law school teaches us a new language that may be incomprehensible to our clients. A lawyer may prefer to use specialized legal terms to impress a client, but the actual effect is likely to be the opposite. A client is apt to distrust a lawyer who rattles off legalese, believing that the lawyer has resorted to jargon in order to distort the truth.

Competent communication must also be open and accurate. No one enjoys receiving bad news, but sooner or later every lawyer must give a client bad news. If the lawyer is straightforward with the client, the client is much more likely to develop respect and trust for the lawyer. Clients do not like bad news, but they will accept it more willingly if it does not come as a complete surprise. If a lawyer's communication with a client has been clear and regular, no bad news should come as a complete surprise.

3.4.1   Good Listening

Listening is as important to building trust as talking. Good listening is more than simply keeping quiet while a client talks. Good listening begins with the ability to listen to a client while keeping an open mind. No client is well-served by a lawyer who is impatient and overly judgmental. A lawyer needs to be able to listen to a client and suspend judgment until all the facts are in. Snap decisions and quick judgments close the mind and interfere with good listening. The good listener learns to wait patiently— not for the client to finish talking, but for the story to unfold completely.

Good listening helps build trust only so long as the client believes that the lawyer is indeed hearing what is being said. Good eye contact and encouraging nods of the head may help persuade the client that the lawyer is listening, but thoughtful and perceptive responses will work even better. The lawyer who can suspend judgment to listen both sympathetically and critically will find it much easier to respond to the client with perception, emotion, and honesty.

Think Twice

This is a point where relying only on our common sense will not be enough. Supervising lawyers frequently identify interviewing as the skill new lawyers struggle with the most. And most often, seasoned lawyers suggest, the reason new lawyers struggle with interviewing is they have a hard time listening to what the client is saying.

Why would this be so? Why is listening to a client any harder or any different than listening to a friend or relative? Think for a moment about just a few of the things that may be happening during a client interview that are not part of a conversation with a friend:

- *The client may be a person the lawyer has never met.*

- *The client may be angry, afraid, or reluctant to talk.*

- *The lawyer needs to assure the client of his or her competence as a professional.*

- *The lawyer needs to form a business relationship with the client.*

- *The lawyer not only needs to learn what happened, the lawyer needs to apply legal doctrine to that information.*

- *The lawyer thinks about applicable legal issues and the law, and is trying to remember it all accurately.*

And while all this and more may be swirling around in the lawyer's head, the lawyer may suddenly wonder whether the advice given the last client was right or whether there will be enough time to finish this interview before going home to make the family dinner.

Our good judgment tells us that listening is important. It will be next to impossible to listen effectively, however, unless we think twice about how challenging it can be to listen in the context of a client interview. It can be quite difficult to concentrate on listening intently when life is so very busy and distracting. But that is what clients expect from us.

3.4.2   Appropriate Comfort

Client trust depends in part on client comfort while working with the lawyer. The lawyer can do much to foster client comfort with three kinds of communication that are particularly reassuring to clients: signals of competence, signals of empathy, and signals of safety.

Signals of Competence. A lawyer sends a signal of competence to reassure a client that the lawyer is a trained professional capable of dealing with the client's concern. A lawyer can communicate competence in a variety of ways, such as explaining the relevant law, talking about past experience with the kind of problem that concerns the client, or suggesting creative solutions to the problem.

> **Example**: Ms. Cullen, I think we may be able to work out a solution to this problem. This is an area of law I'm familiar with, and I think you have more options than you may realize. . . .

Signals of Empathy. A signal of empathy is meant to reassure clients that the lawyer understands and cares about the concerns the client has expressed. Communicating empathy can be a powerful tool, particularly when dealing with a client who has strong emotions about a legal problem. The lawyer can signal empathy by expressly recognizing the client's emotion and then explaining why that emotion seems appropriate.

> **Example:** Mr. Lamar, you seem very upset about what has happened to you, and I can understand that. You've been a good tenant for many years, and now the landlord is refusing to make these repairs. That's got to seem unfair.

Communicating empathy can also reassure the client that the lawyer is listening. A client who doesn't hear an appropriate signal of empathy from a lawyer may feel compelled to elaborate on the emotional content of event until the lawyer recognizes that content.

Signals of Safety. At times, a lawyer can best foster trust by sending the client a signal of safety. Communicating safety is way to reassure the client that the lawyer will remain loyal to the client. The signal of safety is particularly useful when the client is concerned about revealing sensitive or damaging information.

> **Example:** Mr. Lamar, you seem worried about your discussion with the landlord. It sounds like you got pretty angry during that discussion. I want you to feel free to tell me everything you can remember about that conversation. I promise you, I won't be shocked by what you say. I've worked with a lot of clients that got mad at their landlords.

Think Twice

Communicating these signals may also feel reassuring to the lawyer, and some novice lawyers signal more often than needed. A little goes a long way. The danger of self-professed competence is that the reassurance begins to ring hollow fairly quickly. The client who listens to repeated signals of empathy may perceive the lawyer believes the client is right and has done no wrong. And repeated remarks about why the client should feel safe may make it sound like the lawyer believes the client's concerns are irrational.

3.4.3 Faithful Silence

Careless talk about confidential matters is a breach of professional ethics and a threat to the attorney-client privilege. Careless talk about client confidences is also devastating to client trust. Clients have interesting problems and tell lawyers interesting things. It is natural for a lawyer to want to talk about these things—especially with other lawyers. New lawyers need to be particularly wary of this temptation. Legal communities are much smaller than they at first seem to be, and it is surprising how quickly stories spread.

C. OBTAINING INFORMATION

3.5 WHAT INFORMATION DO WE NEED FROM CLIENTS?

What information is relevant to a lawyer? At the beginning of practice, most novice lawyers answer this question too narrowly. This is hardly surprising. Almost everything about our professional training schools us to answer every question we are asked as narrowly as possible. In the classroom, we are challenged to state the precise holding in the appellate court decision and then articulate the few critical facts on which that holding rests. We break down torts and crimes into a small handful of elements and then recite the key facts that prove those elements. Outside the classroom in the world of practice, work with clients is refreshingly wide open. What is relevant is not defined by narrow rules or simple formulas. Instead of narrowing our questions, the work we do with clients asks that we open our minds and broaden the scope of our inquiry.

When we are working with clients, the information that is relevant can be loosely grouped into three different categories: information about the matter, information about context, and information about the client. A lawyer needs a client to provide information in all three categories.

3.5.1 Information About the Matter

This category of information is the easiest to understand. Information about the matter—the case or the transaction that has prompted the client to see a lawyer—are the kind of cold, hard facts that we discussed most often in the law school classroom. For some of us, this may be the kind of information that seems the most immediately relevant to the description of any legal issue. This category includes two kinds of information: "legal data" and "narrative data."

"Legal data" is the information immediately relevant to a client's cause of action or legal problem. It is the easiest information for a lawyer to ask about because everything in our training has taught us to care about this kind of information. Appellate decisions are filled with the information we describe as "legal data." When a client comes to a lawyer with a contract problem, chances are the lawyer's mind fills with questions about offer, acceptance, and consideration. For the most part, the information that answers these questions is legal data.

"Narrative data" is information about the events that gave rise to the client's legal problem or cause of action. In a contract action, narrative data is information about the negotiations leading to the agreement, the drafting and signing of the contract, and the breach of the contract. Simply put, narrative data is the step-by-step account of the events that brought the client to see the lawyer.

3.5.2   Information About Context

"Information about context" is the explanation of the circumstances and background relevant to the client's matter. It is the kind of information that gives greater depth and texture to the flat narrative data that describes the client's legal concerns. For example, whether a client is interested in negotiating a contract with a customer or suing a customer for breach of contract, information about context may include information about whether there is an industry custom about the formation of contracts or whether the client had dealt with that customer before.

3.5.3   Information About the Client

"Information about the client" means something more than the client's phone number or email address. In our breach of contract situation, necessary information about the client would include information about the client's business, but it would also include information about a client's insights, motives, preferences, and concerns. For example, the client may have suspicions about why the customer breached the contract, reasons for wanting to negotiate a settlement with the customer, and insight about whether or not the customer is trustworthy.

3.5.4   Why Is Information Important?

The obvious provides us with part of the answer to this question. The importance of legal and narrative data is self-apparent. If a lawyer is going to represent a client, the lawyer needs an account of the circumstances that gave rise to the need for representation. In most circumstances, the client is going to be one of the most important sources for this information.

Information—about the matter, context, and the client— helps the lawyer assess the client's legal concerns and give effective advice. This same information serves a second purpose. At some point quite early in the work with a client, a lawyer needs to make a decision about whether to accept representation of the client. There is no question that legal and narrative data will help a lawyer make this decision. Listening to information about the context of the matter and about the client may be just as important in assessing whether or not the lawyer can represent the client.

Think Twice

The question that is more perplexing for new attorneys is why any information other than information about the matter is really critical. As it turns out, that information about context and the client may be just as critical for the lawyer's understanding of the legal issues bedeviling the client. Cold, hard data may help the lawyer understand <u>**what**</u> *events have occurred, but background and context information may be more important to the lawyer for understanding* <u>why</u> *these events occurred.*

3.6   TECHNIQUES FOR OBTAINING INFORMATION

Lawyers obtain information from many different sources. The lawyer's own client is one of the most important sources of information. In fact, the client may be the only available source for some of the most important information a lawyer needs. This section discusses how a lawyer can obtain information from a client. Other sections (e.g., Chapter 7) discuss information gathering from other sources.

Typically, much of the initial interview between the lawyer and client is devoted to obtaining information. Your goal is to achieve completion, clarity, and closure. The process of obtaining information does not end with that first interview, however. Across the course of representation, things change. The client's life or business may alter in a way that has a direct impact on the work the lawyer is doing. The client may develop greater trust in the attorney and reveal information not previously discussed.

3.7   BUILDING A NARRATIVE

Particularly in matters that require a lawyer to understand an event, building a narrative is an essential technique for developing information. A nearly complete narrative can be developed with a client with the use of a few helpful approaches.

3.7.1   The Capsule Description

Initial client interviewing is a similar to traveling: if you don't know where you're going, it's hard to get there. It is difficult to conduct a detailed interview of any client until you have some sense of what the interview is all about. Usually an attorney will have information, at a minimum, about the general type of problem that has caused the client to seek out a lawyer. Often, however, a lawyer may know little more than the client has had a problem with a landlord or needs advice about a will and trust agreement.

For this reason, it is often very helpful to ask clients for an initial broad-based description of their legal problems or needs. In a sense, this description is a quick "capsule description" of the client's legal concern. With this summary in hand, the lawyer will have a better understanding of the client's later explanation of events and be able to ask more intelligent and cogent questions.

Think Twice

Care should be taken, however, not to make snap decisions on the basis of a capsule description. A client's one-minute description of a complicated series of events is inherently subjective and necessarily limited. At times, a client will give a quick picture of events that differs radically from the more detailed description.

3.7.2   The Step-by-Step Chronology

After obtaining a capsule description of the legal concern to serve as a guide, it is almost always necessary to ask a client to give a more detailed step-by-step chronology of the events leading up to that problem. Since most people tell stories chronologically, it usually makes sense to ask clients to give an account of what happened from start to finish.

One of the best ways to begin a client's narrative is to fix the time of the first event and simply ask a client to describe what happened next:

> **Example:** Ms. Cullen, you've told me that you're here because you've had problems with your tenant. When did you lease the store?.... What was the first problem?.... What happened next?

Some clients can give a surprisingly detailed narrative description of events if the lawyer simply invites them to do so. Some, of course, are going to need more help. Generally speaking, however, it is worthwhile to permit a client to attempt a description of events with a minimum of prompting or assistance from the lawyer. This may require patient listening but it will be patience that is rewarded. Letting the client tell the story may help put the client at ease and help the lawyer develop a sense of the client's credibility and persuasiveness.

Think Twice

A chronological account of events is often the best choice, but it is certainly not the only choice. For example, a lawyer could ask a client to recount facts topic-by-topic or begin with critical events and move on to less important events. If a client is seeking a lawyer's help with a transaction, there may not be a triggering event, so a topic-by-topic approach may make more sense.

3.7.3　Neutral Prompts

Even the most articulate clients will occasionally need assistance when giving a narrative account of events. One of the most effective ways of assisting a client is offering a "neutral prompt." A neutral prompt is a question or comment that moves the story video forward without suggesting the content of the next scene. Neutral prompts are useful when the client has lost the thread of the narrative and needs help to move forward. Examples of neutral prompts include:

- Please go on.

- What happened next?

- Please tell me more about that?

- What did you say then?

- You just mentioned [Event X]. What happened after that?

These verbal neutral prompts can be very effective in moving a narrative forward and they can also be very effective in reassuring a client that the lawyer is listening to the client and following the narrative. Sometimes a non-verbal prompt may be even more helpful. For purposes of reassuring a client, almost nothing beats a sympathetic nod of the head, good eye contact, and patient silence.

Think Twice

A moment of silence is needed to emphasize its importance ... Okay, why? Many interviewers have a tendency to keep talking, or use a lot of verbal prompts, or avoid periods of silence. Successful interviewers understand the value of quiet. Silence is often very helpful at producing additional, useful information. The client has an opportunity to relax, reflect, and remember more. A few seconds of silence to some seems uncomfortable. Yet, several or more seconds of silence may be all that is needed to get the information you want. Be patient. Be very patient.

3.7.4   Directive Prompts

Directive prompts are comments or questions that move a narrative forward and **do** contain a suggestion about the content of the next event described. When a lawyer asks a client for information about a specific event or subject then that lawyer is using a directive prompt.

> **Example:** Ms. Cullen, did you have a conversation with your tenant about water problems in the store?

Directive prompts are particularly useful to focus the client's attention on a particular issue of concern to the lawyer. They are also useful in moving the narrative to a new event. The risk of using directive prompts is that they do refocus the client. When the lawyer uses a directive prompt to suggest a discussion of a new topic, the client may be upset at being interrupted or also may lose track of the narrative and forget to tell the lawyer something important. The interviewing lawyer may need to return to a topic or time and ask the client to fill in any missing information.

There is also a chance that a directive prompt may cause a client to feel pressured to provide details about the topic the lawyer has suggested, even though the client cannot remember those details. Lawyers should not phrase directive prompts in a way that encourages clients to make up details:

> **Example:** Mr. Lamar, I'm sure your landlord must have assured you the store had no water problems. Please tell me about those conversations?

During the client's narration of events, it is usually wise to use directive prompts sparingly. If the client is narrating events in a reasonably concise and cogent fashion, allow the client to complete the narrative with a minimum of interruptions.

Think Twice

Why would a client make something up just to satisfy the lawyer? Because the client thinks the lawyer knows what should have happened, and thinks that it will be better to go along with the lawyer's "suggestions." And if the lawyer has done a good job of developing trust through signals of empathy and safety, then it's easier for the client to want to agree with the lawyer. Clients often view lawyers as authority figures, which means what you say, imply, or suggest can have a lot of influence on the client's memory and recollection.

3.7.5   Time Posting

As the client moves through a narrative description of events, it is extremely helpful to keep track of the date or time of critical events. Often, the client will supply these during the course of the narrative. If the client does not, the lawyer may simply ask a question such as, "When did that happen?" At the end of the client's narrative, the lawyer will have a rough chronology of the critical events. This will assist the lawyer in structuring the remainder of the interview and it will also flag any significant chronological gaps in the client's narrative.

3.7.6 Recapping

"Recapping" is a powerful tool for building a complete narrative. When a client has finished the narrative, the lawyer may briefly recap or summarize what the client has said. There are two advantages to doing this. First, it gives the client and the lawyer the opportunity to clear up any misunderstanding before the interview continues. Second, recapping is an opportunity for the lawyer to signal competent listening and empathetic understanding of the client's situation.

If the client's initial narrative description is fairly brief, then it may make sense for the lawyer to recap the entire narrative once the client has finished. Sometimes, a client will need to describe a more complex set of events or want to give a more detailed narrative description. In these situations, it may make more sense for the lawyer to recap each topic as the client finishes.

Think Twice

The risk of recapping is that the lawyer will recall the story or describe events differently than what the client said or intended to say. This will require the client to correct the lawyer, which can be difficult if the client perceives the lawyer as the person of authority who must know better about what should have happened. The lawyer needs to carefully and neutrally recap and encourage the client to correct any errors.

3.8 PROBING FOR ADDITIONAL INFORMATION

Once the lawyer has a reasonably complete narrative and chronology, the lawyer can begin to probe for more detailed information. Two particularly useful probing techniques are "flashback" and "slow-motion."

3.8.1 Flashback

Flashback is an extremely simple technique used to probe for background or context information. Quite often, clients will focus on data during their narrative description of events and omit background or context information. A lawyer can use flashback to fill in these gaps. After hearing the narrative, the lawyer can decide what background and context information would be helpful. The lawyer can then identify a specific incident or party and directly ask for background or context information.

Examples:

Mr. Lamar, you mentioned that plaster fell from the ceiling in the store in May. Tell me about the first time you noticed any problems with the roof or ceiling?

Ms. Catron, you said that your customer, Harvester Works, wants to do more business with you. Tell me more about Harvester. When did your company first begin doing business with the Works?

A flashback gives the client the opportunity to provide this kind of background and context information. It is information that can do much to explain the events in the narrative.

3.8.2 Slow–Motion

One of the most common techniques used to probe for additional information is "slow-motion." A lawyer using this technique identifies a particular event from the narrative and then asks the client to recount that event in a very detailed manner. The lawyer and the client can explore the event at greater length, with the lawyer asking progressively more specific, directed questions.

If the client has given only a brief sketch of the event during the narrative, the lawyer may want to begin probing with an open-ended inquiry:

Example: Ms. Cullen, you said you had a conversation with your property manager about repairs he made at the store. I'd like you to tell me everything you can recall about that conversation.

Once the client has given a reasonably detailed narrative description of the event, the lawyer can make some decisions about what further information would be useful. This is the time for the lawyer to use knowledge of legal doctrine and intelligent curiosity to guide further questioning. It is also the time for the lawyer to use more directive prompts and closed-ended questions.

For filling in details about narrative data, background, and context information, the lawyer needs to use who, what, where, when, how, and why questions.

Examples: Ms. Cullen, I have some more questions about the conversation you had with your property manager.

- Where did the conversation take place?

- Who else was present?

- When did the conversation take place?

- How long did the conversation last?

- What did the property manager say about the roof?

- Why did you ask the property manager to make these repairs?

Information about legal data may require more directed questions. Quite often, a lawyer will want information about a key legal point that a client will talk about only in passing or, perhaps, not at all. The lawyer may need to ask about these issues directly:

Example: Mr. Lamar, when did you first notify your land-lord about the problems?

These questions may yield information about an event or set of circumstances that seems particularly relevant to the lawyer. But, for clients, these direct questions can be very disconcerting. A client can easily perceive that the question presumes the client failed to do something they should have done, or that the lawyer wants a favorable answer, or that the client is not being believed by the lawyer.

Think Twice

One of the most common mistakes new lawyers make during client interviews is relying too heavily on these kinds of questions. Most clients feel some discomfort about talking to lawyers. Direct, closed-end questions about legal data can increase that discomfort and make the client feel as if the lawyer is conducting a cross-examination. A little patience can do much to help this problem. Direct questioning of this sort should be put on hold until the client has had a fair opportunity to explain events. It can be surprisingly hard to wait to ask these questions, because they often focus on a critical legal issue and they can be an efficient way of narrowing legal claims and defenses. Asking these questions at the appropriate time— after some trust has been established and after the client has given a narrative of their own—and asking them in a naturally curious, nonjudgmental way will help obtain accurate answers.

3.9   DIFFICULTIES IN OBTAINING INFORMATION

Clients are often the first and best source of information for lawyers. They are only human, however, so they are not perfect sources of information. At times, a client may at first be reluctant or unable to give the lawyer important information. This section discusses techniques that a lawyer can use when faced with some of the more common difficulties in obtaining information.

Loss of memory is another common obstacle a lawyer faces while obtaining information. A lawyer may want information about something that took place months or years before. Details that may seem critically important in the law office may have seemed trivial at the time they transpired. There is often no reason for a client to recall some events because the client foresaw no need to remember what happened at a later time. Whatever the reason, it is the rare client that remembers everything the lawyer wants to know.

There are a number of ways to help a client revive a dim recollection. One of the best places to begin is to remember that while lawyers are intently focused on the written and spoken word, many other people are not. Rather than attempting to prompt clients to remember words, it is frequently more useful to help clients remember situations and events.

Three common techniques for refreshing memory are described below: describing the setting, searching for a triggering detail, and citing other sources. A lawyer should keep in mind, however, that clients are human, and like all of us subject to all the vagaries of memory. Even the most skillful lawyer will find some recollections that simply cannot be refreshed. Pushing a client too hard can only cause a lapse of trust or a lapse of integrity.

3.9.1   Describing the Setting

Frequently, a client may initially recall little more about a meeting than the fact that the meeting occurred. The lawyer may be most interested in learning what was said at the meeting, but pressing the client for details of the conversation will probably be futile. Visual images can often be a springboard to better memory. Consequently, the lawyer can ask the client to recall as much as possible about the setting of the meeting. Questions about the setting of a meeting, for example, include:

- Where was the meeting?
- What time of day was it?
- Who was present?
- Where was everyone sitting?
- Who spoke first?

By encouraging the client to recall details about the physical setting of the meeting, the lawyer may foster recollection of the conversations during the meeting.

3.9.2   Searching for a Triggering Detail

Sometimes memory can be triggered by a single unusual detail. If the lawyer is aware of something that might trigger the client's memory, a question can be formed to make use of that detail. For example, "Isn't that the meeting when Mr. Calahan lost his temper?" or "Wasn't that meeting on your birthday?"

More often, especially at an initial interview, the client will need to be the source of the triggering detail. Whether the client remembers a detail that sparks the memory may depend on the lawyer. Any lawyer can ask the client, "Do you remember anything at all about that day? Anything unusual?" The question will not yield a lot of information unless the lawyer has the patience to wait for the client to answer, and the client feels sufficiently at ease. If the lawyer is patient and the client at ease, however, it is surprising how often this simple question can yield worthwhile information.

3.9.3 Citing Other Sources

A great deal of information—particularly where business or government is concerned—is set down in writing. A lawyer may also have information from witnesses other than the client. Often, information from these other sources can be used to refresh a client's memory. Sometimes the simplest way to restore a client's memory is to tell the client about the information available and see if the client can add anything. For example, if the client's memory about a meeting seems exhausted and the client has provided the lawyer with a copy of the minutes of the meeting, the lawyer can question the client about events that are recorded in the minutes. "Now the minutes you gave me say that this was the meeting when Mr. Calahan wanted to re-negotiate the terms of his contract. Tell me about that."

A client who has provided the lawyer with information about an event, such as minutes to a meeting, may want to defer to the minutes instead of trying to recall the meeting. It is often useful to have the client give his or her recollection of the event first, however. A lawyer in possession of an alternative source of information may also be tempted to use it as a first tool to prompt the client's memory. Typically, it is best to begin with other methods of refreshing a client's memory, since many people are reluctant to admit to a recollection at odds with a written record. Finally, lawyers should also remember that in most jurisdictions, writings used to refresh witness' recollections are subject to discovery production during litigation.

3.9.4 Sensitive Subjects

Sometimes lawyers want information that clients are reluctant to divulge. This may be information that concerns a sensitive or personal topic or this may be information that the client believes jeopardizes a position. Either way, the client may not have enough trust in the lawyer to reveal the information.

Often the best solution for the lawyer is to wait until the client feels more trust. If the lawyer does a good job fostering trust, the client may feel it is safe or appropriate to reveal the information. Sometimes postponing discussion of sensitive issues until later in the same interview will be enough to give the client confidence to speak freely. If not, the lawyer may want to wait to revisit these topics until a later meeting with the client.

This approach may not always be possible. If a client is reluctant to talk about sensitive issues, there are things a lawyer can do to put that client at ease. First, the lawyer may want to build trust by reassuring the client of the lawyer's fidelity.

> **Example:** Ms. Cullen, I understand your reluctance to talk about this issue, but I want you to know that I have a duty to keep confidential everything you tell me.

Alternatively, it may help for the lawyer to explain why it is important for the client to reveal the information:

> **Example:** Mr. Lamar, I know this isn't easy to talk about, but I need this information in order to do a good job working for you. When I sit down to talk with the other side, it's important I know as much as possible about this situation. You don't want me to be surprised.

By building trust and explaining the need for the information, it is often possible to encourage clients to talk about sensitive issues.

Think Twice

When a client seems reluctant to talk about a topic, it is easy to believe the client is hiding information—or even misrepresenting information—because "the truth" would be contrary to the client's interests. It is important to resist this conclusion at an early stage in the lawyer-client relationship. A client may have many other reasons for being reluctant to talk about something with a lawyer he or she has just met. The client may feel the information is too personal, too embarrassing, or simply none of the lawyer's business. Asking a question that suggests the lawyer believes the client is hiding adverse information can badly damage the client's trust in the lawyer and jeopardize the attorney-client relationship. It's usually better to explain your need to learn about all the facts— good and bad ones.

3.9.5   Agenda Differences

A client may feel a particular event or issue is extremely important and want to devote a great deal of time talking about that topic. This may create problems, particularly if the attorney feels that other issues or events merit more attention. An attempt to steer the client toward another subject may worsen the difficulty. The client may feel that the lawyer has underestimated the importance of the topic and resist any attempt to change the subject.

A lawyer faced with this kind of difficulty should offer reassurance that the client's concerns are taken seriously and also offer appropriate empathy. Quite often, a client will insist on continuing discussion of an emotional issue because the lawyer has not signaled any understanding of the client's distress. Once the lawyer has reassured the client, the client may feel more comfortable moving onto other issues. This technique can be coupled with an explanation about the importance of discussing additional issues and events.

> **Example:** Mr. Bingham, I understand you are very upset about the way your supervisor treated you. I know how difficult it can be to work for a boss that treats you that way. I'm glad you've told me about this problem, and I know it's something we'll talk about more. I also need to spend some time today hearing about other things that happened to you. During the half-hour we have left, can you tell me about . . . .

3.9.6   Waiting to Decide

For better or worse, quite a bit that happens in the law school classroom prompts us to make decisions quickly. This may be a good habit in the classroom, but it can be disastrous in the office. A quick decision can interfere with listening; it is hard to hear when your mind is already made up. The lawyer who keeps an open mind is the lawyer who listens best, and the lawyer who listens best is invariably the lawyer who is the most successful in obtaining information from a client.

Sometimes, a lawyer may be unable to agree with or perhaps even understand a decision that a client has made. When a client tells a lawyer about an action that seems foolish or wrong, the temptation to respond judgmentally should be resisted. The more appropriate response is to seek additional information about the context or additional information about the client. This may both foster greater understanding of the client and greater trust between the lawyer and client.

D. ELICITING DIRECTION

One of the most important things a lawyer needs from a client is direction. From the first meeting with a client through the termination of the lawyer-client relationship, a lawyer needs to build an understanding of what it is that the client needs and wants, and regularly make sure that that understanding remains accurate.

3.10 WHY IS DIRECTION IMPORTANT?

An understanding of a client's goals will help the lawyer in two ways. First, provided that the client's goal is lawful and ethical, that goal should serve as the lawyer's principal source of guidance in completing work for the client. Second, it is worthwhile for the client to articulate goals and for the lawyer and client to reach an express understanding of those goals. This will help the lawyer make later decisions about appropriate legal advice and may also help prevent the client from forming unrealistic expectations about what the lawyer can achieve.

Think Twice

Some of this may seem self-evident, but it is surprising how often a new lawyer may neglect to promptly elicit the correct direction from a client. For example, a client meets with a novice lawyer to talk about an eviction notice. The attorney begins by asking the client many questions to obtain information needed to defend against the eviction. The client grows increasingly frustrated and finally interrupts the lawyer to explain that she no longer wants to live in the apartment. It's not hard to understand how this mistake was made: the client asked for legal advice about eviction. The assumption that the client wants to avoid eviction is a natural one, but it is inappropriate. It is the lawyer's responsibility to elicit direction from the client, and the first step in eliciting that direction is explicitly asking what the client wants.

3.11   WHAT IS DIRECTION?

As discussed in the previous section, the direction that a lawyer needs from a client has a lot to do with the client's goals—what it is that the client wants or needs. These goals may have much to do with successful resolution of the matter that has prompted the client to seek legal help. On the other hand, a client may also have goals that are important for the lawyer to understand, and yet not directly tied to that matter.

3.11.1   Immediate Goals

"Immediate goals" are the desires a client has related to the solution of some particular problem or concern. Put simply, an immediate goal may be the negotiation of a particular transaction or a specific verdict in a lawsuit. A lawyer needs the client to articulate immediate goals to first determine whether they can be achieved and, if so, to guide the lawyer's activities and efforts on the client's behalf.

Immediate goals have a lot to do with the substantive outcome of the concern that brings the client to the lawyer. Sometimes the client may define the immediate goal narrowly, for example, in terms of dollars obtained, contracts formed, or documents drafted. Sometimes the client may define the immediate goal more broadly, in terms of the client's sense of a just or acceptable outcome. Often, a client will articulate an immediate goal subject to certain time constraints. For example, a client might tell a lawyer to complete a particular transaction, but only if it is possible to do so before the end of the year. The time constraint "before the end of the year" is a critical part of the client's immediate goal.

3.11.2   Overarching Goals

In addition to immediate goals, all clients also have "overarching goals." These are the goals that the client will want to achieve even after the lawyer has helped achieve the immediate goals. A client may have an overarching goal such as maximizing profit, maintaining a working relationship with the opposing party or avoiding publicity.

A lawyer needs to develop an understanding of a client's overarching goals, as well as immediate goals. Some avenues to a client's immediate goals may run afoul of overarching goals. A lawyer who fails to understand the client's overarching goals runs the risk of completing work on the client's matter seemingly successfully, only to discover the client is dissatisfied with the overall resolution.

3.11.3   Process Preferences

There may have been a time when lawyers could take for granted the legal process to be used to achieve client goals, or could make decisions about which process to use without consulting the client. Those times have come and gone. Today, clients can make more choices about legal processes and about lawyers than ever before—and today, clients are increasingly asking to make those decisions themselves.

Alternative dispute resolution and rising legal costs have certainly played a part in this. There are a growing number of business and corporate clients who not only want to decide whether to arbitrate or litigate a matter, but also want to decide whether to file a summary judgment motion or conduct exhaustive legal research. Factors other than cost also shape client process preferences.

Business clients may have preferences influenced by their vision of their own corporate style or culture or by their level of risk aversion. In much the same way, individuals may have ethical, emotional, or personal preferences with respect to particular types of legal process. For example, either a corporation or individual might object to an overly aggressive approach to litigation—not for reasons of cost, but because that approach would create unwanted ill will. A lawyer needs to talk expressly with clients about these types of issues.

Think Twice

What can go wrong with discussing goals? At some point in your career you are likely to have a client who wants you to do something that is illegal or unethical. Your

response is quick and easy: "No. Absolutely not." Why would a client ask you to do something like this? The client may not realize it's wrong; or the client's competitors may be doing the same thing; or the client may foresee great benefit from this if you are willing to take a risk. You cannot.

Or your client may want you to do something you don't want to do. And you can refuse to do it. You don't have to do a deal or resolve a dispute for clients unless you want to represent them. It's much better to learn this early on in the initial interview then later on in the relationship.

3.12   ELICITING DIRECTION FROM A CLIENT

As odd as it may seem, it is not unusual for a lawyer to fail to ask a client for direction or to delay asking for direction, to the client's—and lawyer's—detriment. Unfortunately, simply saying to a client, "By the way, what are your goals?" is unlikely to be enough.

3.12.1   Techniques for Eliciting Direction

There are three cardinal rules for eliciting direction from a client: discuss the issue expressly, broadly, and frequently.

First and foremost, a lawyer must discuss direction, goals, and preference with a client *expressly*. The lawyer's assumptions about what the client wants have questionable value, and the lawyer who acts on those assumptions invites not only client dissatisfaction but malpractice suits. A lawyer needs to know what a client wants, and the only way to find out is to ask expressly.

Second, a lawyer should discuss direction *broadly*. The client may not volunteer any information about overarching goals or process preferences. Concerned with completing transactions quickly or caught up in the heat of contentious lawsuits, it is not unusual for lawyers to discover that clients have not thought through their overarching goals. The lawyer must be sufficiently astute to raise these issues for the client's consideration. It is not enough to talk only about the client's immediate goals. A lawyer may elicit direction in much the same way information is obtained from the client: Begin with an open-ended question raising the issues and then follow up with more specific questions about immediate and overarching goals, as well as process preferences.

> **Example:** Mr. Lamar, you've told me that you want to sue your landlord to force her to make repairs to the building. Let me ask some additional questions about what is important to you. How important is it for you to remain in the building? ... Would you feel comfortable continuing to lease space from a landlord you had sued? ... You've mentioned you are extremely busy with work at your store. This lawsuit will require some of your time and attention, too. Can you spare that time right now?

The third cardinal rule is to discuss direction *frequently*. Clients' lives and businesses change; so too, do their goals and preferences. What seemed most important to the client at the initial meeting with the lawyer may later become only a secondary consideration. Some clients may volunteer information about these sorts of changes, to be sure, but it is the lawyer's responsibility to update this understanding about what it is the client wants.

3.12.2   Limits on Client Direction

It would be easier to be a lawyer if we could refer all the hard decisions to our clients. The reality is, however, that we can't. There are many decisions that a lawyer will typically make and, in fact, may be inappropriate to ask a client to make. These boundaries may differ from client to client. Some clients—particularly those with a great deal of experience dealing with lawyers—may want to give direction to the lawyer on a variety of issues that other clients prefer to leave to the lawyer's discretion.

The lawyer should elicit direction from the client, but the lawyer should not necessarily accept that direction at face value. Sometimes the client may offer direction that the lawyer believes is ethically wrong. The lawyer should not follow directions that would violate the law or the rules of professional responsibility. If the lawyer believes that the client has goals that seem to the lawyer to be unethical or immoral, then the lawyer may also wish to refuse the client's direction.

Beyond ethical reservations, the lawyer has a responsibility to alert a client if the client's overarching goals seem inconsistent with the client's immediate goals and process preferences. The lawyer also has the responsibility to "reality test" the client's immediate goals. If those immediate goals are not realistic, then the lawyer should discuss these reservations with the client. This process of client decision-making is discussed in greater depth in the next chapter, "What a Client Needs from the Lawyer."

Think Twice

All this makes sense, so why is it that these "direction" conversations with clients go awry? Consider the human dimensions. The client can be upset, angry, or downright scared, making it difficult to set aside those feelings and think and act rationally. So the client may appear to listen to what the lawyer is saying in the initial interview but then prove too troubled to process it. And some clients will be so overwhelmed by what is happening to them that they really do not want to discuss events in detail, much less contemplate what the future may hold.

These clients may feel it's easier to try and ignore it all, but in many situations, they can't so instead they try to shift this responsibility to the lawyer. Obviously, clients ought to know what they really want and need, and have a firmer understanding of those goals than their lawyers would. But sometimes clients may seem unable to articulate their goals because they can't think clearly enough, or because they think the lawyer will have a better answer.

It takes patience to probe and a reasonable degree of skepticism about what clients really mean when they say what they want or need. The thoughtful, caring lawyer will take the time to reassure them, to try and reduce the impact of their emotional malaise, and to gently help them reach a reasonable position.

E.   FORMING A BUSINESS AGREEMENT

The hardest subject for many new lawyers to discuss with clients is fees. Yet every lawyer in private practice needs to be able to talk confidently and responsibly about fees. Every lawyer—whether in private practice or not—also needs to talk with clients about the practical limitations of legal representation. Discussion and accord about these issues is necessary for a successful business agreement between lawyer and client. Section 2.6 explained fees, costs, and retainers, and is worth a review.

3.13   RESPONSIBILITY ISSUES

The business agreement between a lawyer and client needs to cover more than the payment of fees. The lawyer and the client also need to reach an understanding of issues such as:

- The identity of the individual lawyer or lawyers who will actually perform the work on the client's behalf.

- The responsibilities the client may have, such as helping to obtain necessary information or documents in the client's possession.

- The reasons for which either the client or the lawyer can terminate the agreement.

- The method by which fee disputes or other disagreements can be resolved, such as the inclusion of a pre-dispute arbitration clause.

This list is not, of course, complete. A lawyer should give attention to additional issues that need discussion and agreement at the outset of work for any new client and, in all likelihood, at the outset of new work for any existing client. These are issues that need to be considered by lawyers even when they are handling matters on a pro bono basis.

3.14   WHY IS A BUSINESS AGREEMENT WITH A CLIENT IMPORTANT?

The work lawyers do for clients is the basis of their livelihood. The business agreement is the contract between lawyer and client. Early discussion and agreement with respect to business issues will help prevent serious problems of misunderstanding and dissatisfaction during work on the client's matter, and will help make it easier for a lawyer to collect fees.

From the client's standpoint, no one wants to agree to buy anything without knowing what the cost will be. The client purchasing legal services has a right to understand the cost of those services and the contractual obligations of the attorney-client relationship. This will allow the client to make informed decisions about hiring a lawyer and will also allow the client to make more realistic decisions about immediate goals and process preferences.

3.14.1 How Should a Lawyer Discuss Business With a Client?

Many new lawyers find it difficult to talk about the business aspects of our profession with clients. A good starting point for new lawyers is to remember that a lawyer owes the client the same duties of candor and competence whether talking about the law or talking about fees. A client is entitled to open and straightforward discussion of the business aspect of the attorney-client relationship.

3.14.2 Talking About Fees and Costs

There is a wealth of literature on marketing of legal services full of suggestions about how to "sell" fee arrangements to clients. That advice varies from practice area to practice area and, fortunately, is a topic beyond the scope of this chapter. Regardless of what kind of private practice a lawyer has, however, there are three principles that should guide discussion of fees and costs:

Be candid. Explain fully and accurately the fee arrangement (hourly, contingent, flat, or a combination of these) and other costs.

Make sure the client understands this explanation.

Give the client the chance to ask questions. People paying money for services have a right to ask questions. Client questions are an opportunity to clear up possible misunderstandings that could be devastating later in the relationship.

A client has the right to expect that a lawyer will follow these three guidelines. Doing anything less invites unpleasant, and perhaps insurmountable, problems later in the attorney-client relationship.

Think Twice

For a variety of reasons, many new lawyers seem inclined to be apologetic with clients when discussing fees. A lawyer is a professional who earns a livelihood by selling legal services. There is no reason to apologize for that fact. But even good lawyers have difficulty following this advice. Why? One reason is this is a discussion about money, which can be a sensitive topic for many people. There are plenty of people who can discuss a lot of private matters, but when it comes to costs, salaries, and finances, prefer to divert the discussion to other issues.

Another reason talking about fees can be difficult is that the lawyer is interested or eager to represent the client, and worry that talking about fees may discourage the client from going forward. Perhaps the less time spent talking clearly about fees and expenses, the less chance the client will bolt to another, less expensive, lawyer.

It's no wonder that one of the most common complaints clients have with lawyers relates to fee discussions. They may rightly or wrongly blanch at some of the fees we charge, but more often than not clients complain that they didn't know what to expect. A good lawyer has to explain fees so the client understands what to expect and then re-explain them to make sure the client fully understands.

3.14.3   Express Agreement and Authorization

Before doing anything on a client's behalf, the lawyer should make certain that the client has hired the lawyer and agreed to the terms of representation. The best way to make certain of this point is to ask the client directly.

Example: Ms. Cullen, I've explained my fees to you and talked with you about my retainer agreement. I need to know if you want me to represent you. If you do, you should sign the retainer agreement.

The lawyer's notes of the meeting should also reflect this discussion and agreement.

3.14.4   Written Representation Agreement

The best way to finalize the business agreement between the client and lawyer is to put it in writing. Section 2.6 explained the requirements and advantages of doing so. A written agreement defines the scope of the lawyer's work for the client, helps the client understand the nature and cost of the lawyer's services, and reduces the chances that future billing problems will arise.

F.   THE FIRST MEETING WITH A CLIENT

First impressions are important. The first meeting between the lawyer and a new client is the lawyer's opportunity to assess the client and determine whether it makes sense to accept representation of the client. It is the client's opportunity to learn whether it makes sense to hire a lawyer and whether this is the lawyer to hire.

3.15   PREPARING FOR THE MEETING

A lawyer usually does not have a great deal of information about a new client prior to the first meeting. Typically, the lawyer or someone from the lawyer's office will have spoken to the client to arrange the time and place for the first meeting. During this conversation, the client may have given some information about legal concerns. Some lawyers have legal assistants screen clients more thoroughly before the first meeting. If this is the case, then the lawyer can make a more detailed plan for the initial interview. If not, there are still things the lawyer can and should do to prepare for the first meeting.

Review available information about the client. At a minimum, the lawyer will know the client's name, and this gives the lawyer a basis for making a preliminary check for conflicts of interest by reviewing past and current files. Many lawyers make a routine practice of searching for information about a client on the web prior to a first meeting. Some of your clients will have looked you up on the web as well.

Review available information about the client's concern. The lawyer will typically have some information about the reason the client is seeking legal advice. With this information, the lawyer could, for example, briefly research the basic elements of the legal claim, as well as the common defenses to the claim.

Plan questions. With some information about the client's concern, the lawyer can begin to outline the topics that will need to be covered during the meeting.

Create an agenda. For new lawyers especially, it is helpful to outline not only topics for information-gathering, but all other issues to be covered during the first meeting. The lawyer can look over the retainer agreement and any other documents the client will need to review during the first meeting.

3.16   THE SETTING FOR THE FIRST MEETING

Part of successful preparation for any meeting with a client is arranging to have an appropriate place to talk with the client. Often, the client will meet at the lawyer's office. This is undoubt-edly more convenient for the lawyer, but may be inconvenient or pose difficulties for the client. If it does, the lawyer can meet at the client's home, office, or some mutually convenient place. Wherever the meeting occurs, the lawyer should make sure that the interview will take place at a location with:

Privacy. It will be difficult to talk with a client in any location where there is a chance of being overheard. Like-wise, the meeting will be more successful if the chances of interruption are minimized. For example, if possible, the lawyer should avoid telephone calls, text messages, or other interruptions during the interview.

A place for both the client and lawyer to sit and write. A lawyer can use a laptop or pad to write on if conducting a meeting at a client's place. In-office interviews eliminate this concern, but create questions about who should sit where. Some lawyers believe that sitting behind a desk during an interview seems remote or even pompous. They may sit on the same side of the desk as the client, offer the client a seat at the side of the desk, or conduct the interview at a table. Other lawyers feel that this is too informal or invasive and may be intimidating to the client. Lawyers should be thoughtful about these issues, and there is probably no single solution that is best. The key is to provide a comfortable environment that will allow *both* the client and the lawyer to do the work needed during the meeting.

Materials to keep notes. Few of us have photographic memories, so note keeping is a necessity for most. Clients may also wish to take notes during the meeting, so it is a good idea to keep a spare pad and pen or pencil available for client use.

Copies of any necessary documents. The lawyer should be certain to have a copy of the retainer agreement, as well as any other needed forms such as information releases.

G.   STRUCTURING THE MEETING

3.17   A SUGGESTION FOR STRUCTURE

Different clients have different concerns, and good lawyers keep their plans and agendas flexible to accommodate these differences. Consequently, you can use this list as a starting point for preparing an agenda appropriate for the client you are interviewing:

1. *Introduction.* After welcoming the client, the lawyer can briefly describe the agenda for the meeting and the amount of time that is available. This gives the client a sense of what will happen. Many clients also appreciate a brief discussion of fees, so they at least know whether they are being charged for the meeting.

2. *Capsule description.* The lawyer can ask the client for a brief overview of the reason the client is seeking legal advice.

3. *Brief review of immediate goals.* The lawyer can then also ask the client for a brief overview of what the client would like the lawyer to do about this concern.

4. *Step-by-step chronology.* After the lawyer has a concise picture of the client's concerns and goals, the client and lawyer can then develop a more complete narrative of relevant the relevant events or circumstances. When appropriate, the lawyer can recap this narrative.

5. *Probing via "flashback" and "slow-motion."* The lawyer can then seek additional information on a topic-by-topic basis.

6. *More complete discussion of direction.* Once the lawyer has obtained the necessary information, the lawyer and client can have a fuller discussion of immediate and over-arching goals, as well as process preferences.

7. *"Next-step" planning.* At this stage, it usually makes sense for the lawyer to give the client some suggestions about what work the lawyer needs to do next or would like to do next. It is usually too soon to give the client a complete description of legal options, but the client needs to have some sense of what the lawyer can do.

8. *Business agreement.* The lawyer can explain the fee structure and agreement, and give the client a chance to ask any questions. If the client chooses to retain the lawyer, then the lawyer can obtain authority from the client to do "next-step" work.

9. *Arrange next contact.* No client should leave a lawyer's office without knowing when the next communication with the lawyer will be. After talking about what will be done next, the lawyer should make a commitment to the client about the next contact.

10. *Explain what will happen.* The lawyer needs to explain what the lawyer will do before the next contact, what the clients should or should not do, what events may transpire, or what else may happen. Lawyers cannot often immediately solve client problems or fully answer all their questions, but client concerns can be reduced.

11. *Provide appropriate legal advice.* While the first inter-view is typically too soon to fully address a client's legal concern, lawyers may be able to provide some advice and a good deal of legal information to a client during the first conference.

12. *Appreciate the experience.* It's easy to forget our earlier advice to enjoy your life as a lawyer. Remember that your new client is a person who provides you with an opportunity and a challenge, and not that you just have yet another problem to deal with or resolve. As your professional life fills up with clients, it is harder to take a moment and appreciate

the honor and privilege it is to be a lawyer. It's worth taking that moment.

Think Twice

In our experience, these are the two most common mistakes new lawyers make during initial interviews:

One: Not encouraging the client to talk during the early stages of the interview. Understandably concerned with building trust and obtaining necessary information, many new lawyers spend far more time talking than the client during the first portion of the interview. As indicated above, many clients will appreciate some preliminary guidance from the lawyer about the interview process, but it is important to give the client an opportunity to talk.

Two: Failing to give the client any reassurance, particularly near the end of the interview. We know that we cannot give our clients guarantees or make promises about results. Frequently, in an attempt to avoid raising client expectations, new lawyers will conclude an interview without any words of assurance or even consolation. It's far better to tell clients that you take their concerns seriously and will do your best to help them.

Chapter Four
COUNSELING: WHAT CLIENTS NEED FROM US

Bromidic though it may sound, some questions don't have answers, which is a terribly difficult lesson to learn.

—*Katherine Graham*

A. WORKING AS A LAWYER: A RANGE OF PERSPECTIVES

Chapter Three discussed what a lawyer needs from the client. In this chapter, the focus shifts to what a client needs from the lawyer. As the lawyer-client relationship develops beyond the initial stages, the lawyer's role becomes more active and, consequently, the client expects to see tangible benefits from the lawyer's services. One of the most important things a client expects from a lawyer is sound legal advice. This chapter discusses the process of advising clients and assisting clients in making decisions.

4.1 WHAT IS LEGAL ADVICE?

When a client seeks legal advice from a lawyer, the client has the right to expect the lawyer to do four things:

- Make an assessment of the client's legal problem or concern.

- Suggest options for dealing with that problem or concern.

- Predict the advantages and disadvantages associated with each of those options, including the likelihood of success.

- Assist the client in making decisions about those options.

B. ASSESSMENT

Clients seek legal assistance for two primary reasons: they have an idea or plan and seek legal help to pursue this objective

---

95

or they have a legal problem that needs resolving. Before providing the proper legal advice, the lawyer needs to identify the legal issues or concerns.

Clients who come to a lawyer seeking advice often have related problems and concerns that a lawyer can't address. An injured client has physical problems and perhaps mental or emotional problems, as well as financial problems. A business client may well have a need for accounting and marketing information. At times there will be a bright line between a problem that calls for a lawyer's help and a problem that needs the attention of another profession, but there will be occasions when clients may not realize the complexity of their problems or projects and may believe the lawyer can resolve everything. In addition to identifying specific legal issues, the counseling lawyer may also need to identify other issues and recommend the client seek help from others, or refer the client to other professionals. The lawyer can then work at the same time on related issues or work with other professionals to help the client.

4.2   WHAT IS ASSESSMENT?

The process of assessment involves more than listing the issues of concern to the client. Of course, the client and lawyer must work together to identify these issues, but the lawyer must also work to do two additional things. First, the lawyer must determine which issues need legal attention. Second, the lawyer must determine whether it is possible to represent the client with respect to all of these legal issues, or whether there are issues on the list beyond the lawyer's professional capability.

Clients seldom arrive at the lawyer's office with a detailed list of legal problems, accurately categorized by type, all aligned perfectly with the lawyer's area of expertise. More typically, clients come to a lawyer with either a goal they would like achieved or a description of problem they would like resolved. In either situation, the client's concern may potentially trigger several legal, as well as non-legal concerns. The lawyer needs to identify and separate these issues and ultimately make a decision with the client regarding which problems or projects will be the subject of the lawyer's advice.

Example: Ms. Overholt, you've told me that you're planning on purchasing this land and building a distillery. You have concerns about negotiating and drafting the purchase agreement. I have experience in real estate law, and can help you in that area. It seems to me that you may also need a license to run a distillery. While I'm not familiar with licensing procedures for distilleries, our firm has the expertise to help you. I'd like to talk with another lawyer here in our firm who can help with that situation.

Example: Mr. Bingham, you've told me that your employer fired you. It sounds like you may have a claim for wrongful termination, and we should talk about that further. You've also mentioned that you're very concerned about being unemployed. I wish I could do something that would help you with that concern right away, but of course I can't. You may want to file a claim for unemployment benefits and talk with some job counselors.

This stage of assessment may identify some issues that are obviously legal ones, and some that are just as obviously non-legal. It's the issues that fall in between that create concerns about what a lawyer can or should do. An effective way to handle these questionable areas is to raise them with the clients. After all, it's their life and they should be made aware of their options and what they can or should do.

Think Twice

That all seems pretty straightforward: talk to the client and let the client decide. But some cases raise delicate and sensitive issues that make it difficult to discuss assessments. How is it best to handle the married couple who were both physically injured in an auto accident but one of whom has an addiction problem. Or, the CEO who seeks legal advice on behalf of the company but who is engaged in sexual harassment and appears to be in need of counseling. Some clients will be open to a wide-ranging assessment discussion and some will only want to focus on their purely legal issues. As a practical matter, it may be up to the lawyer to decide what is appropriate to discuss, but, if in doubt, all issues should be raised with the client, as highlighted below.

4.2.1   Why Is Assessment Important?

There are three reasons why assessment is an important part of legal advice.

First, assessment identifies the legal issues that become the subject of the lawyer's representation of the client. Identification of these issues helps frame the business agreement between the lawyer and the client and also serves to focus the direction the lawyer will need from the client. This certainly does not mean that the lawyer should be blind to all other legal concerns. It does mean, however, that the work the lawyer chooses to do for the client should be oriented toward the resolution of these identified issues.

Second, assessment also identifies other legal issues that may need attention from another lawyer with a different area of expertise. No lawyer is capable of handling every brand of legal deal or dispute. Consequently, sometimes the most helpful advice a lawyer can give a client is a referral to another lawyer.

Third, it is important for lawyers to expressly recognize some of the problems that a client mentions even when there are no good legal solutions for those problems. One of the most important things you can tell a client is: "You do have a problem, but I'm afraid it's not the kind of problem a lawyer can help you with." Expressly recognizing a client's non-legal problem is one way to communicate empathy, and a lawyer's failure to at least mention the problem may make the lawyer seem cold and inhuman. In addition, even though it may seem perfectly obvious to the lawyer, it is helpful for a lawyer to expressly tell a client that he or she will not be helping with a particular problem because it is not a legal problem. Making this kind of statement will help avoid client dissatisfaction in the future and may prompt the client to seek alternative solutions for the problem.

Think Twice

Sometimes new lawyers believe that they have no responsibility to tell clients about legal problems unless the client asks for assistance with those problems, particularly if those problems are outside the scope of the lawyer's professional competence. This view is extremely short-sighted. An internist who detects symptoms of glaucoma has a responsibility to refer the patient to an ophthalmologist. In the same way, a litigator who "diagnoses" a potential tax problem should make sure the client is aware of the problem and make an appropriate referral. Failure to identify these other legal concerns is not simply a disservice to a client; it may also be malpractice.

4.2.2 How Should a Lawyer Assess a Client's Legal Concerns?

Capable and effective assessment depends on a lawyer's ability to identify problems both inside and outside the lawyer's particular area of expertise. This means that it is a lawyer's responsibility to be familiar with a broad range of legal issues, and to keep abreast of new case law, legislation, and legal developments in the jurisdiction. Good assessment skills depend on more than the lawyer's store of knowledge, however. These skills are also dependent on the lawyer's ability to listen and talk to clients about legal problems and concerns.

4.3   LISTENING TO THE CLIENT

As is true when interviewing a client, careful listening is also an extremely important factor in making a competent assessment of a client's legal concerns. Listening would be easy if clients came to our office and said things like: "I have a breach of warranty claim and a possible quantum meruit claim I'd like you to take a look at." They don't, and consequently a lawyer's listening needs to involve more than making an accurate and complete list of the problems the clients mention. A client will, however, often make a statement about what the client believes the legal problem or concern to be.

The first step in careful listening is to take this statement seriously and discuss it with the client. Knowledgeable clients who work with lawyers frequently may be better able to identify and explain their legal issues. Other clients will be unable to do anything more than describe what happened or what they hope will happen.

The second step in careful listening is to take the client's statement as nothing more than what it is—the client's best guess about the legal problem. Relying on the client's statement as an accurate assessment of legal needs may be disastrous, no matter how experienced the client. Clients cannot fairly be expected to identify all relevant legal concerns and expressly ask for help with each. The lawyer should listen to the client's narrative description of events and goals and determine if there are issues that need attention, even though the client has not identified these issues as concerns.

> **Example:** Ms. Montoya, you've told me about the car accident you had last month and the problems you've had at your job as a result. You said you wanted to bring a lawsuit against the other driver, and we've talked about that. It also sounds to me like your employer has asked you to do work that has made your injury worse. I'd like to talk with you about that, too.

Identifying legal issues should seem like a familiar skill—it is one of the abilities most frequently tested on law school exams. And like answering a law school exam, a lawyer should, at a minimum, mention each additional legal issue to the client. Whether the lawyer undertakes to advise the client about every legal concern depends on the client, the nature of the concern, and the lawyer's own expertise.

4.4   TALKING TO THE CLIENT

Careful listening is critical, but it is seldom enough. It will almost always be necessary for the lawyer to elicit additional information from a client about problems the client has mentioned, as well as problems the lawyer suspects may exist but the client has not mentioned. Additional probing is likely to be essential.

> **Example:** Now Ms. Montoya, when I asked you about your earnings the last three years, you mentioned you didn't have any tax returns. This is something I need to ask you about.

Did you mean that you didn't have copies of tax returns or did you mean that you didn't file tax returns for those years?

Needless to say, unmentioned legal problems may involve sensitive or embarrassing issues. A lawyer should deal with these concerns carefully, as with any sensitive issues.

C. OPTIONS

4.5 CLIENTS NEED CHOICES

In many situations, the difference between good lawyering and adequate lawyering lies in the ability of the lawyer to generate additional options for the client. The ability to generate choices for clients can spring from many sources. Many lawyers rely on a solid knowledge of the law coupled with years of experience in practice. Novice lawyers must substitute thorough research and creative thinking for experience, supplemented with a willingness to seek help when needed from more experienced lawyers.

Think Twice

The generation of options requires the lawyer to not only know the law and the client's goals, but also to be reasonably creative about what best serves the client's interests. Often, the lawyer can generate a potential "list" of options and begin to determine which need to be explained to the client. This explanation process can also be quite challenging because it requires the lawyer to explain the options neutrally and accurately.

4.6 PRESENTING OPTIONS TO THE CLIENT

A client cannot be expected to make an effective choice among options unless the client truly understands those options. Put another way, even the most creative and productive thinking will be of little use to the client if the lawyer does a bad job explaining the options born of that thinking. The acid test for presenting options to a client is this: Has the lawyer given the client enough information so that the client can be an effective decision maker? If not, then the lawyer needs to expand the explanation of that option.

This section reviews some of the most important points a lawyer needs to raise when talking with a client about options and choices. One of the most important items is not included, however. A lawyer not only needs to describe options, a lawyer must also give the client some sense of the likelihood of success of those options. This topic is covered separately at Section 4.7.

4.6.1 Explain Each Option Fully

Having created a brilliant list of options for a client, it is not enough for the lawyer to simply name the options and ask the client to make a selection. One of the easiest mistakes to make while describing an option is to assume that the client understands the intricacies of the legal process. If a lawyer is listing "litigation" as an option, then the lawyer needs to explain what that option means for this client in this case—and the lawyer needs to make that explanation in a language comprehensible to the client.

We all know enough not to throw around terms like "res ipsa loquitur" or "original issue discounts" when talking with clients who are not experts in the law. This is straight legalese, and clients resent having it poured down their throats. But we also need to remember that "legalese lite" can be equally offensive and baffling to clients. A lawyer's description of "litigation" may do a client little good if the description is full of terms like "work product" or "summary judgment," or based on inaccurate assumptions.

> **Example:** Mr. Lamar, if we sue your landlord she will probably want to take your deposition. You've told me you've never had your deposition taken so let me explain what a deposition is. I will go with you to the deposition which is likely to be held at the office of your landlord's lawyer. The lawyer will ask you questions about what you know. There won't be a judge there, but there will be a court reporter who will take down all the lawyer's questions and all your answers. You'll be under oath to tell the truth. The deposition may take several hours. I will explain everything in more detail later when I prepare you for your deposition.

It is of course critical that lawyers avoid talking down to clients. Condescension is also offensive, and some clients have a great deal of familiarity with any number of legal terms of art. A client who knows what a deposition is does not need a full explanation of the process. What we do recommend is that the lawyer remember who the client is and what the client's level of experience is, and make sure that the description of options is appropriate for that client. One of the best ways to help that happen is to invite questions from the client about each option described.

Think Twice

It's easy to forget that using legal terms becomes second nature to us very quickly. We have seen a new lawyer tell a client that if the defense to an eviction was not successful, the sheriff would come with a "writ of execution," and watched as the client's eyes widened in horror. A client may feel embarrassed to ask for the definition of a legal term. Or they may have different definitions of "legal" terms. Another novice lawyer asked a client if she had a lease. To the client, a lease was a formal year-long written agreement; to the lawyer, it meant any type of lease term. Make sure you and your client both have the same understanding in mind and that your client knows you welcome questions about any words you use.

4.6.2   Explain How the Option Fits the Goals

Clients also need to hear why the lawyer believes a particular option is a realistic choice for the client. The lawyer should take the time to explain how the option fits with the client's immediate and overarching goals and the client's process preferences. This may seem obvious to the lawyer, but it may not be as immediately apparent to the client. It is also helpful for the lawyer to give this explanation, because it gives the client an excellent opportunity to correct any misapprehensions the lawyer may have about the client's goals.

Example: Ms. Xiong, I've told you what arbitration is. Let me explain why I think it may be an option for you. You've said that it is important to you to resolve this dispute quickly, and you feel that any further negotiation with your tenant would be a waste of time. One of the advantages of arbitration is that it usually takes much less time than a lawsuit and is less costly.

4.6.3   Talk Openly About the Downside

Clients also need to hear about an option's disadvantages. These disadvantages, drawbacks, and downsides must be discussed openly and completely before the client makes a decision. Lawyers need to remember that the client's definition of a disadvantage may not coincide with the lawyer's own. For example, a client may believe that disclosure of personal medical history is enormously invasive and embarrassing. The lawyer may have considered the production of medical records as a fact of life in litigation, and failed to talk about it with the client. Complete discussion of client goals and complete description of options will help avoid these kinds of problems.

> **Example:** One of the problems with suing the coal company is that lawsuits are public. If we sue the coal company, Mr. Peevyhouse, your neighbors could find out about the lawsuit and the problems you had with the coal company. Information about your lawsuit will be accessible on-line and might even be reported in the newspaper or on television. Publicity could be helpful, but I can see it might cause problems for you. We need to talk about that.

4.6.4   How Much Will It Cost? How Long Will It Take?

No client should ever have to raise these questions. A lawyer should give a client as full and accurate estimate as possible of the cost of an option and the amount of time the option will take to complete. Without this information, a client cannot make effective choices. To be sure, it will seldom be the situation, that a lawyer will know the precise answers to these questions. The client needs to know that the lawyer's answers are estimates, and if those estimates are little more than professional guesses then the client needs to know that too.

> **Example:** Mr. Peevyhouse, I can't tell you exactly how long a lawsuit might take. It may take two years or more before we can go to trial, and if we win and the coal company appeals, it may take another year or even two before you get a final decision from the courts. Now, there are things we

will try to do to speed the process. We can try to convince the company to settle, or we can try to convince the court to decide in your favor without a trial. But if we decide to sue the coal company, I want you to understand that it may take a very long time.

When it comes to costs, more and more clients are insisting on something more than guesses, however. Clients today are far more sensitive to issues relating to legal fees and far more knowledgeable. Many institutional clients, such as insurance companies or corporations, insist on detailed estimates of fees before agreeing to hire counsel. One lawyer might choose to be responsive to this request and view it as an opportunity to involve the client in making decisions about the legal work. Another lawyer might see this kind of client concern as a nuisance. It will be easy for the client to choose between the two.

Think Twice

So why is it that a recurring complaint by clients is that they were later surprised by unanticipated fees or negative results? Why didn't the lawyer discuss those matters? At the beginning of the client relationship, the lawyer has a tendency to be supportive of the client's case and to avoid talking about how expensive the work may become, in part, to avoid losing the client to a less costly, more optimistic lawyer. You don't want to unnecessarily scare a client, but you do need to be open and frank about options and costs.

D. PREDICTIONS

Not all options are equal. Some fit better with a client's goals, some entail fewer disadvantages, and some are more likely to succeed. One of the most important things a client needs to know is which options are more likely to produce successful results. For the client to be an effective decision maker, the lawyer needs to provide this information.

4.7 PREDICTING SUCCESS

Lawyers cannot write guarantees, and almost all clients understand and accept this. Even the most experienced lawyer cannot give a client a truly accurate assessment of the odds of a particular option resulting in a successful outcome. Clients do need information about an option's relative likelihood of success, and at least some of this information must come from the lawyer.

When lawyers assess an option's likelihood of success there are a wide variety of factors to take into account:

- Has the option proved successful in similar situations in the past? Does case law suggest the option is likely to be viewed favorably by the courts or other decision makers?

- Has the option been successfully used in other transactions or deals?

- Does the option seem to produce an equitable result? Does it seem fair? More equitable than other alternatives?

- Does the option seem grounded in good public policy?

- Who is likely to oppose the option? Are the opponents willing to compromise? Is their opposition founded on strong legal, equitable, or policy arguments?

Weighing these factors to produce an assessment of the likelihood of success is an art, and it is an art largely learned in the studio of experience. A new lawyer may want to double-check his or her assessments with another, more experienced lawyer before giving those predictions to the client. Even an inexperienced lawyer, however, can help a client weigh these factors objectively to estimate which options are relatively more likely to produce successful results, and to estimate whether chances of success are fairly good or fairly remote. All lawyers should remember that their client's views on some of the factors influencing success (are opponents willing to compromise, for instance) may be more useful than the lawyer's own.

4.7.1 Describing Success

An estimate of the likelihood of success is not enough. A client also needs to hear a description of success. Too often, lawyers fail to give clients the information necessary to understand what success means. Civil litigation is a perfect example of this problem.

There is nothing like the thrill of winning a jury trial—for the trial lawyer. Many clients, however, find civil litigation and a verdict at trial quite disappointing. Why? Part of the explanation is that clients are strongly motivated by justice, and even a successful verdict at trial may not give a client a satisfying experience of justice. Part of the explanation is that often a civil jury verdict does not result in any immediate tangible benefit for a client. Victorious defendants face the possibility of appeal; victorious plaintiffs face the possibility of appeal and the difficulty of collecting judgment.

This doesn't mean that litigation isn't a good option for clients. Sometimes it is. It does mean that part of what a lawyer needs to do is describe what success means. The client needs to hear a description of the immediate results success may yield, and the client also needs to hear a description of the impact success may have on the client's goals.

Very few legal solutions fix all of a client's problems. Most legal solutions do not achieve client goals, instead they make achievement of those goals easier or possible. Clients who do not understand this limited quality of legal success have difficulty making effective choices. For example, many good settlements have been passed over by clients who mistakenly believed that successful verdicts would bring a greater sense of justice and vindication.

Think Twice

Once again, it's all too easy to avoid candid predictions or to say one thing but be heard saying something else. The client may well ask and ask again: "Well, fine, but tell me whether I really do have a good case?" The lawyer may wish to avoid undermining the client's confidence, and be tempted to agree that the case is a good one. The danger is that the client interprets that to mean that the lawyer will win the case, which is not what the lawyer intended to say. The lawyer and client need to have an open discussion so that both understand each other and the probabilities of success, as discussed further below.

4.8   DEVELOPING A LANGUAGE OF PREDICTION

The language of prediction needs to balance competing concerns of accuracy and flexibility. Clients want a lawyer's predictions to be as close to certain as possible, because clients have to make difficult choices and they want as much assurance as possible that their decisions are correct. Lawyers want flexibility because lawyers make predictions in a world where outcomes depend on variables that lawyers cannot always control or even identify. Often, a discussion about prediction results in the client pressing for more certainty than the lawyer has given and the lawyer creating more flexibility by hedging on the original answer. This kind of discussion can be frustrating for both the lawyer and the client.

4.8.1   Establish the Necessity of Flexibility

A lawyer can avoid this dynamic by telling the client that accurate predictions are not possible, and explaining why that is so. Some clients may need to hear this message more than once, but every client should hear this message before any detailed discussion of the likelihood of any option's success.

> **Example:** Ms. Traver, you've asked me whether you think the marketing company will accept our licensing offer. I can't tell you the answer to that question because I don't know the answer. It may depend on whether the company would prefer an outright purchase to a licensing arrangement. That's not something we know right now. That being said, I can tell you . . . .

If the lawyer establishes why flexibility is necessary at the beginning of the discussion, it will help prevent later hedging that is troubling to the client.

4.8.2   Give the Client Reasonably Definite Information

Telling a client "There is a 43.6 percent chance of winning this lawsuit" would be ridiculous. Lawyers cannot make predictions to that level of certainty. On the other hand, telling a client "I have no idea whether you'll win this suit, your guess is as good as mine" is unfair to the client. Lawyers can make better predictions than that, and have a duty to provide the client with reasonably definite predictions that the client can use to make decisions.

One area where lawyers can offer reasonably definite information is the relative ranking of options. A lawyer may not be able to quantify the exact odds of success, but the lawyer should be able to give the client information about which of a set of options is most likely to yield success.

> **Example:** We can make the offer now or wait. I can't predict the exact odds of our offer being accepted. I can tell you, though, that our offer is more likely to be accepted now than it would be if we made it after two more months of negotiation. Here's why I believe that. . . .

In most situations, a lawyer can also give a client reasonably definite information about whether chances of success are good or remote.

> **Example:** I think there is a reasonable chance that we will win this motion. There are some valid reasons why we should not lose. Here's why I believe that. . . .

Explaining the factors underlying the prediction gives the client a basis for assessing the accuracy of the prediction.

Think Twice

It can be hard to say no to a client, and a client may, of course, push for a more definitive prediction. Before quantifying any prediction, a lawyer should consider whether the answer will really be sufficiently accurate to improve the client's decision-making ability. If the lawyer believes a more exact prediction is possible, the lawyer may want to give the client a range of probabilities.

> *What are our chances of winning the appeal? I can't tell you exactly. I can tell you that I think our chances are better than one in five, I don't think our chances are as good as one in three. This appellate court has reversed similar cases to ours. I believe our chances depend on . . . .*

Identifying the factors that may determine the outcome will give the client a greater ability to assess the prediction.

E. MAKING DECISIONS

4.9   THE LAWYER'S ROLE IN DECISION MAKING

There is a great deal of writing about the lawyer's involvement in client decision making. Some lawyers believe that it is dangerous for a lawyer to make suggestions to a client because the client will be swayed by the lawyer's recommendation, and substitute the lawyer's judgment for the client's own. Others believe clients are largely incapable of making their own decisions about complicated legal matters and it is the lawyer's duty to "guide" the client to the right decision.

This issue of lawyer recommendations has taken a central position in what is and what is not appropriate client counseling. We believe that often the central question is not who should make the decision—or even whether the lawyer can make a recommendation to clients. The central question should be whether the lawyer has provided the information, opportunity, and time necessary for the client to be an effective decision maker.

Our experience and our colleagues' experience—in a wide variety of practice settings with corporate clients, with indigent clients, with small businesses—leads us to believe that a client who is an effective decision maker is capable of listening to a lawyer's recommendations without being bowled over. Our experience also leads us to believe that with appropriate information from the lawyer—information about assessment, options, and predictions—most clients can be effective decision makers.

Make no mistake, we believe that clients need to make decisions for themselves. They know, or should know what is best for them. It can be preposterous for a lawyer to presume what is best for a client. However, clients may find themselves in situations—legally, emotionally, financially—that limits their ability to make a wise decision.

In the course of a lawyer's work on any given matter, it is likely that there will be a wide variety of decisions that need to be made. In general, the more serious the decision and the more central the decision to achievement of the client's goals, then the greater the need will be for the client to make the decision. The less important or critical, the more likely it is appropriate for the lawyer to effectively decide, especially on procedural issues.

4.10 CLIENT DECISIONS, LAWYER DECISIONS

Clients will need to make decisions for themselves, but should they be expected to make all the decisions? Certainly not. In the course of handling a client's legal problem or concern, there are some decisions that are clearly the lawyer's responsibility. Typically, there are additional decisions that the client will wish to delegate to the lawyer.

The line between lawyer decisions and client decisions is neither straight nor unvarying. It is easy to articulate the types of decisions that fall far from the line on either side. For example, typically, the client needs to choose whether or not to file a lawsuit. The client needs to choose whether or not to accept an offer to close a deal. Some authors have characterized these decisions as strategic. These are the types of decisions the client must make to direct the lawyer's work.

On the other side of the line are the decisions lawyers can make on their own. Some authors have described these decisions as tactical. A lawyer will typically decide, for example, how to cross-examine a witness or when to make a counter-offer during face-to-face negotiations. Often clients may have little or no input into these types of decisions.

Closer to the line, it becomes harder to say whether a decision is the lawyer's to make or the client's. Where that line is drawn will often depend on the client's view of the lawyer's role. A client who has hired a lawyer to be a technician may want the lawyer to make all decisions within the lawyer's area of expertise and ask for very little lawyer input on matters outside the area of the lawyer's technical competence. On the other hand, a client who wants the lawyer to serve as counselor may welcome more participation from the lawyer with respect to the entire range of decisions the client needs to make.

These are issues that each lawyer must sort out with each client. Though this sorting process must continue throughout the course of representation of the client, it makes sense to discuss some of these issues with the client during the early stages of representation because this will help clarify the client's expectations and help define the work the lawyer will do.

Think Twice

A consistent pattern that emerges throughout the entire client counseling process is the need for ongoing and even repetitive discussions between the client and the lawyer. Why repetitive? Because clients change their mind, the costs and expenses involved in the deal or dispute increase, the focus of the client wanes as a deal or dispute drags on, and other matters become as or more important in a client's life. Revisiting past discussions to make sure the client still is interested in the same future outcomes is a wise counseling approach.

4.11   HELPING THE CLIENT REACH A CONCLUSION

Typically, during the early stages of representation, the lawyer will need the client to make a decision directing the lawyer to follow one course of action rather than another. By the time this point is reached, the lawyer should have given the client sufficient information so that the client can act as an effective decision maker. The lawyer should have given the client an assessment of the legal position and described various options for the client, including the cost and likelihood of success of each option.

At this stage, some clients are ready to choose one or more of the options. On the other hand, some clients may be uncertain, unable to select an option. If so, the lawyer may be able to assist the client in making a decision. As a matter progresses, the client will typically have to make other decisions. The process the client and lawyer have used to make decisions, and decide who makes what decisions, early in a matter may form the basis for decision-making later on. The following sections describe some of the techniques a lawyer can use to help a client make a decision.

4.11.1   Match Goals and Options

One of the most useful things a lawyer can do during the decision-making process is to match options with client goals and preferences. Usually a particular legal option will be more likely help the client achieve one goal, and less likely to help achieve another. A different option may be more likely to help the client achieve this other goal. Matching options with goals can help the client make a decision. It may also help clarify misunderstandings the lawyer has about the client's goals, and help sharpen the lawyer's sense of the relative importance the client attaches to the different goals and preferences.

> **Example:** Mr. Peevyhouse, you've told me that you would like to recover as much money from the coal company as possible. Suing the company for fraud is probably the option that gives you the best chance of recovering the most money from the company. On the other hand, you've also told me that you want to finish this matter just as soon as possible. Trying to negotiate a better settlement is likely to take much less time than pursuing a lawsuit to trial. . . .

Think Twice

We don't mean to suggest that this option process goes smoothly or even easily. Some clients will change their mind during the same interview with you; others will quickly decide, perhaps prematurely, and later find it difficult to tell you they are really unsure what to do; and others will need time and more time to decide what they want. You'll need to help them through this process with patience and understanding.

4.11.2   Shortening the List of Options

Some clients find it difficult to pick a single option from a list of many. These clients are, however, often able to strike some options off the list. Shortening or winnowing down the list in this way can help decision-making because it will focus the client's attention on the remaining options.

Some lawyers, reluctant to have clients make decisions too quickly, refrain from asking the client to select a single option. Instead, these lawyers ask the client to strike unacceptable options, and then talk further with the client about the remaining choices. This may give the lawyer a better chance to learn about the client's goals and preferences, and gives the client an opportunity to make more considered decisions.

4.11.3 Reframe the Choice

Once a list of options has been narrowed to two or three, it is frequently helpful to reframe the client's choice. Rather than asking the client to choose between two legal courses of action, the lawyer can identify the options with the client goals they serve and ask the client to choose between the goals.

> **Example:** Mr. Peevyhouse, we need to decide between going ahead with a lawsuit or trying to negotiate a settlement. I think the choice you need to make is between your feeling that you want to have this over and done with quickly and your hope for a larger recovery. You need to decide which of those goals is more important to you.

Reframing the choice this way usually helps clients clarify their own understanding of their goals and then reach a decision. Reframing the choice this way also illustrates why this is a decision the client must make and the lawyer cannot.

4.12 CHOOSE TWO FOR NOW

The discussion of decision-making is written with the assumption that when a client makes a choice, the client is selecting one course of action, one single option. This is sometimes true, but often it is possible for a lawyer to follow one course of action and reserve another as a backup plan or even pursue several courses of action simultaneously. Obviously, if this is the situation, it makes no sense to press the client to choose a single option. The lawyer may need to explain that pursuing multiple courses of action may, however, make accomplishment of one of the options less likely.

> **Example:** Mr. Hakkim, we can go ahead and file the lawsuit against the company and then try to negotiate a settlement. It may be that filing the lawsuit will make the company more willing to negotiate a settlement. In this case, I think it may make settlement more difficult. . . .

Lawyers also need to remember that client decisions may not last forever. Lives change, business plans change, and when they do, clients change their minds, as mentioned previously. This is one reason that it is important to remember, as discussed in Chapter Three, that obtaining direction from a client is a process that continues throughout the course of representation. It is also a reason to build in plenty of flexibility into any option the client and lawyer decide to pursue.

Think Twice

A lawyer who recommends a decision to a client must keep the client's goals and preferences foremost in mind. That's not easily done. Abraham Maslow observed that if the only tool you have is a hammer, then every problem starts to look like a nail. It's also true that all problems start to look like nails if the tool you like using best is a hammer. Lawyers need to be particularly mindful of this phenomenon. If a negotiated settlement is the option that works best for a client, the lawyer who loves trial work needs to take care not to let that love influence the recommendations given a client. And the negotiating lawyer who fears going to trial needs to have a law partner or another retained lawyer available to try the case.

F. PREPARING FOR THE MEETING

Clients come to lawyers seeking legal advice and they usually hope to obtain it just as soon as possible. Sometimes it is possible to give clients the advice they seek at the first meeting with the client. More often, the lawyer will need additional time for investigation, planning, and thinking. When this is the case, it will be necessary to have a subsequent meeting with the client.

A meeting to advise a client is, in some ways, no different from any other meeting with a client. You may want to review the discussion in Chapter Three about the first meeting with a client, if you didn't memorize it yet. There is no standard formula for a meeting to advise a client, but we do offer the following suggestions for preparing for this type of meeting.

4.13 WHAT A LAWYER NEEDS FROM THE CLIENT

Seek information, direction, a business agreement, and trust—just like we suggest in Chapter Three. Without information and direction, it will not be possible for the lawyer to think productively about client options. A business agreement is necessary because developing options for a client may take a substantial amount of time and effort. It is important for the lawyer and the client to have reached some agreement before the lawyer begins this work. Finally, it makes little sense to try to advise a client who feels no trust in the lawyer.

4.14 THINKING AND PLANNING

As emphasized earlier, clients need choices and it is often up to the lawyer to provide those choices for the client. Thinking creatively and productively—matching what the lawyer knows about the client's concern, the client's goals, and the law—is a critical part of the process of advising the client. Unless the lawyer is experienced in dealing with concerns similar to the client's, this process may take time and the lawyer should make sure the client can afford to have the lawyer take that time.

Think Twice

The timing of these various processes can create a counseling conundrum. It may take time and effort to generate realistic choices, and the lawyer may want to be paid for this planning and thinking. But, this work may not yield realistic options, and a client will be reluctant to pay for something that yields nothing. The lawyer may well decide to initially put in extra work—and not ask for a fee— because the lawyer hopes this will prompt the client to further retain the lawyer. The counselor will need to make choices about how best to generate choices for the client.

4.14.1 Legal Investigation

Legal investigation is another critical part of preparing to advise a client. The lawyer should do the legal research necessary to learn what the traditional approaches to the client's concern have been, and what new approaches might be plausible.

Increasingly, records of past approaches taken in similar situations are accessible. Sometimes this record is found in appellate decisions; sometimes, in agency rules; sometimes, in settlement reports; sometimes, in past agreements between the parties; sometimes, on the web; sometimes, only in the memories of other lawyers. A review of these sources will also help the lawyer begin to estimate the likelihood of success of the available options.

The depth and amount of investigation will depend in part on the lawyer's own expertise, but also on the agreement between the lawyer and the client. A lawyer should not devote more time and expense to investigation than the client has authorized.

4.14.2   Fact Investigation

At times, it may be necessary to do fact investigation to prepare to advise a client. A lawyer may want to interview other witnesses or obtain financial records or other documents. The process for doing this is set out in Chapter 7. This investigation may help the lawyer fill in gaps in the information obtained from the client. It may also help the lawyer begin to move beyond "lawyer" approaches to the client's concern. The depth and amount of investigation will again depend on the agreement between the lawyer and the client, as well as the lawyer's own expertise. It is particularly important that the lawyer have the client's express agreement before contacting any other witnesses during a supplemental fact investigation.

4.15   CHECKING YOUR WORK

New lawyers should remember that experienced lawyers are often a very valuable resource of information, plus a source of new friends to replace those lost during law school. A lawyer who has not dealt with a concern similar to the client's may want to discuss particular options with a more seasoned attorney. More experienced lawyers can be particularly helpful in providing guidance about the likelihood of success of different options. Depending on the depth of discussion, the lawyer may want to have the client's permission before talking to a colleague. If the lawyer seeks advice from an attorney outside the lawyer's firm, care should be taken to safeguard the attorney-client privilege.

4.16   AGENDAS AND LISTS

Before meeting with the client, the lawyer should prepare an agenda for the meeting that, at a minimum, lists the different options to be discussed. The lawyer should consider giving the client a copy of this agenda. For some clients, it may be helpful to have the lawyer make a list or chart matching the different options and goals. In fact, some corporate clients routinely ask lawyers to prepare elaborate "decision trees" matching each option with the likelihood of success and the client's goals.

It is sometime possible—and often tempting for both the busy lawyer and the busy client—to try to make decisions over the phone or via email. When the decision to be made is a critical one, however, meeting in person is usually advisable.

Think Twice

The extent of this planning process depends on the nature of the deal or dispute. How important is it to the client? How much is at stake? What resources does the client have? Will the fees have any impact on the outcome? Some cases will require extensive planning work, while others will only need minimal efforts.

G.   STRUCTURING THE MEETING

4.17   A SUGGESTED STRUCTURE

Once again we remind you, as we did in Chapter Three, that different clients have different concerns, and good lawyers keep their plans and agendas flexible to accommodate these differences. Consequently, you may use this suggestion about structure as a guideline or checklist for preparing an agenda appropriate for the client.

1.   *Update.* As time passes, things happen. But many lawyers conduct subsequent meetings with clients as if facts and plans were set in stone at the first meeting. Find out if something new has happened or if the client's goals have changed.

2.   *Assessment.* A lawyer needs to give a client an assessment of the client's legal situation. It usually makes sense to do this before discussing the client's options.

3.   *Description of options.* Some lawyers like to give clients a quick overview of all the different options and then discuss each separately. Other lawyers prefer simply to move

through options one by one. The lawyer should give the client the opportunity to ask questions about each option, and should discuss the cost of each option and likelihood of success.

4. *Review of options.* After a full discussion of the individual options, it is generally helpful to briefly recap the list. For many clients, it is helpful if this recap includes a reference to the goals the option is best able to help achieve, the likelihood of the option's chances of achieving those goals, and the cost of the option.

5. *Decision.* After the client has discussed the available options, the client will typically need to choose one or more. If the client is not ready to make a decision, the lawyer can help by matching goals and options, narrowing the list, or reframing the choice.

6. *Discussion of next step.* After the client has made a decision, the lawyer and client should discuss what the lawyer plans to do next to implement the decision.

7. *The next contact.* Before the close of the meeting, the lawyer should tell the client when the client will next hear from the lawyer.

8. *The future.* The lawyer needs to explain what the lawyer will do before the next contact, what the client should do, what events may transpire, or what may not happen.

9. *Reassurance.* It is critical for the client to continue to be reassured that the lawyer will continue to do her or his best to represent the client.

10. *Implementation.* At some point, the lawyer will have to do something on behalf of the client. The remainder of this text deals substantially with what, how, and when to implement legal advice.

Think Twice

Lawyers tend to be decisive people. Many of us make decisions for ourselves quickly and easily. While meeting and working with clients making decisions, one of the mistakes new lawyers make most commonly is expecting our clients to be like us. While helping clients make deci-

sions, it is important for the lawyer to be patient and to remember that the client may feel a great deal of anguish about his or her decision. It is also important to remember that while we may want a decision made by the end of the meeting, it may not be necessary for the client to do this. A topic for discussion may be how much time is available for a decision to be made and how much time the client wants to take to make a decision.

Part Two
PLANNING AND NEGOTIATIONS

Chapter Five
PLANNING THE TRANSACTION

My Master was yet wholly at a loss to understand what motives could incite this Race of Lawyers to perplex, disquiet, and weary themselves by engaging in such a Confederacy. . . .

—Jonathan Swift
Gulliver's Travels

A. INTRODUCTION

5.1 THE OTHER SIDE OF PRACTICE

Fiction shapes our vision of reality. A half-century of media, movies, books, and television programs have largely defined our conception of what it means to be a lawyer. Say the word "lawyer" to people today, and most will picture a lawyer made famous by the media or a Hollywood star who portrays a lawyer on television or in the movie—typically in some courtroom drama.

That vision is, however, only half of the story. Many lawyers have never set foot inside a court or hearing room and never plan to. These are the lawyers that do the legal work needed for creating and running businesses, corporate mergers, real estate sales, contract drafting, and a variety of other tasks. Some attorneys call this work "corporate practice," but that is a misnomer, because this work is done for individuals, partnerships, and sole proprietorships just as often as it is done for large publicly traded corporations. Some attorneys call this work "office practice" or "advisorial practice," but those dreary names fall far short of capturing the challenges and excitement inherent in this work. In the end, "transactional practice" is the best from a batch of choices, but is itself misleading, because this work involves a far greater range of activities than negotiating and crafting deals.

5.2 THE NATURE OF THE WORK: TRANSLATION, DEFINITION, AND TRANSACTION

By whatever name it is called, much of lawyering involves work that has little to do with the resolution of disputes. The breadth of this practice defies easy categorization, but in the main, legal work outside the realm of dispute-resolution involves translating the law, creating and defining relationships, and structuring transactions.

Think Twice

It's estimated that 20% of law graduates work for businesses and organizations, but not as lawyers. They may serve a variety of roles, from CEO to Sales Manager. Their training as a lawyer undoubtedly helps them succeed and they may well use some of the lawyering skills covered in this book, but they would not necessarily fall within the work described in this chapter.

5.2.1 Translation: Bringing the Law to Clients

One of the most important tasks any lawyer can perform is to make the law accessible to clients. As the law has grown more complex, it has become increasingly difficult for clients to have a first-hand understanding of the rules, regulations, and statutes that govern their actions. Consequently, one of the big parts of any lawyer's job is finding and explaining to a client the law that bears upon that particular client's situation.

The importance of this task is heightened when the client needs legal advice in order to guide future behavior. A large part of transactional practice involves "translating" a sophisticated body of law and advising clients about that law so that the clients can make effective decisions. Clients come to lawyers for advice about tax laws, securities regulations, estate planning, or intellectual property. In fact, in the day-to-day practice of law, many lawyers who consider themselves advocates find that they spend a great deal of time translating the law and advising clients outside the context of a particular dispute. For example, a small business owner might seek advice from an employment lawyer about the Americans with Disabilities Act; a corporation's general counsel might call an antitrust lawyer for an opinion about the Robinson–Patman Act; a tenant in a housing project might consult a legal aid lawyer about lease provisions. All of this work involves "translation" of complex bodies of law and regulations, and all of this work could be described as "transactional," because none of it necessarily involves the resolution of existing disputes.

5.2.2   Creation and Definition: Making the Law Work for Clients

Transactional practice also often entails the creation of new relationships or the definition of existing relationships. The web of the law is filled with categories of different types of relationships between people: agent and principal; landlord and tenant; licensor and licensee; settler, trustee, and beneficiary; employer and employee; lender and borrower; buyer and seller. At each juncture, the creation and definition of these relationships is work often done by transactional lawyers.

When these relationships are created or defined, a client will typically seek help from a lawyer in understanding the rights and responsibilities the law imposes. The lawyer may need to "translate" the relevant law so that the client can make effective decisions. That translation is, however, only part of the lawyer's work. There is more to transactional practice than telling the client the law and then reaching for the appropriate forms. An important part of the lawyer's job involves developing a deep enough understanding of the client's goals to offer meaningful advice about how the law may help the client accomplish those goals. Rather than trimming the client's goals to fit the law, the creative lawyer will work to tailor the law to fit the client's needs.

For example, a client who wishes to start a business and comes to a lawyer asking for information about forming a corporation certainly needs to understand the requirements of incorporation, and may also need advice about the rights and responsibilities of directors and shareholders. "Translating" corporate law for the client is a part of the lawyer's work, but only a part. That same client may be better served by the lawyer who takes the time to explore the client's goals, and then works with the client to determine whether it might be wiser, for example, for the client to form a limited liability partnership rather than a corporation.

Creation and definition of relationships usually entails drafting documents that spell out the rights, responsibilities, and limits of the relationship. Whether that document is a lease, a will, an employment manual, or a contract, the transactional lawyer must make sure that the document comports with the existing law governing the relationship. And whether the client is an individual, a small business, or a multi-national corporation, the transactional lawyer must insure that the document will give the client useful guidance during the course of the relationship.

5.2.3   Transaction: Using the Law to Work With Others

Sometimes a transactional lawyer is called on to create or define a relationship that a client wishes to create or define largely for its own purposes. For example, an employer may ask a lawyer to draft a manual that spells out the rights and responsibilities of the workplace. A large manufacturer may want legal help in creating policies governing the distribution of its products. While the interests of the employees or purchasers are important, in these types of situations the employer or manufacturer may be able to create or define relationships unilaterally.

More often, transactional lawyers find themselves called upon to create or define relationships in which other parties have a voice in the costs, benefits, and design of that relationship. Every transaction involves this sort of negotiation. Mergers, securities offerings, real estate purchases, employment contracts, sales of goods—all of these require the parties involved to reach mutually agreed-upon resolutions of a whole host of questions about legal relationships. The transactional lawyer is responsible for making sure that the right questions are asked and, to the extent possible, that those questions are answered in a way that accomplishes the client's goals.

When other parties come to the table, the challenge of transactional practice increases exponentially. To complete a transaction successfully, a lawyer must be able to translate the law for a client and create and define a new relationship. That lawyer must also be able to work with other parties who have interests and goals at odds with the interests and goals of the lawyer's clients. The ultimate challenge of transactional lawyering is convincing a variety of parties to balance competing interests in a fashion that serves the interests of the lawyer's client. To do this, the transactional lawyer must not only be an effective negotiator, the transactional lawyer must also have a deep understanding of the client's goals.

Think Twice

Law schools are partly to blame for the view that lawyers largely are involved in resolving disputes. The focus of much legal study is based on case law development and analysis. Take contracts: The course books are really case-books filled with mistakes lawyers have made in drafting and enforcing agreements. It makes more sense to some that if you want to learn contract law, you'd be better off studying model contract agreements and how they are created and made enforceable. That is the work of transactional lawyers. Then you could study relevant case law dealing with problems and disputes which can be avoided by good lawyering.

B.   DIFFERENCES AMONG DISTINCTIONS

5.3   IT'S THE SAME, BUT IT ISN'T

In some sense, all law is much the same and lawyers have more in common with each other than with anyone else. Being an advocate is more like being a transactional lawyer than being a doctor, stockbroker, locksmith, or wedding planner. Still, there are important differences between the work of the advocate and the work of the transactional lawyer. These distinctions shed some light on the different sets of skills necessary to be an effective transactional lawyer.

5.4　I GOT HERE AS SOON AS I COULD, AND I'M NOT PLANNING ON LEAVING ANY TIME SOON

The first set of distinctions between advocacy and transactional practice concerns the points in time in which the client seeks assistance from the lawyer. Every lawyer who has tried lawsuits, arbitrated disputes, or negotiated settlements has, at one time or another, thought: "If only this client had called me sooner, none of this ever would have had to happen." These thoughts are commonplace because, quite often, a client will not sense a need for legal assistance until a dispute has arisen—for example, the client is sued. The lawyer who is summoned once a dispute has flared is in the position of a fire fighter. The dispute may be a manageable blaze or an enormous conflagration, but either way, a crisis has occurred and it is the lawyer's job to help the client extinguish that crisis.

By contrast, the transactional lawyer is often in a position more akin to a fire inspector. The client summoning a lawyer before a dispute has arisen is not interested in putting out fires; instead, the client wishes to prevent fires altogether. Like a fire inspector, it is the transactional lawyer's job to seek out potential trouble areas, and suggest changes (through creative planning or drafting) that will prevent future problems. To be sure, good litigation practice also requires some of these same skills, since sound strategic planning is important in solving crises. Transactional practice is more heavily reliant upon these skills, however, since good transactional practice is built upon a lawyer's ability to see trouble before it happens and help a client take steps to forestall that potential trouble.

The advocate arrives when the client calls for assistance in resolving a crisis. At the end of a trial, a litigator may be called upon to work on an appeal; or after an arbitration, a lawyer may assist with enforcement of the award. But, for the most part, an advocate's work is done once the crisis is resolved.

Transactional lawyers not only arrive on the scene earlier than advocates, they stay around longer. Since transactional work is not focused on the resolution of a dispute, there is no "natural" stopping point for much of the work transactional lawyers do. There are certainly exceptions to this rubric; at the end of a negotiated deal, a client may no longer need or want legal assistance. More often, however, a client will want continued advice and assistance from a transactional lawyer across an extended period of time. Consequently, the transactional lawyer must be able to foresee future problems and help solve them.

5.5 BEYOND COURT–MADE PROCESS: EXCUSE ME, COULD YOU DIRECT ME TO THE FEDERAL RULES OF TRANSACTIONAL PROCEDURE?

There aren't any. And that fact—perhaps as much as any other—makes for the difference between the life of the transactional lawyer and the life of the advocate. When the advocate submits a dispute to the jurisdiction of the courts or initiates an arbitration proceeding, the applicable rules of practice and procedure dictate to that lawyer the conduct and structure of the case. Those rules determine the when, where, and how that dispute will be resolved. The world of the advocate involved in litigation, arbitration, or administrative proceedings is bounded by rules that govern lawyer, party, and decision maker behavior.

No such rules exist for the transactional lawyer. To be sure, the transactional lawyer must answer to the same ethical standards as the advocate, but read through those rules and see how many seem to have been drafted with only the advocate in mind. To be sure, the transactional lawyer must heed the statutes and cases that govern the relevant legal concerns of the client—but these laws do not govern lawyer behavior. When a client asks for legal advice, there is no rule that tells the transactional lawyer that the client's question must be answered in thirty days. When two parties agree to the terms of a contract, there is no rule that tells the transactional lawyer the size or type of the font for the contract. If a deal turns sour and negotiations become bitter and hostile, the transactional lawyer cannot ask a judge to sanction opposing counsel.

All this can be very freeing. Transactional lawyers can mold the law to shape clients' needs unfettered by rules that mandate process. This leaves much room for innovation and creativity. It also leaves much room for headaches and frustration.

Think Twice

A popular law school myth holds that the life of the transactional lawyer is much less hectic than the life of the advocate. A little thought about the difference between the two practices dispels that myth. If a client comes to a litigator and asks the lawyer to sue someone and collect a judgment before next Thursday, the lawyer can patiently explain that America's court system doesn't work that quickly. The client may not like the explanation, but the client will blame the system for the delay, not the lawyer. On the other hand, a client who comes to a transactional lawyer and asks that a contract be drafted before next Thursday need not listen to explanations about the wheels of justice grinding slowly. If this lawyer can't do the work, the client can find someone else who will. Ultimately, transactional law is a process that is driven and administered by the participants, not by some outside authority— and it has all the joys and frustrations of a process that is self-driven and self-administered.

5.6 VOLUNTARY EXCHANGES: I DON'T HAVE TO IF I DON'T WANT TO

In the final analysis, the most important distinction between transactional work and advocacy is that the participants in a transaction are often all there voluntarily and, typically, any of them can leave whenever they want to. The realm of advocacy is far different: at least one and sometimes all the participants are there against their will and, typically, none can leave without the assent of the judge, arbitrator, or the other parties. It is this distinction that makes for much of the charm and challenge of transactional practice.

The right to walk away is an enormous power (and discussed in Chapter 8). In most transactional settings, it is a power that each of the participants has. In almost every transactional negotiation, any of the parties to the deal could simply decide to take their capital, their business, their services somewhere else and walk out of the room. In litigation, if a party walks away from a settlement negotiation, that party walks straight into the courtroom. In transactional work, the alternative to the transaction is either no deal or another deal with someone else.

An advocate works—in a sense—to make the other side go away. A transactional lawyer must work—in a sense—to keep the other side at the table, at least for a while. Consequently, it is not enough that the transactional lawyer have a good understanding of the client's goals. The transactional lawyer also needs to be attuned to the interests, motivations, and goals of all the other parties at the table.

C. TRANSACTIONAL GOALS

5.7 DOING TRANSACTIONAL WORK: TAKING GOALS SERIOUSLY

The skills that a transactional lawyer uses in practice are not that different than the skills an advocate uses. Like the advocate, the transactional lawyer interviews clients, advises clients, researches the law, negotiates with other parties, and drafts agreements. Like the advocate, the transactional lawyer must be a good listener, a thoughtful and knowledgeable interpreter of the law, a creative and lucid drafter, and a persuasive and patient negotiator. But because of the differences between advocacy and transactional practice, there are distinctions in the skills needed to be an effective practitioner. The most important of these distinctions centers around the understanding the transactional lawyer must have about the goals and motivations of the different parties to a transaction.

Think Twice

Lawyers who have engaged in both types of practice perceive additional similarities between transactional lawyers and trial advocates. While there may be no formal rules of evidence, deal makers question their clients and cross-examine other clients and their lawyers. And while there is no judge or jury, transactional lawyers tell stories and engage in summation presentations trying to persuade the other side to reach a decision favorable to their client.

5.7.1 Immediate Goals: Clarify and Condense

A great deal of transactional work involves intensive work with clients—a cycle of interviewing, advising, and drafting— that is repeated until the clients' goals are accomplished. Time, patience, and sanity are best preserved when the lawyer has a solid understanding of what it is that the client wants. Pity the new lawyer who drafts an opinion letter or email for a client and then is told by the senior lawyer on the file: "This is fine, but it doesn't address two of the real issues the client has, and this last section answers a question the client didn't ask." This kind of misunderstanding usually occurs when the lawyer has a firm grasp of the legal matters, but only a vague sense of the client's goals.

The best way to obtain a solid sense of the client's immediate goals is to ask the client. Unfortunately, simply asking, "Oh client, what are your immediate goals?" seldom yields enough information. Instead, the transactional lawyer needs to ask a whole gamut of who, what, where, and when questions. The lawyer writing the opinion memo should, for example, ask:

- Who will be reading this opinion?
- What kinds of decisions will they be making on the basis of this document?
- Where does this memo fit in with other legal or business advice the client may already have?
- When does the client need this opinion? When will it be used?

As these questions are answered, the lawyer can begin to clarify the understanding of the client's immediate goals. And as that understanding is clarified and condensed, it is usually true that the work the lawyer does for the client will be more efficient and more valuable.

5.7.2 Overarching Goals: Learn and Serve

A civil dispute may well involve a crisis, and crises can be easy to understand. Clients don't like crises; clients want crises solved. Clients call lawyer advocates to deal with crises, and are happy once the crises—and the lawyers—are gone.

Transactional practice presents a different calculus of desire. Clients typically do not seek out a transactional lawyer for crisis management. Instead, clients hire transactional lawyers to do work the clients have chosen to do in order to promote long-range or overarching goals, although some of these goals may need to be addressed with great dispatch. Often, the true measure of the value of the transactional lawyer's work is whether that work has helped advance the client's overarching goals. The lawyer who drafts an employment manual for a client may have helped that client achieve the immediate goal of creating written policies for the workplace. Whether that work is of any value, however, will depend on whether the employment manual accomplishes overarching goals such as harmony in the workplace or minimization of litigation and arbitration.

It takes time—and often experience or intuition—for a lawyer to understand how the work the lawyer is doing for the client fits into the client's long term plans, the client's business, the client's life. While the question "why do you want to do this?" is hardly out of place in the advocate's office, it must become a staple of the transactional lawyer's practice. That question is usually the first step on the road to understanding the client's overarching goals.

One of the joys of transactional practice is that a lawyer may well work with many of the same clients across several years. As the lawyer accumulates experience with a client, the lawyer's understanding of the client's goals will deepen, and the lawyer will be better able to tailor legal work to meet the client's interests, needs, and goals.

Think Twice

Lawyers usually enjoy and hope for repeat business. Litigators prefer to be retained again by a client who has another dispute. That will more likely occur if the litigator has won the previous case. Transactional lawyers tend to be retained to continue their good work, as long as it meets the needs of the client and does not foster disputes that require the hiring of litigators. The nature of these different practices often affects the extent, depth, and length of relationships between clients and lawyers.

D. THE ROLE OF THE CLIENT

5.8 PROCESS PREFERENCES: PASSENGER, DRIVER, OR MAP–MAKER

Since there are no rules for transactional procedure and since participation in most transactions is completely voluntary, the client's level of participation in transactional work can vary enormously. Advocates know that during discovery or a hearing there are times in which the client's participation is not simply desirable, but actually required by law. In transactional work, the client's level of participation in the process is largely left to the decision of the client and the lawyer. Consequently, the transactional lawyer must spend more time with the client learning about the client's own process preferences.

In transactional practice, it is possible for a lawyer to serve a wide range of functions—driver, map-maker, or passenger. The lawyer who fails to understand a client's process-preferences risks inevitable client dissatisfaction and a possible malpractice claim.

Some clients come to lawyers with a firm idea of what it is they want to accomplish. These clients need lawyers who can function as *drivers* steering through difficult patches of road, suggesting alternative routes, finally bringing the client safely to a destination that client has determined. Pursuing a patent for a client fits this function.

Other clients may need lawyers to function as *map-makers*. These are the clients that need a wider range of assistance from their lawyers. The new business owner who comes to a lawyer to ask for assistance negotiating a commercial lease may also need the lawyer to point out the need for the client to do some tax planning. In fact, this client may not only need the lawyer to do this, but may expect it.

Sometimes the transactional lawyer is along for the ride, and provides legal advice to a client who is doing the driving and navigating. Just as some clients are sophisticated parties to arbitration or litigation (finance or insurance companies, for example), some clients are sophisticated parties to transactions. These clients may neither expect nor want questions from lawyers about the whys and wherefores of a particular transaction. For example, a client may hire a lawyer to complete a particular type of real estate transaction, having already made informed decisions about whether the transaction serves immediate and overarching goals. Persistent and repeated questions from the lawyer about whether the client's decisions are well-grounded may only serve to convince the client to hire a different lawyer next time. This client needs neither a map-maker, nor a driver. This client simply needs a valuable *passenger*—a lawyer with the technical expertise to implement decisions the client has already made. In transactional practice, this is a reasonable process preference and it is the lawyer's responsibility to ask the questions necessary to learn about this process preference.

5.9 THE OTHER SIDE: ALL THE SAME ISSUES SQUARED

The transactional lawyer needs a solid understanding of the client's goals and preferences. When dealing with other parties with competing interests, the transactional lawyer needs as firm an understanding of the other side's goals and preferences. That understanding is helpful to the advocate, but critical for the transactional lawyer. In a transaction, a party will be present only as long as that party sees participation in the transaction as consistent with the party's goals. A transactional lawyer needs to understand those goals. Absent that understanding, the transactional lawyer lacks the basic information necessary to keep the other side at the bargaining table while still protecting the client's interests.

How does a transactional lawyer learn about the other party's goals? Fact investigation can yield some information about other's immediate and overarching goals, but it is often possible to obtain that information directly from the other party's lawyer. Can lawyers get that information from opposing counsel? At first glance, it seems the answer must be no, but in a sense, negotiation is the opportunity to do exactly that. The transactional lawyer must use negotiation as an exchange of information, as well as an exchange of positions.

5.10 MAKING PROBLEMS INSTEAD OF SOLVING THEM: WHY DON'T MY CLIENTS SMILE WHEN I WALK IN THE ROOM?

Lawyer jokes aren't just about litigators. Just as some clients resent having to hire lawyers to resolve disputes, some clients may dislike transactional lawyers. Clients may mutter to themselves, or we hope, discuss with us concerns about:

Deal Killing. Clients may perceive that lawyers view themselves as deal killers instead of deal makers. The lawyer who is overly negative about a situation or who continually raises roadblocks instead of suggesting bridges to close gaps may rightly be perceived as interfering with the process instead of constructing a deal.

Nitpicking. The lawyer who focuses on what seems to the client to be petty issues and details that can only be revealed by a legal microscope may view the lawyer as being focused on irrelevant matters. This is not to say that a devotion to minute details may not be critical to the success of a project, but a lawyer who seems overly obsessed with these details may not be what the client needs or expects. The danger is that the lawyer who dwells on the minutia may lose sight of the broader goals of the transaction, to the dissatisfaction of the client.

Legalese Speaking. The lawyer who drafts terms that only another lawyer can understand may cause the client to wonder if the lawyer speaks the same language as the client. Drafting legal provisions may require the use of legalese, but the terms should also be drafted plainly enough so all can understand.

Disaster Predicting. It is appropriate and necessary for lawyers to point out to clients worst case scenarios and to draft accordingly. For example, good lawyering involves discussing with the client the inclusion of a pre-dispute resolution clause, like an arbitration clause, in an agreement to resolve any future dispute. However, the lawyer who is primarily worried about unlikely potential disasters and tries to negotiate for every possible contingency or drafts a lengthy arbitration agreement will wrap the client in a tangle of red tape and may unnecessarily interfere with the completion of a deal.

All these and other concerns can be avoided by understanding the proper role of the lawyer and by open communication between the client and attorney. The goal of the lawyer is to help the client and not create unnecessary problems. It should be the client's choice, in consultation with the lawyer, how this can best be accomplished.

Think Twice

What can get in the way of communications between lawyers and clients? Why do problems arise between transactional lawyers and their clients? Successful, busy deal makers are, well, busy and, often, very busy. And many will be too busy to take the necessary time to communicate with their lawyers. Lots of things can happen that affect the development of a relationship or the construction of an agreement, and not all of it is communicated to the lawyer responsible for crafting the underlying documents. So, it's incumbent on the lawyer to periodically check with the client to see what has changed and what is likely to change.

E.   THE ROLE OF THE DOCUMENT

5.11   DOCUMENTING THE TRANSACTION: HOW WILL WE KNOW WHAT WE DID—NOW AND FOR THE FUTURE?

Transactional lawyers plan for the present and the future by preserving the terms of the transaction or relationship in writing, or, more typically, in electronic bits and bytes. How they go about doing this depends upon the several factors: the type of transaction, the nature of the relationship, and the immediate and overarching goals.

5.11.1   Clarification and Preservation

Written contract? We know what we've agreed to and we won't forget.

Unlikely or impossible. That's why smart lawyers record the transaction or relationship so the parties of today and the participants of tomorrow all have the operative document. This document may be short, long, or excessively detailed. A purchase agreement could be contained in a few sentences (the offer, acceptance, and arbitration clause). An employment contract may be several pages in length and refer to other documents including an employer/employee handbook. A corporate acquisition agreement may contain hundreds of pages of provisions. However long, or short, it is wise, if not necessary, to record the results of the transaction or relationship.

5.11.2   Planning for Future Disputes

We don't need anything in writing, we trust each other.

Likely, but maybe not forever. Ordinarily, for the parties to reach an agreement they will have developed a trusting relationship. The nature of the trust will vary depending how well and how long they know each other and for some transactions the extent of the trust will be minimal. And, maybe for some parties, they can and will be able to trust each other's spoken word.

As we already suggested, and as you surmised, transactional lawyers plan ahead and predict the future. They can predict that a percentage of the transactions will result in disputes between the parties. Often, these disputes arise from the document recording the agreement; and, so it is critical that this document be drafted as accurately and completely as possible. We know that some transactions result in future litigation; what we don't know is which agreements and what parties will end up with a dispute. If we did, our predictions would guide the terms of the agreement, or, whether it is worth it to consummate a deal.

5.11.3   Resolving Future Disputes

Well, if a problem arises, we'll sort it out when it does.

Think again. It is at the very start of a relationship that parties typically get along the best. They like what they did, and often like or respect each other. It is when a dispute arises, that their relationship becomes strained. Planning to resolve a dispute before it arises is usually a lot easier than trying to get warring parties to reach another agreement, this time, to end the dispute.

Plus, there is often no legitimate business, legal, personal, or other reason for one party to a dispute to try to resolve it promptly or even fairly. A delinquent party is not anxious to be told exactly how much is owed immediately. A defaulting party may not want to have an arbitrator or judge quickly decide whether a breach occurred. These parties want delay and obfuscation.

Transactional lawyers protect their clients' interests by including in an agreement a pre-dispute resolution clause, so the parties will know how to resolve their dispute and do not have to later argue about that issue. The most common clause is a pre-dispute arbitration clause, which may also include a pre-dispute mediation agreement. These clauses provide parties with a clear, affordable, and fair way to resolve future problems, even for those parties who only foresee peaceful prospects ahead.

Think Twice

And it's for these very reasons that transaction lawyers need to know how disputes are best handled. How might the claim be initiated? What might be the defenses? What types of discovery may be needed. Is an arbitrator better than a judge or jury? Just as trial lawyers seek help from transactional lawyers when drafting a complicated settlement (particularly regarding tax consequences), transactional lawyers work with advocates in crafting pre-dispute resolution clauses.

5.12 DRAFTING THE AGREEMENT

The process of recording the agreement includes two primary concerns: content concerns and composition concerns.

5.12.1 If Only I Knew What to Draft

You do, or you will, or you should. Obviously, the specifics of what to include or exclude depends on the specifics of the agreement. Some general considerations that apply include:

Follow the Law. That's why you are a lawyer and are drafting an agreement. You know what is legal and what is not enforceable. You know how another lawyer may attempt to get out of an agreement.

Be realistic. Include everything you believe needs to be included, but not necessarily everything you or your client can think of. A contract that overreaches creates problems; a draft that includes terms that were not negotiated invites trouble.

Be accurate. Draft what the parties agreed. You may be tempted to draft a term that favors your client even though the parties agreed otherwise. Being true to the agreement is not only the right thing to do it is required practice.

Be complete. Include all what the parties agreed, and if there are other drafting issues that need to be considered (and there often are) raise them with your client and the others for discussion.

Predict the Future. Intended and unintended events and consequences may occur, or they may occur to you, and you have to consider drafting for them. It often is impossible to draft around every possible contingency, but drafting for significant, foreseeable events is smart lawyering.

Be precise and clear. Say what the parties meant, and make sure your client, when reviewing the draft, understands it to say what was meant. The other lawyer will do the same. Sometimes, the parties will not—and cannot—agree on something, and a provision may have to be omitted or drafted ambiguously.

Make it workable. A legal wordsmith could spend a lot of time drafting the perfect, ideal agreement and get an "A" in legal drafting, but a lengthy document chock full of legalese will often not work for the parties. Documents are working agreements, and should be drafted to be easily read and easily used.

Satisfy Your Client and the Parties. The final product should reflect what the client wants and needs to have happen. Thorough client interviewing, effective client counseling, and successful negotiations should result in a draft that accomplishes your client's goals and the goals of the other party as well.

5.12.2   I Know How to Compose It

The key to successful composition is having your client (as well as the other parties and the other lawyer) congratulate you on a well drafted agreement. The five most common complaints clients have with documents lawyers draft are:

It's written in a foreign language. Documents should be composed using understandable language and common words. But lawyers are tempted to overuse legalese and complex presentations. As lawyers, we learn hundreds and thousands of legal words and phrases and they often need to be included in a document, or we may want to show off and include them. Legal words and phrases need to be translated so non-lawyers can comprehend what they mean.

I can read it, but I still can't figure it out. Agreements should be drafted using simple sentences, topical paragraphs, active voice, and proper grammar. These approaches make it a lot easier for clients to understand the provisions and make them a lot more comfortable with the agreement.

It's way too long. Being concise and precise are hallmarks of good drafting. Legal documents may need to be longer than clients prefer because so much has to be included. If that is so, that needs to be explained to them.

I can't find anything. A well structured document that has headings, subdivisions, numbering, and other structural devices makes a document, however short, a lot easier to use.

I paid you all that for this? A well-structured, understandable document that contains good grammar and punctuation and is concise and comprehensive may cause a client to think that the lawyer may not have earned the fees charged to draft the document. The availability of form documents and computer accessible drafts may prompt clients to believe all the lawyer had to do was push a button and—presto—the document was done. Lawyers need to make sure that clients understand the hard work, education, and preparation required to produce the document.

5.12.3   Much More on Drafting

Detailed advice, explanations, and examples of good drafting appear in *Synthesis: Legal Reading, Reasoning, and Writing* by Deborah Schmedemann & Christina Kunz (2007).

Chapter Six
PLANNING FOR DISPUTE RESOLUTION: WHAT ARE WE TO DO?

Burning with curiosity she went in after the rabbit down a hole under the hedge, never once considering how in the world she was to get out again.

—Lewis Carroll

Alice's Adventures in Wonderland

A. INTRODUCTION

6.1 PLANNING WHAT TO DO

It has happened. Your client is involved in a dispute and comes to you for help. You may already know what lawyers initially need to do to help. They need to:

- Assess the dispute
- Determine the remedy
- Seek relief
- Select a dispute resolution method

B. ASSESSING THE DISPUTE

6.2 DISPUTE RESOLUTION PLANNING

A lawyer representing a client involved in a dispute needs to consider the nature of the dispute. The first assessment is whether the client has a claim to make or must respond to a claim brought by someone else. If the client has a claim then affirmative steps may need to be taken. If a client only has a defense, the client may not need to do anything but wait, or the client may need to take affirmative action to preserve or enhance the merits of the defense.

6.3 I WANT TO DO SOMETHING ABOUT THIS

Not every problem lends itself to legal resolution or legal action. For example, even nasty behavior that causes tangible hurt to a victim will not be actionable in tort if the law does not recognize a duty on the part of the perpetrator or does not recognize the resulting injury as significantly concrete to justify legal relief. To take a fairly obvious example, if Chris and Lou develop a personal relationship and Lou dumps Chris, there is unlikely to be any cause of action for intentional infliction of emotional distress (Lou has no duty to stay with Chris) no matter how sad Chris becomes (romantic heartbreak is not sufficiently tangible), even if Lou terminates the relationship with harsh words.

Real life presents even more complex situations. What if Lou, knowing Chris has just finished treatment for alcoholism, delivers a case of favorite beer and a tirade complaining about that Chris is repulsive? Will Lou be liable if Chris downs a case of beer, drives into a school bus, dies, and kills several children? To Chris's estate? To the childrens' families? To the school district for damage to the bus? To the state for road repairs necessitated by the crash? Substantive tort law provides the answers to these sorts of questions and varies among jurisdictions, requiring the lawyer to obtain sufficient facts and then conduct appropriate research, the depth of which will vary according to the novelty of litigation, the stakes involved, and the ability and willingness of the client to pay.

To take the preceding "breaking up is hard to do" scenario one step further, consider how a few changes in the facts can have major legal consequences. If Chris and Lou were not merely in love but married, the law regulates their relationship much more closely. If they break up, they will need the government's "permission," obtained via divorce, and each may have a claim against the other for a share of property, child support, or maintenance. Whether the client is Chris-the-jilted-lover or Chris-the-abandoned-spouse will have a dramatic impact on the appropriate lawyering response.

6.3.1   Should I Do Something About This?

Even if the law provides a right of relief, reality may not. For example, a tortfeasor may lack financial resources. Even in cases of relatively great harm, it may simply not be worthwhile to pursue a civil judgment against an impecunious defendant. "Spite" litigation—pursing a legal claim just to make life difficult for the defendant without any realistic hope for recompense—is both ethically suspect and out of reach for any but the most well-healed spite litigants.

However, some litigation against judgment-proof wrong doers is objectively justified. For example, if the tortfeasor has caused numerous accidents in many states and continues to drive without a license or insurance, this person is a menace endangering the lives of the innocent. A relative of a recent victim may want a lawyer to urge government prosecutors to act or to seek an unsatisfied judgment as grounds for contempt of court resulting in imprisonment in order to remove the defendant driver from the road. More benignly, the plaintiff may wish to force the defendant into a settlement that requires treatment for alcohol abuse, the underlying cause of the automobile accident.

6.3.2   What Type of Claim Should Be Brought?

The substantive law has much to say about what claims can actually be brought. You will need to attend your other classes or research those areas you missed when you were enjoying yourself away from your classes.

Think Twice

The first question an advocate must consider is this: will my client be able to enforce a judgment or award against the defendant/respondent? In other words, can my client collect what is owed or obtain the sought-after relief? Most losing parties pay what they owe and do what they are told by a court and that avoids this issue. They do so because they have the financial wherewithal or, more often, have liability insurance, and they prefer to comply with a civil judgment rather than face the consequences of not doing so.

It would be unusual, although not unethical, for a lawyer to pursue a legitimate case where the defendant will totally ignore the judgment. Collection lawyers who obtain default judgments hope the client will collect on them someday. And a client with financial resources or a point to prove can try to obtain a judgment on principle.

It may be disappointing to think that our civil justice system might not be about actual justice or fairness unless the defendant/respondent is flush or has insurance coverage. But there is little value in winning a case for a client if the victory is hollow. Plus, there needs to be a way for the winning lawyer to be appropriately paid. Rational parties are not going to pay a lawyer unless they also get compensated. And rational private lawyers—unless proudly engaged in doing pro bono work—cannot keep their office open without cash flow.

C.   DETERMINING REMEDIES

6.4   WHAT REMEDIES CAN BE SOUGHT?

The law recognizes the following remedies:

6.4.1   Money, That's What We Want

The client who has been wronged may want the wrong to be righted by monetary compensation. A money judgment or award requires the losing party to pay money to the victor. Our society and the law generally have a preference for monetary relief because this type of relief normally resolves matters, and because many people are content with money. Most people pay their debts, at least after they have lost fair and square, so the victimized party is usually compensated.

6.4.2   Stop, in the Name of the Law

A client may want to stop someone from doing something or to require that person to do something else. This is, as you know, known as equitable relief. This form of relief involves a court order requiring a party from refraining to do something (stop dumping sewage in the river) or to affirmatively do something (fix the colonial war fence you ran over in the monster truck). In modern America, the courts of law and equity are merged virtually everywhere.

Modern lawyers may find it better to think in terms of "compensatory" relief (rather than legal) and "injunctive" relief (rather than equitable). Injunctive relief is normally only ordered when monetary relief is ineffective or problematic. Injunctive relief requires more judicial effort to enforce compliance and may require ongoing judicial involvement.

6.4.3   Just Decide

A related equitable remedy is "declaratory" relief, which results in a judge or arbitrator deciding the status of something. For example, declaratory relief may determine who owns real estate or whether an insurance policy covers a specific loss. A declaratory judgment can have monetary ramifications and can be enforced by an injunction.

6.4.4   Pay My Lawyer, Too

A party may also seek to recover costs and attorney's fees incurred in pursuing claims and defenses. The losing party usually has to pay the winning party for some costs and expenses involved in a case, though typically not attorney's fees. Recoverable costs include expenses such as filing fees, discovery expenses, expert witness fees, and related transaction costs.

Attorney's fees are not recoverable except in four limited situations: (1) if a statute allows for the recovery of attorney's fees, (2) if a contract or an agreement between the parties allows them to recover these fees, (3) if a party acts in such bad faith that a decision maker determines it is an appropriate remedy, or (4) if a substantial public interest demands payment (for example, winning a class action). The prevailing party in these four situations is entitled to the recovery of reasonable attorney fees. The winning lawyer has to provide the court with sufficient and accurate fee information and documentation.

6.5   LEGAL AND PRACTICAL LIMITS ON SEEKING RE-LIEF

Legal doctrines place limits upon available remedies in addition to the economic reality of seeking certain types of relief. For example, the statute of limitations may prevent a claim from being brought if it is too old. Or, an injured party may forego a remedy if to do so would cause unnecessary family strife or severe adverse community responses.

Think Twice

For most parties that have been injured or damaged, our civil justice system compensates their loss with money. That's why there appears to be this emphasis on dollars and cents. And because the legal profession is also a business, lawyers need a source of fees as well. The available remedies dictate what can be practically and successfully litigated or arbitrated and who recovers how much.

There are cases where money is not the primary focus, including public interest litigation and constitutional and civil rights cases. But those are few in number compared to the typical disputes faced by parties.

D. SEEKING RELIEF

6.6 WHAT THE CLIENT WANTS

Anyone who has a legal claim for relief can do something about it. The party must be involved in an actual controversy with an opponent and must seek a recognizable judicial remedy. We lawyers call this "standing." But not everybody can get what they want. An outraged citizen cannot sue the president to "do something about ethnic bloodshed abroad."

People can join together to do something. More than one person or entity can be joined together in one action to seek relief against defendants individually or all together. Lots of people can also get together in a class action. A representative plaintiff or plaintiffs can represent numerous unnamed class members. Class action litigation can be complex, difficult, and risky. Federal Rule of Civil Procedure 23 and similar state court rules establish criteria for class litigation.

Class actions may provide relief to victims who otherwise would remain victims. Class actions when properly administered by counsel and the courts can vindicate the rights of a large number of people who have losses significant in the aggregate but individually too small to justify the costs of litigation. Class suits have been criticized as encouraging the named plaintiffs and counsel to use this device to pocket a sizable settlement and substantial counsel fees while selling out the class interests. Class actions can also result in questionable settlements because of the extensive transaction costs of defending them and the sheer risk of an adverse judgment.

6.7 WHO WILL PAY?

Any person or any entity that is legally responsible can be a proper defendant or respondent. However, not everyone who does something wrong can be civilly liable for wrongdoing, not even in this country. The reach of the law determines who may be held accountable for their actions. You learned in contract law that relief may be sought against a party who breached a contract. You learned in tort law that anyone breaching a legal duty of care may be sued. You will learn in practice that your client will usually want to go after someone who can pay them. Adam Smith was right.

Some potential defendants may not be worth suing. They may be unable to pay damages and consequently will be judgment proof. Others may be entities with which the claimant may wish to do future business. Still others may be business people, friends or family with whom the plaintiff wants to maintain a relationship.

Think Twice

Civil disputes commonly revolve around who is legally irresponsible or accountable for someone else's injury or damages. Who committed the tort? Who breached the contract? Who is ultimately legally responsible? These questions are the grist of civil litigation and arbitration. As described in the previous sections, even in America, there may no recognizable cause of action for conduct that your client believes is reprehensible and unjust. Life is unfair, and not all that is unfair is illegal. That is the difficult conversation you'll have with some of your clients.

With other clients, the contrary conversation will occur. A defendant or potential respondent will not believe that they can be sued or held accountable for what they consider to be someone else's irresponsibility. They will be appalled at the reach of some claims and remedies and will rail at the overly litigious society America apparently has become. That is an equally difficult discussion.

E. SELECTING A DISPUTE RESOLUTION METHOD

Parties involved in or anticipating a dispute have a number of methods to choose from to resolve their problems:

- They can negotiate on their own and settle their disputes.
- They can have an impartial forum and decision maker decide their case.
- They can have a neutral person mediate their dispute.
- They can have someone provide an opinion or an evaluation of their case.
- They can create their own dispute resolution process.

6.8   NEGOTIATING YOUR OWN ACCORD

Parties can negotiate on their own or through their attorneys to reach an agreement. Chapters Eight and Nine describe this process in detail.

6.9   AVAILABLE DISPUTE RESOLUTION FORUMS

There are at least three different impartial forums that can decide disputes: *judicial, arbitral, and administrative.* We exclude fields at dawn.

You may or may not have a choice where to bring or defend a case. A binding arbitration clause may require that a claim be filed with a specific arbitration organization (e.g. National Arbitration Forum, American Arbitration Association, or JAMS) that will administer the case and appoint an arbitrator who will conduct the hearing. The law may require that you bring a claim in an exclusive forum. You have to file a bankruptcy petition in federal bankruptcy court, a divorce action in state court, and a workers compensation claim in a state administrative forum. If there is a choice, you will need to consider the ability and jurisdiction of the forum to decide the case. More on that in Chapter Eleven.

6.9.1 Enforceability

The initial issue you must resolve is to make certain that a judgment or award you win will be enforceable. It does your client little good to win something that is unenforceable. It does your client less good to have the losing party rightfully refuse to pay money. Proper jurisdiction is what makes your judgment or award enforceable. If the forum has jurisdiction to hear and decide the case, your decision will be enforceable. All that time you spent studying jurisdiction may be worth it after all.

A related issue you must consider is *where* you will seek to enforce the judgment or award. It will do you no good to seek to enforce your victory in a place where it is unenforceable. In this country, judicial, arbitral, and administrative decisions made by a forum with proper jurisdiction will be enforceable everywhere.

Jurisdiction and venue laws determine enforceable judicial and administrative judgments. The Federal Arbitration Act allows a party to force a recalcitrant party to arbitrate and to enforce an award if the agreement is in writing and involves interstate commerce. State arbitration laws have similar provisions for enforcing and policing arbitration agreements and outcomes.

In other countries, treaties and conventions determine the reach of enforceable judgments and awards. Most countries readily recognize and enforce arbitration awards and judicial judgments entered in the United States. You need to do legal research and planning to determine these issues before you seek any remedy for your client anywhere. You may become an international lawyer before you know it.

6.9.2 Litigation

Lawsuits may be brought in federal or state court, whichever has jurisdiction over the defendant. You will recall that the federal courts resolve disputes involving federal statutes and the federal constitution, disputes between citizens of different states in excess of $75,000, and federal cases such as civil rights, patent disputes, and bankruptcy. State courts are courts of general jurisdiction and hear the vast majority of disputes.

You may also recall that a plaintiff can serve a summons and complaint on the defendant who can reply with an answer. Litigation proceeds with the parties conducting discovery and bringing motions with the case eventually resulting in settlement or a trial (only 2% of the time at most). Parties have a right to a jury or a bench trial. Federal and state constitutional and statutory provisions provide parties with the right to a jury trial in most civil cases, particularly those involving money damages. Other cases, including injunctive relief cases, are tried in a bench trial. Any party with grounds may appeal to an appellate court.

Litigation is usually the remedy available to the parties if they are unable to agree to another dispute resolution method. Litigation is often the last resort parties rely on to have their dispute resolved because the trial process can be very expensive, slow, time consuming, and painful. Only lawyers think it's a really fulfilling process.

Parties may decide to litigate and then agree to submit their dispute to a private judge who makes a decision after a trial. Parties may prefer a private judge instead of a public judge because the private judge may have experience resolving the type of dispute and the trial may be able to be scheduled much more quickly than a public trial. In some jurisdictions, the decision by the private judge (special magistrate or referee) can be enforced as if it were a judgment and can also be appealed.

6.9.3   Arbitration

An arbitration resolves a dispute between parties by the issuance of an award by an arbitrator after a hearing. One type of hearing is called a document hearing in which the parties submit their case to the arbitrator in writing through documents, records, and affidavits. Another type of hearing is called a participatory hearing in which parties present evidence through witnesses and exhibits and make arguments before the arbitrator.

Arbitration proceedings operate under rules administered by the arbitration organization conducting the arbitration proceeding, e.g., The Code of Procedure of the National Arbitration Forum. The parties select an arbitration organization before or after the dispute. The organization appoints the arbitrator and administers the arbitration procedure.

Arbitrations begin by a claimant filing a written claim with the arbitration organization and serving it on a respondent, who answers and may counterclaim. Arbitration proceedings are less formal than judicial proceedings, with limited discovery and motions and less strict rules of procedure and evidence. The arbitrator or panel of arbitrators decides a case by issuing a written arbitration award following the hearing.

The award in a binding arbitration proceeding is final and binding, although it can be reviewed by a judge who can modify, vacate, or confirm it. An arbitration award is as effective as a judgment entered after a judicial trial. Arbitration awards are legally enforceable in all fifty states and in the federal courts.

A non-binding arbitration proceeding operates similarly to a binding arbitration process, with the exception that the award is only advisory and not final. A court may mandate parties use non-binding arbitration before proceeding to trial. Any party can refuse to accept the arbitral decision and have the dispute resolved through another dispute resolution method.

Costs of arbitration include the filing fee and the fee for the arbitrator. Arbitration transaction costs are commonly substantially less than litigation transaction costs, including lawyer fees, because the arbitration process is less time consuming, more streamlined, and less complex than litigation.

6.9.4 Administrative Hearings

Administrative hearings typically resolve disputes involving governmental agencies or statutory remedies. A party may file a petition with an administrative tribunal, and an administrative judge holds a hearing and decides the case. The availability of discovery and the use of motions may be limited.

Controversies resolved through federal and state administrative hearings include workers compensation claims, unemployment compensation claims, tax claims, social security claims, welfare claims, licensure disputes, and other rule based claims.

Administrative claims may also involve regulatory procedures. Parties involved in a dispute regarding the enactment or enforcement of government regulations may appear before administrative bodies to present their case. Examples include utility rate setting cases and environmental cases.

6.9.5   Forum Choices

For most disputes, your client will not have a choice of a forum. The substantive and procedural laws may force them to litigate or seek relief in an administrative proceeding. If there is no prior agreement, then the choice is really made by the legislature and the courts. Statutes impose administrative law remedies, or, by default, constitutional provisions make courts available. In that sense, parties who do not plan ahead "choose" litigation as their dispute resolution method.

But if you step back in time before a dispute arises, the potential parties may have a choice on how they want their potential disputes resolved. Parties in a legal relationship, e.g., a contractual agreement, could plan ahead anticipating a dispute. They could decide early on how they prefer any dispute between them to be resolved. Arbitration provides them with an option.

This arbitration choice may not be discussed by the parties for the same reasons that pre-nuptial agreements are rare among couples (compared to the number of marriages that occur). No one wants to think what could go wrong; no one perceives anything will go wrong; everyone hopes things will go well and plans accordingly. But, rational parties will consider a pre-dispute arbitration clause.

Think Twice

So why not select a forum after a dispute arises, if a choice is available? The existence of a dispute means the parties are not getting along well and may even harbor bad feelings. It's difficult to get adversaries to agree on anything, let alone a dispute resolution method. Plus, since most disputes involve money or, more accurately, the collection of money from someone who does not believe they should have to pay, there is no incentive for the recalcitrant defendant/respondent to want to have the dispute resolved. Who is anxious to be told they have to pay a certain amount promptly? And so, choosing a forum after a dispute has arisen becomes doubly difficult.

6.10 MEDIATION

Mediation involves disputing parties resolving their differences with the assistance of a mediator who facilitates a settlement in a private, confidential setting. Participants in mediation include the parties, their attorneys or representatives, and an impartial mediator. Mediators can clarify what the parties want, focus on their needs and interests, exchange information, evaluate the strengths and weaknesses of a case, and suggest alternative ways to reach an accord.

Parties may mediate voluntarily by agreement entered into either before or after a dispute arises, or as mandated by a court. Mediation only results in a settlement if the parties mutually agree to a resolution. Mediation may take only a couple of hours, several hours, or a number of days, depending upon the complexity of the issues and the position of the parties. The cost of mediation includes the mediator's hourly fees and, in most mediations, an administrative fee.

Parties may use mediation by itself or before resorting to other forums to resolve a dispute. Parties may first attempt to mediate the dispute, and if that fails, they can then litigate, arbitrate, or administrate. The neutral who mediates the dispute with the parties is usually not the judge or arbitrator, but may be. The mediation process may not resolve the entire dispute, but may resolve some substantive and procedural issues.

The most common form of mediation involves one neutral mediator. Mediation may also be conducted by a team of mediators, and this is called a moderated settlement conference. Team mediation may be useful in complex cases or situations where the involvement of additional individuals may accelerate the mediation process. A combination mediation and arbitration proceeding is known as a med-arb proceeding, with mediation occurring first followed by arbitration, if necessary. You will learn much more about mediation in Chapter 10.

6.11   CASE EVALUATIONS AND OPINIONS

Parties may find it useful to obtain an independent evaluation of their case. There are three primary ways parties can obtain an evaluation from other persons.

6.11.1   Early Neutral Evaluation

This process involves a neutral who, early in the dispute resolution process, obtains information from the parties and evaluates the case. The recommendations of the neutral may become the basis for resolution by negotiation or mediation, may narrow the issues to be resolved, or may suggest a dispute resolution method or combination of methods to use. The neutral may also act as a mediator or arbitrator. Fact-finding can be useful in resolving complex scientific, technical, or economic issues.

6.11.2   Minitrial

Minitrial is a proceeding where each party makes a short presentation before a panel which then issues a written or oral evaluation of the case. The panel may consist of one or more neutrals or one neutral and a representative from each party. The non-binding decision may resolve the dispute or may be a basis for negotiation or mediation.

6.11.3   Summary Jury Trial

A summary jury trial is what it sounds like: the parties present a summary of their evidence and arguments to a mock jury. The jurors may be selected from a jury pool or may be obtained from a jury consulting organization. The jury, after hearing the evidence and presentation, deliberates and returns a recommended verdict. This advisory verdict provides the parties with a basis to predict what a jury would do after a complete trial. The lawyers may question the jurors about their verdict and learn why the jurors reached the decision they did. The verdict may also be a basis for negotiation and mediation.

Think Twice

These alternative dispute resolution methods can be quite effective but their transaction costs and related expenses usually limit them to cases that involve significant issues or parties who have substantial resources. It ordinarily is not economically practical to use these methods in smaller scale disputes.

6.12 CREATING YOUR OWN DISPUTE RESOLUTION PROCESS

Parties involved in a dispute can create their own dispute resolution system instead of using an existing process. They can reach an agreement that provides the details and mechanics of the system to be used. This power to decide their own fate is based upon contract law and applicable federal and state statutes, including the Federal Arbitration Act. The parties need to consent to whatever system they wish to use, and their contractual agreement binds them to this process and makes the result enforceable.

The type of system used depends upon the needs of the parties. The parties may select one method or a combination of methods. For example, parties can agree to mediate, and if mediation is unsuccessful, agree to submit the dispute to binding arbitration. Parties may prefer to use these fast, affordable, private, and fair resolution methods.

Parties may and typically do agree on a process before a dispute arises, known as a pre-dispute resolution agreement (e.g. a pre-dispute binding arbitration clause). These agreements are quite common. Or parties can fashion their own process after a dispute arises, known as a post-dispute resolution agreement. These agreements are less common because it is difficult for disputing parties to agree on a process, as explained previously.

F. DISPUTE RESOLUTION GOALS

6.13 GOALS OF DISPUTE RESOLUTION METHOD

Parties should consider the following goals in designing or selecting a dispute resolution system:

Speed. How quickly do the parties need a resolution? How long can they wait?

Cost. What can the parties afford? What are the transaction costs? For example, in litigation, parties will legally or practically need to have an attorney represent them. In arbitration or administrative hearings, the parties may be able to represent themselves.

Exchange of Information. How should information be disclosed and exchanged between the parties? Is formal discovery necessary?

Discovery. In litigation, discovery includes depositions, interrogatories, document production requests, and admissions. In arbitration and administrative hearings, discovery may be reasonably limited, or the parties can agree to use specific discovery devices.

Availability of Motions. Do the parties need to bring motions to resolve part or all of a case? In litigation, there are hundreds of motions that can be brought. In arbitration and administrative hearings, only a limited number of motions are possible or necessary.

Hearing and Trial Procedures. All forums generally allow opening statements, direct and cross-examination of witnesses, submission of exhibits, use of expert witnesses, and closing arguments.

Decision Maker. Who should be the decision maker? Should it be an expert, like an arbitrator or administrative judge? Should it be a public judge? Should it be laypersons on a jury?

Finality. Should the decision be final and binding? Should there be broad appeal rights? Should there be limited circumstances to challenge the decision?

Privacy. Do the parties want the proceedings private? Do they prefer a public trial?

Enforceability. How will the final decision be enforced? Mediation settlements can be enforced as contracts. Arbitration, administrative, and judicial decisions can all be enforced as judgments.

Fairness and Satisfaction. Whatever the method used, the process must be fair and one in which the parties can be satisfied with the process if not with the result.

6.14 MANDATED ALTERNATIVE DISPUTE RESOLUTION

Alternative dispute resolution (ADR) is a popular description of non-litigation methods used to resolve disputes. It would be more accurate to describe these procedures as "advanced" methods. The most common ADR methods are mediation and arbitration, as previously described.

A growing number of federal and state court systems mandate parties to use mediation or non-binding arbitration before they will be allowed to go to trial. A growing number of legislative enactments substitute ADR methods instead of litigation to resolve problems. For example, the new federal healthcare initiatives promote the use of ADR methods. Administrative agencies may require the parties to attempt to mediate a problem before a hearing is conducted.

These developments are occurring for a number of reasons. ADR methods are usually much faster and much less expensive than trial. The use of ADR may result in a resolution that better meets the needs of the parties and that may not be available through a judicial or administrative decision. The transaction costs and attorney fees involved in ADR are significantly less than judicial proceedings. For many disputes, the litigation system can cause more problems that it resolves. Through ADR, parties can participate and construct a resolution of their dispute.

Think Twice

Dispute resolution methods ought to be fast, affordable, and fair. To the extent they are not, that presents a real barrier to justice for many parties. Justice that is delayed, expensive, and problematic is not justice, especially for those that have to wait or pay for it. Your goal as a future advocate is to influence, shape, and reform our civil justice system so that civil justice is truly available and affordable for all.

Chapter Seven
INVESTIGATIONS: OBTAINING INFORMATION FROM THOSE IN THE KNOW

The best way to win an argument is to begin by being right.

—Jill Ruckelshaus

A. INTRODUCTION

7.1 SCOPE OF INFORMATION

This chapter concentrates primarily on the informal gathering of information from sources other than a client or opposing party. During the interviewing, counseling, and planning stages of a deal or dispute, you will need to seek and obtain information from others and about others. Subsequent chapters explain how to discover information from opposing parties during litigation.

Information is available from three primary sources: the internet, documents, and people. The internet permits web-based searches for almost anything imaginable both in the public domain, and to a somewhat lesser extent, in the private domain. Documents include sources of available printed, recorded, and electronic information. People include anyone who might know something.

B. THE WORLD AT YOUR FINGERTIPS

7.2 INTERNET SEARCHES

It seems almost like magic. A few relevant search terms and a few keystrokes and—abracadabra—there's your answer. While it's not quite that easy, you can acquire an awful lot of information you need to uncover on your computer using a variety of internet investigation techniques. A lot of cyber research is fast, easy, and free.

Where to begin your investigation depends on what you are looking for. How to continue that investigation depends on what you find. When to stop depends on how successful you are. Internet searches can be amazingly productive or a bottomless black hole with endless and exhausting possibilities. Knowing when to stop is as important as knowing where to look.

Your goal is to obtain accurate, reliable and authoritative information and your searches should focus on sources that provide that information. There are more than enough sources out in cyberspace chock full of data, but many should be avoided. You can evaluate a sites usefulness for legal work by noting who is the originator of the site, who wrote the content, and when was the information published.

The following section discusses alternative sources of online investigative databases and information. The order in which you use them depends on what you need to uncover.

Think Twice

Before you begin to search the web you may prefer to use a new email address to reduce chances of spam and phishing. You can obtain a free web-based email address by using one of the search engines identified below.

7.2.1 Search Engines

Several search engines can be used to handily locate information. You may have a favorite site which you can start with and use others as needed. The most common sites are currently Google, Bing, AlltheWeb, AltaVista, Hotbot, Metacrawler, Yahoo, and Search.

7.2.2 Informational Sites

Other web sites can provide you information you never knew you wanted or needed. Wikipedia has become a go-to source of information and is sometimes even cited in judicial opinions. Or you could ask Ask.com about About.com. while searching for

Answers.com. Other websites (besides Wikipedia) that relate to the law include megalaw.com and lawguru.com.

7.2.3   Specific Informational Sites

You can narrow your search to more specific sites that contain more relevant information. There are a host of government, public, and private sites that exist, and, to give you some idea of the potential sources, here are a few frequently used ones, as well more obscure ones:

Public Records Search Directory at www.searchsystems.net

Reference, Facts & News Free Resource at www.refdesk.com

Government Information at www.usdoj.gov

Sources of Public Information at www.gao.gov/special.pubs

U.S. Census Bureau data at www.census.gov/main

Corporation Information at www.corporateinformation.com

Google Maps at www.maps.google.com

Obscure Government documents at www.governmentattic.org

Law Enforcement Documents at www.thesmokinggun.com

7.2.4   Social and Business Portals

Typically, you are looking for specific information about a person, place, or thing. A source mentioned above may be a good starting place, but it may need to be supplemented. You may search for information about an individual on social networking sites or public interest or private data bases. Facebook, Linked In, Myspace, You Tube, and Bebo may yield fascinating information, and some of it may be helpful. There may be a blog that has even more information, or you may consider searching or joining a chat room, bulletin board, forum, message board, list serve, discussion room, or another social or professional networking site.

7.2.5   Commercial Databases

You can search for current commercial sources by using the search term: online databases for investigative use. Some common fee based web sources are:

Accurint—data records on individuals and businesses

Hoovers—international data on companies, industries, and executives

Dialog—covering business, science, engineering, finance, and law

Dun & Bradstreet—research on companies, executives, and industries

Factiva, from Dow Jones—business news and information

Thomson Reuters—news about legal, financial, media, health, science

Think Twice

There is so much information available online that it can be overwhelming. You need to focus on what you need to know and select those sources that are likely to be informative. Of course, it's possible to surf without a particular plan and hope to stumble across some informational gem, but mining and surfing are always more efficient if you use a systematic and thoughtful approach.

By the time you read this, there will undoubtedly be technological developments that make something we suggest laughable or outmoded. You ought to look for and be alert to better ways to locate web based reliable information, with any luck, for free.

The low cost and relative ease of web searches make this method of investigation tantalizingly seductive. It's important to supplement web investigation with some of the other techniques discussed in the following sections.

7.2.6 The Right Stuff

Now you have some ideas, coupled with your own experiences, about where to look online. Next we discuss what to look for.

C. RELEVANT MATERIALS

7.3 DOCUMENTS AND ELECTRONICALLY STORED INFORMATION

What you need to know may exist in some written, printed, electronic or recorded form. How to uncover this information depends upon its type, source, and format.

7.3.1 Types

There are two basic types of information: materials another party has created and materials developed by others about relevant issues. The former includes specific information someone involved in the case has written or developed, for example, the proverbial "hot document" which reveals damaging information. The latter involves general information about a matter related to the case, such as an article written about a party, statistics gathered about a particular field, or data publicized by a specific industry.

Two common forms of communications include emails and text messages. You can use an email search website to discover email addresses of individuals. If you receive an email, you can retain an online reputable company to conduct a reverse email search. Similarly, with cell phone messages and texts, you can obtain help from a legitimate online company to track these sources.

Think Twice

The Federal Rules of Civil Procedure and many state court rules use the phrase "electronically stored information" to refer to virtually all types of electronic information and documents—ESI for short. We'll use that term, as it has already acquired that meaning.

7.3.2 Sources

The two primary sources for documents and electronically stored information are private and public information. Private information may only legitimately be obtained with the consent of the holder of the information or through a subpoena. For example, a business may only be willing to reveal information it has because it wants to or because a court orders it to. A private corporation may provide copies of bills and invoices only to individuals involved in the transaction. A bank may not reveal any of its records without a subpoena. Or, there may be a website out there that has somehow obtained the private data and published it.

On the other hand, public information should be readily available on request. For example, you can take a bus to the library to research information or ask for help, you can stay at home and use your computer to search online for data as previously explored, or you can contact a governmental agency for information. The Freedom of Information Act and comparable state statutes are powerful tools for dislodging public information.

Public information may have a high degree of credibility because it is generated by disinterested persons and made for some purpose usually unrelated to your case. Although some public records are poorly conceptualized (they give you every imaginable statistic except the really useful information), badly organized (they have the information but it is hard to decipher), or inconveniently stored (the required record is misplaced), many are useful and easily accessible. Public information can be cheaper than seeking information from resistant witnesses and opponents. Public information can also be used as a check on the degree to which counsel is receiving complete and correct information from witnesses and opponents.

7.3.3   Format

The availability of documentary information may depend upon its format. It may appear in written form in an article or book. It may be retained as a separate piece of information or as part of a file or report. It may be a digital photograph. It may be stored electronically in a computer database, or exist only as a recording on a hard drive. Uncovering where it resides is the first step, obtaining it comes next.

Electronically stored information will appear in its native format, which may or may be readily available. The data may need to be re-formatted or transferred to another system. ESI metadata also tells a lot about the origins and history of a document. Section 14.6 explores the world of electronically stored information (ESI) in more detail.

Think Twice

Think back a few years ago to the devices available that produced electronic documents and materials. And think about the various formats that are no longer used or even available to hold or display that information. You almost

have go to a museum to see them. Currently, native for-
mats and metadata raise some complicated issues regard-
ing what to uncover about ESI. Section 14. 6 explains how
these concepts affect formal discovery. They affect infor-
mal investigations differently. To the extent you need to
know more, you'll have to do your own research, on line,
on a search engine, or in Wikipedia.

7.4 THINGS

Things are where you find them. If they are commercially
available, you can buy one. If they are public property, you can
view them. If they are on private property, you will need the
consent of the owner to see them.

Objects that are relevant to a case investigation often require special attention. With some things, you may need the
original, if it is still available. With other things, a duplicate or
similar model will suffice.

You may want to inspect it or test it. You'll need to services
of an expert to help. Section 14.9 explains this.

D. THE HUMAN TOUCH

7.5 PEOPLE

There are four principal categories of people who may know
something useful:

- Friendly witnesses

- Neutral witnesses

- Adverse witnesses

- Experts

You or your client are very likely to know them. You can
keystroke their name on Google or another search engine and
often learn a lot about them. And then there are those social
network sites like Facebook that may have even more interesting
revelations.

Think Twice

Identifying witnesses or sources who have relevant infor-
mation is often a key to a successful outcome. People are

often an excellent source for confirming what a client told you in your interview or for obtaining factual support before negotiating a deal or resolving a dispute. It's very helpful before contacting a potential witness, and certainly before talking to them, to craft a plan on how best to do so.

7.5.1　Friendly Witnesses

Broadly defined, a friendly witness or source is anyone who likes your client. These people include family (well, most of them), friends, acquaintances, and colleagues. A friendly witness is also someone who may not know your client but who supports your client's position.

Other witnesses can be equally friendly and useful. Regulators of a particular business, although forbidden by law from playing favorites, may be inclined to help by providing information to people they believe are deserving of the information.

One of the best aspects of friendly witnesses is that they will be cooperative and relatively easy to contact in seeking information. All you need to do is tell them who you represent and what you want, and they will tell you what they know or where you may find what you want. It's not always that easy, but it is a lot easier than dealing with the other types of witnesses.

7.5.2　Neutral Witnesses

A neutral witness or source is (obviously) someone who is (ostensibly) impartial. The major difference in dealing with neutral witnesses is the way you approach them and the manner in which you attempt to obtain information. Neutral witnesses will usually not be as cooperative, receptive, or available to provide information. You are, after all, asking them for a favor for a total stranger (your client).

7.5.3　Adverse Witnesses

An adverse witness or source dislikes your client, wants your client to lose something, or both. The most obvious problem with this type of witness is that the witness may be unwilling to talk or cooperate with you. You know you can always subpoena them in litigation (as you can with any other witness including a neutral or friendly witness) to talk with you or bring materials to a deposition. With a dispute, it may be to your client's advantage for you to contact them to obtain information informally; and, with a deal, there are no subpoena rules available to use.

There will be some adverse witnesses you will not be able to informally contact. An adverse party represented by an attorney cannot be contacted directly except through their lawyer. Adverse witnesses who are managing agents of a party or who may be closely affiliated with the party also cannot be contacted without permission of opposing counsel. To do so would violate the rules of professional conduct prohibiting you from making such ex parte contacts.

7.5.4   Experts

You may need an expert to help you interpret or create information or provide you with an opinion. You may need an expert for a transaction (for example, a tax accountant), and you may need an expert for litigation (for example, a scientist). You can contact experts to determine their availability, interest, and fees. Experts usually expect to be paid by the hour or a set fee, plus expenses, often with a retainer.

The most effective way to locate an expert is through referrals from other counsel, clients, associations, other experts, or on line referral services. It is wise to research experts before contacting them to determine their experience, reputation, and special knowledge. You can obtain this information from your referral source, information on the web, periodicals, media information, and an internet or paper trail of their publications. You also want to consider (when you contact and interview them) their cooperativeness, working style, punctuality, personality, and cost. There is no substitute for a reasonable, affordable expert who works well with others.

After you retain experts, you can meet with them or provide them the information they need to be of assistance. If you are involved in a transaction, you will need to tell them what they need to know. If you are involved in litigation, what you tell your expert may depend upon what role they will play in litigation.

Information disclosed to an expert who will testify at trial is subject to discovery, as explained in Section 12.5.

Think Twice

You can contact experts to help you understand a technical, scientific, medical, engineering, financial, accounting or other topic relevant to your deal or dispute. You may also present to experts an opinion or conclusion that supports your side of a deal or dispute, and see if they agree with you. If not, find out why and perhaps search for another expert who may have a different view.

7.6   COOPERATION WITH WITNESSES

You can increase the cooperation of a witness or source by following certain interviewing approaches:

Be kind, respectful and courteous. You made need to be persistent, but trying to bully people into providing information is almost always counter-productive. Being impolite and rude to a reluctant witness will simply accelerate the end of the interview.

Select a convenient time and place for the witness. Make it as convenient as possible for the neutral witness to provide information. Make things as easy as possible by going to them instead of asking them to come to your office, sending someone to help search for materials or copy documents, agreeing to meet after business hours or on weekends, and reimbursing them for reasonable travel expenses.

Be punctual and brief. You should avoid wasting their time and use as little of it as necessary.

Make the person feel good about cooperating. Unless you are a Hobbes fanatic, approach witnesses as if they were good people who are willing to help. They usually will help if they feel they are doing something beneficial for someone else, their job, the public good, or themselves. So tell them how talking with you benefits your client, how it is part of their job responsibility, how it helps promote societal interests, or how it benefits them. A neutral witness may have a self-interest of which they may not be initially aware. For example, an uncooperative neutral witness may provide evidence in litigation regarding artwork after being advised that an adverse result could cast doubt on the authenticity of the witness' own valuable art collection.

Empathize with the witness. Identify with appropriate attitudes and positions and listen approvingly.

Personalize the client. Describe your client as an individual who needs help and the assistance of the witness.

Rely on altruism. A polite appeal to altruism may go a long way. Most humans have a bit of it, no matter what neoclassical economists may say. For example, telling a witness that an injured client has only limited insurance and needs to prevail to obtain full compensation may help.

Consider who is present. The presence of someone else besides the witness may make it more difficult for the witness to recall accurately and without unnecessary influence. Alternatively, some witnesses may be more willing to talk if someone else they know is present.

Provide a reluctant witness with a reason to talk to you. Start by asking why the person is refusing to cooperate. This information may help you understand the person's position and may help you craft a reason the witness should talk with you.

7.7 DIFFICULT WITNESSES

You should not shirk from pursuing the difficult witness. You are unlikely to convince an adverse witness or source to switch sides, and attempting to do so may further alienate the witness. You may, however, be able effectively to use additional approaches to gain information:

Appeal to the person's natural inclination to want to tell the truth. Say: "I understand you don't want to talk to me, but you do want us to know what really happened, don't you?"

Let the difficult witness persuade you of the correctness of the opposing position. Try saying: "Tell me what you know and my client may not pursue this matter."

Let the witness rant and rave. Encourage them to tell you what happened and disclose their biases and prejudices. Say:

"I need to know all the bad things about my client. What do you know?"

Appeal to their self-interest. Say: "You may want to talk to me if you knew what some people have said about you. I heard you were a...."

Focus on their involvement. Say: "You may want to tell me some things that directly involve you. Let me ask you a few questions to clarify your involvement."

Appropriately explain the consequences of not cooperating. There is a time for appropriate threats. For example, you could explain that not talking with you now means that you will have to subpoena the witness to appear at a deposition. Further explain that the timing and location may then be a greater inconvenience.

Think Twice

Not surprisingly, witnesses are people and are consequently influenced by the same things that generally influence people. How best to approach and talk with a witness is largely a matter of an understanding of human motivations. The approaches outlined here reflect those notions. Your instinct or hunch on how best to proceed, if different, may work well. You may want to follow your own judgment with a particular witness.

7.8 WITNESS PAYMENTS

The general rules are these:

- The expenses that may be reimbursed for a lay witness are reasonable costs for travel.

- A lay witness cannot or should not be paid for giving information or for testifying.

- Expert witnesses may be paid for their professional services, with an hourly or flat fee, plus reasonable costs.

- Some witnesses may expect to be reimbursed for their personal time spent being interviewed, such as individuals who are often eye witnesses (e.g. police).

E.   HOW TO OBTAIN INFORMATION

7.9   ASK. LOOK. DEMAND

What you need often involves contacting a person. If you want what someone knows, you obviously have to talk with the person. If you want electronically stored information, documents, or other materials, you may need the cooperation of someone who has them. To get what you want, you can:

- Ask for what you want

- Look for what you want

- Demand what you want

Think Twice

Lawyers have a wide range of different approaches and ideas about all facets of practice, including investigation strategies, depending on their professional and personal experiences. What one lawyer thinks a good idea, another scoffs at. You'll have to make your own decisions in particular cases about which of the approaches in this section will work best for you or seek advice from a more experienced lawyer or professional investigator.

7.9.1   Asking

You can start by asking questions of everyone connected with the matter who is willing to talk. When involved in a transaction, the lawyer can ask about other prospective parties, the goals of the deal, the client's situation, previous similar dealings, or standard practices in the industry. When engaged in dispute resolution, the lawyer can ask questions of persons with knowledge of the dispute. Sometimes this is the only way to obtain critical information, since the participants may know things that were never recorded in any other medium. Sometimes, further inquiries may reveal the existence of documents and other things.

7.9.2   Looking

The adage "seek and you shall find" is good, practical advice for legal practice. Whether counsel is reconstructing an event giving rise to a dispute or attempting to determine whether

Purpleacre is really worth the multi-million dollar price tag, there may be no substitute for simply going, seeing, and digging around. Where possible, counsel or an assistant should get in the car, take a drive, and view the property in question, visit sites of events, review physical material, and study other relevant things.

Often, looking can be done informally because the material to be examined is in plain view or available to the public. Sometimes, special arrangements may need to be made (e.g. a tour of a factory or plant subject to possible sale). With voluntary transactions other parties will be inclined to cooperate in order to facilitate a legal project. Other times, particularly in disputes, looking is not as easy as a simple walk-by but will require the consent of the other side and perhaps the instigation of a formal discovery request.

Another option is to use an internet map website. You may be able to get a camera based street view of a house or property, and while you may not learn as much as you would with an in-person visit, you can make this search easily and anonymously.

7.9.3 Demanding

If information is not forthcoming voluntarily, a lawyer can always demand the information. In transactional work, the demand may prompt the other side to cooperate if it is in their best interest because otherwise the deal may not be completed. In disputes, the threat of a demand without serving formal documents may be sufficient to gain cooperation. If not, discovery methods may obtain information from a party or a subpoena may obtain the information from a third party. See section 14.11. Information in government hands may be demanded pursuant to the Freedom of Information Act or similar state statutes. See section 14.12.

7.10 THE HOW, THE WHEN, THE WHERE, THE WHO

Not all legal precedent is created equal, nor is all prospective information. Some information is more germane to determining legal rights or responsibilities. Similarly, all sources are not created equal. Some sources are more important because they are more likely to possess relevant information.

Before beginning investigation, you should develop a plan or agenda for discovery, taking note of the time and resources available to you. One of the most common mistakes new lawyers make is beginning fact investigation without a plan. Typically, this results in investigation following the path of least resistance, with contact being made first with the easiest sources. This may prove workable, but it often means that witnesses need to be interviewed again after more critical sources have finally been contacted or—worse—that the available time or resources for an investigation have been devoted to obtaining less than critical information.

7.10.1   The How

Face-to-face interviews of course allow the interviewer to observe the witness and develop a more personal relationship with them. Telephone interviews can be much more efficient and economical and still provide sufficiently useful information. You may also be able to use a software application that produces video conferencing calls (like Skype) so you can talk to and see the witness. This obviously requires the witness to have the computer devices to make this happen.

7.10.2   The When

Effective investigators generally conduct their initial and subsequent investigations in descending order of importance. The most valuable information and sources should be pursued immediately both to ensure obtaining accurate information (e.g., before prospective opponents contact the source and create inter-ference) and to ensure the information is not eroded in some way. Information and sources should also be preserved before something expected or unexpected happens. A key witness may later be unavailable and should be talked to early in the investi-gation. An important witness may die and valuable information lost unless preserved.

7.10.3   The Where

The best location for an investigation depends upon the circumstances. A witness who is favorable and is willing to talk may be willing to come to the lawyer's office for an interview. A lawyer will usually need to go see a neutral or adverse witness. If a witness will be referring to documents and other things that are best illustrated on site, that location will be preferable. Sometimes a neutral interview site is required for purposes of accommodating schedules or avoiding attention. A witness may want to be helpful but may not want to be seen. Usually interviews should be conducted in an accommodating location, but sometimes interviews should be conducted in an intimidating atmosphere. It all depends on the witness, the allegiance of the witness, the nature of the information sought, and related factors.

7.10.4   The Who

While we have focused on the lawyer as the person obtaining the information, it is often more productive and less costly for others to be information gatherers. An experienced investigator, retained independently or employed by the law firm, can often be more effective and efficient. This investigator may be more available, knowledgeable, and better equipped to obtain the information, and may also do a significantly better job than an attorney because some investigations require the gathering of physical, technical, and scientific information. Investigators who are also experts in using internet searches and technological devices to legitimately obtain relevant information are worth their weight in computers.

Experienced investigators may also be better able to interview witnesses and more efficiently record stories and testimony. Other people besides the primary lawyers may be less expensive. Investigators who charge a lower hourly or set fee or paralegals or associates in a firm who have low hourly fees may be more economical.

Another consideration relates to the possible impact on the use of the information sought. If an attorney interviews a witness or negotiates with a prospective defendant, these conversations may become part of a dispute. If this occurs, the lawyer may be disqualified from continuing to provide representation if the lawyer will also be a witness about the point in contention. To avoid this prospect, lawyers should either avoid these sorts of interviews or contacts entirely or be accompanied by a non-lawyer. If testimonial conflicts later ensue, the non-lawyer can provide the needed testimony without necessarily disqualifying the lawyer.

Think Twice

We each have different talents. Witnesses interviewing in particular is a skill that some do better than others. You can learn a lot about the process in this chapter and after interviewing witnesses but you may reasonably conclude that having a trained and professional investigator do this work may be better for your client. And you should not feel less of a lawyer for doing so. Indeed, for the reasons suggested above it may be the best thing for your deal or dispute if you do not get involved in the investigation. But you still need to know how they do things, so please read on.

7.11   INTERVIEW APPROACHES

Three common interviewing techniques for witnesses are:

- Creating a narrative
- Asking specific questions
- Asking closed end "cross-examination-type" questions

These techniques may be and usually are mixed during any one interview. Your goal is to achieve completion, clarity, and closure. A narrative approach has the witness relate in story form what the witness knows. Specific questions clarify information, add details, and elicit new information. Cross-examination questions pursue evasive answers, resolve conflicting information, test the perception of the witness, and search for impeachment. These approaches are identical or similar to interviewing approaches used in client interviews and depositions, discussed in Chapters Three and Thirteen. Suggestions contained in these chapters relating to clients and deponents also apply to the questioning of witnesses.

7.11.1   Interview Techniques

Investigators may assist a witness in accurately remembering and correctly reciting information. Or, investigators may attempt to influence responses a witness gives during an interview. These approaches recognize that witnesses may not have seen or heard everything, may have forgotten some things, or may be mistaken regarding their perceptions. Techniques that some investigators employ to influence witnesses include:

Word choice. The selection of certain words may create a more helpful and persuasive witness story and statement. The suggestion or inclusion of adjectives and impact words may strengthen a witness' version. For example, adding "very" to modify the word fast will make an obvious difference, and substituting "screamed" for "said" may also make a difference.

Leading questions. Questions that suggest an answer may encourage the witness to agree with the suggested answer.

Filling in details. An interviewer may tell the witness what happened so the witness will include that information in a story they may otherwise have forgotten.

Other versions. An investigator may tell the witness what other witnesses have said to influence the interviewee. For example, an investigator may say: "Two other witnesses have told me the light was green, what color did you see?"

Disagreeing with the answers. The interviewer may explain why what a witness has said may be inaccurate, implausible, or mistaken in an attempt to change the mind of the witness.

Composing a statement. After an interview, the investigator may draft a witness statement and compose it in as favorable a light as possible for a client.

These techniques must be used carefully to avoid unfairly influencing the witness. It sometimes is a fine line between what is appropriate and what may be unethical or illegal. If in doubt, the investigator must avoid improper techniques.

7.11.2 Advising Witnesses

An attorney cannot provide legal advice to a witness unless the attorney represents the witness. It is improper and a conflict of interest for an attorney to provide legal advice to a non-client witness. The most tempting advice to give a witness is not to talk to anyone else about a situation. But it is unethical to tell a witness to refuse to talk and also a mistake. It is a tactical mistake to create an impression that the investigator has something to hide and has to rely on withholding information in an attempt to gain an advantage.

A lawyer may properly and carefully, without providing legal advice, explain the consequences to a witness of talking or not talking to the other side. A lawyer cannot suggest or tell a witness what to do and should expressly tell the witness this. A lawyer may provide general information to witnesses informing them about their rights, and witnesses may rely upon this explanation in making their own independent decision.

Think Twice

Investigative techniques dramatically depicted in the movies or on television may be fun to watch, but most are seldom useful for lawyers practicing in the real world. Those strategies are often inappropriate or illegal or reflect bad tactics. And remember in criminal cases, things are far different. In civil cases, you need to be careful in dealing with witnesses and what you say to them. Some advocates pretend to themselves that their interview is being secretly recorded and some day they will be asked to explain and account for what happened. Doing the right thing is always the best advice.

7.12   PRESERVING THE INTERVIEW

An investigator needs to decide before, during, or after an interview whether and how the information should be preserved. It may be unnecessary to record information obtained from a friendly witness who will always be available. It may be necessary to preserve information from a neutral or adverse witness who may be unavailable or who may later change their story. Three common ways to make a record of information obtained are:

- A file memo
- A witness statement
- A contemporaneous recording

7.12.1 File Memo

The file memo may contain several parts:

- The date, time, and place of the investigation along with contact information for the witness.

- A summary of the information obtained.

- A description of the demeanor and credibility of the witness and the importance and implication of the information.

- Additional relevant comments produced in the interview.

The lawyer-investigator should be involved in the drafting of these memos and their content and comprehensiveness. File memos are usually not discoverable because they contain private information for transactions or constitute work product for litigation, as explained in Section 12.4.2. Care needs to be taken in drafting a file memo to determine whether all or part of the memo may be later discoverable.

7.12.2 Witness Statements

Witness statements may include the following components:

- The identity of the witness, including name, address, phone, email address.

- Statements in the first person, with the statement written as if the witness was telling the story.

- The witnesses' own words and expressions, reflecting how they told their story.

- Clear and understandable language that is not ambiguous or confusing.

- Information that is sufficiently complete to reflect what the witness knows.

- Selective information that supports the story most helpful to a client.

- A concluding statement that the witness has read and understands the statement and that the statement is true and accurate.

Other considerations affecting the content of the statement include:

Timing. A witness statement may be composed during or after an interview. Completing the statement in the presence of the witness is the most efficient and economic procedure. Completing the statement later requires the investigator to meet with the witness again and may permit some event in the interim to cause a witness to change a story.

Format. Witness statements are often handwritten or printed documents. The investigator who drafts the statement is better able to suggest the structure, the words used, and facts included. A witness statement may also be composed as a sworn affidavit or declaration. This may encourage the witness to be sure to tell the truth or increase the impeachment value of the statement.

Review. A witness should read a statement for accuracy and completeness and to correct any mistakes. This avoids later efforts by the witness to recant the story and reduces a claim against the investigator for unfairly influencing the witness.

Adopting the statement. It is usually best for a witness to sign a statement, and they may need to initial each page in a multi-page statement. If the witness refuses to sign a statement, the witness may be willing to initial the statement. Alternatively, the investigator can read the entire document to the witness and have the witness sign a short statement that the document is accurate as read.

7.13   RECORDING THE STATEMENT

Recording the interview may be preferable to composing a written file memo or a printed witness statement. The two most common forms of recording are an electronic recording and a court reporter statement. Electronic recording may be made by any kind of audio recorder or by a video camera. A court reporter statement is a transcript prepared by a reporter who accompanies an investigator and who contemporaneously records the interview.

In most jurisdictions it is permissible to electronically record a face-to-face interview without the knowledge or consent of the interviewee. It is permissible in all states to electronically record a face-to-face or telephone interview if both the interviewer and interviewee consent. Some states prohibit a lawyer from recording interviews or telephone conversations without the other party's consent; other states permit recording as long as one party consents.

A recorded interview has the advantage of preserving the exact words of a witness and the complete story. An audio recording captures the voice inflections and sounds of the witness. A video recording reproduces everything that is said and done. The growing availability of personal digital assistants and cell phones that have video capabilities make video recording more accessible and available. And the popularity of social network sites makes people more familiar and comfortable with video recordings. But, if these electronic devices make the witness uncomfortable or apprehensive the witness may well decline to be interviewed or may withhold useful information.

Think Twice

What to preserve and how to preserve witness information depends upon how the information helps your deal or dispute or how it hurts the other side. It is a truism that you should only preserve information if it will help your client succeed or win. You do not have preserve or record everything or even most of everything. You need to be selective in retaining information from witnesses.

Chapter Eight
NEGOTIATION PREPARATION AND PLANNING: WHAT DO I WANT, WHAT DO I KNOW, WHAT DO I DO?

We arg'ed the thing at breakfast, we arg'ed the thing at tea, And the more we arg'ed the question the more we didn't agree.

—*Will Carleton*

Betsey and I Are Out

A. INTRODUCTION

8.1 THE STAGES OF NEGOTIATION PLANNING

Negotiation is an important part of the work of nearly every practicing lawyer. Lawyers negotiate on behalf of clients to create transactions or to resolve disputes. Virtually every client problem, virtually every client goal creates an opportunity for a lawyer to resolve the matter through negotiation.

Like all other lawyering skills, a lawyer's success will depend in large part on the willingness to do the work necessary to prepare. A successful negotiation is typically the result of a thoughtful plan. Good negotiators ask themselves three sets of questions to prepare for a negotiation:

- What does my client want? What does the other side want? To answer these questions, the successful negotiator needs to understand both parties' immediate goals, over-arching goals, and process preferences.

- What do I know? What do I need to find out? What will the other lawyer try to find out? The answers to these questions require making a plan to exchange information by disclosing and seeking information from the other side during the negotiation.

- What should I do during the negotiation? What will the other side do during the negotiation? To answer these questions the successful negotiator should analyze effective approaches and factors that influence the negotiation.

In addition, the responsible negotiator needs to:

- Assess ethical issues and concerns.

This chapter focuses on each of these four areas in the context of planning and preparing for negotiation. The following chapter explores the negotiation process itself.

B. ESTABLISHING GOALS: WHAT DOES MY CLIENT WANT? WHAT DOES THE OTHER SIDE WANT?

8.2 NEGOTIATION GOALS

The first step before beginning a negotiation is to understand the goals of the client, as well as the interests and needs of the other side.

8.2.1 Goals of the Client

What is it that the client really wants and needs from the negotiation? What are the client's immediate and overarching goals? In a straightforward negotiation to purchase goods, it's tempting to think that the buyer's goal is simply to pay as little as possible, and the buyer's goal is to receive the largest possible payment. Think back to the discussion of client goals in Chapter Three. Client goals in a transaction for the sale of goods would certainly include obtaining a favorable purchase price—that is an excellent example of an immediate goal. Those immediate goals will shape the offers and demands made during the negotiation.

It is also essential to understand a client's overarching goals and process preferences. A client may, for example, be more concerned about an overarching goal to establish a long-term business relationship rather than the immediate goal of getting the best price possible in the present negotiation. In a litigation context, a client's willingness to settle a lawsuit may be motivated by a strong process preference to avoid trial.

A client in a negotiation may have goals that are tangible and goals that are intangible. Tangible goals could include making money, obtaining position or power, or persuading the other the other party to do something. Intangible goals could include a desire to preserve dignity, achieve justice, improve community cohesion, seek revenge, vindicate a principle, or simply be heard. It is often more difficult to learn a client's intangible goals than the tangible ones, but a client's satisfaction with a negotiated outcome often turns on how well the lawyer has understood that client's intangible goals.

A wide variety of factors—cultural, social, ethnic, economic, and religious—may significantly influence client goals. For example, many clients behave primarily as entrepreneurs with the goal of maximizing profits in the marketplace. Other clients are not motivated primarily by money or do not act as competitively. A lawyer may need to cultivate awareness of these factors in order to understand the client's goals. This task can be complicated by the fact that client goals may shift during the course of representation. Life goes on, the odds of winning at trial change, business opportunities open and close, injuries heal or fester, personal and community situations change. The good lawyer communicates regularly with the client in order to learn about these influential shifts.

Think Twice

It's easy to overlook or underestimate the influence that one or more of these factors may have in a negotiation. The client may not be aware of these influences or be willing to talk about them. A client may want to keep something private—an upcoming business deal. Or a client may be too embarrassed to discuss something— feelings of revenge. The lawyer may need to raise these possible influences with a client to see if they exist. And that can be difficult because they can be delicate and sensitive issues.

8.2.2   Perceptions of the Other Side

It is just as important to understand the other's side's goals. To accomplish this, it is often useful to first think about how the other side perceives the situation giving rise to the negotiation. Perceptions that parties have can dramatically affect negotiation goals, and the two sides to a negotiation may have dramatically different perceptions of the situation. Consider these two examples, one involving a transactional negotiation and the other, a settlement negotiation.

In a sale/purchase transaction, a buyer and seller may have significantly different perceptions about the value of a piece of land. A variety of objective and subjective perceptions may influence the parties:

Buyer	Seller
This land is going to be worth a lot more in the future.	This land is worth more now than I thought it would be when I bought it.
I can resell this land for more money tomorrow.	This property is not going to be worth any more tomorrow than it is today.
I have always wanted to own this piece of land.	I want to get rid of this and buy something else.
I can get this land rezoned and make a huge profit.	I tried getting it rezoned, and it can't be done.
I can keep some of this land for my own use, and sell part of it for the same price I'm paying for all of it.	No one else has offered me anywhere near this amount of money.
This land will skyrocket in value when the adjacent land is developed.	The bridge and highway are not going to be built making this land almost useless.

In litigation, adverse parties may have markedly different views about the case. The following reflect the views what a plaintiff, who was injured in a golf cart accident, and the defendant golf course, who owns and leased the golf cart, might have in a personal injury lawsuit:

Plaintiff	Defendant
I expect something I lease to be safe and the defendant owes me, a consumer, special care.	The cart was recently inspected and was in excellent shape.
We carefully used the cart the same way other golfers use it.	The driver didn't know how to drive the cart and should have been more careful.
Special brakes should be placed on such carts, but the golf course is too cheap to do so.	The brakes didn't stop the cart because the tree did first.
If the defendant wants protection he should sell insurance with the cart. I would have bought some.	She sues me instead of her friend who was driving because I have money.
This has never happened to me before, and I'll never be the same.	This has never happened on our course before, and the bad publicity has hurt my business.

These differing perceptions may be based on objective data, speculation, personal experience, or hopes and dreams. The other side's perceptions may be accurate or fanciful, and may be challenged or changed during negotiation. While preparing for the negotiation, it's useful to consider what those perceptions might be in order to understand what the other side's goals are likely to be.

Think Twice

It can be easy to dismiss the other side's perceptions because they run counter to what a client perceives and because they may be based on irrational or unreasonable perceptions. Parties to a negotiation are unlikely to readily admit they are being influenced by anything other than rational, reasonable positions. They may even believe that their emotions have no impact on their decision making. In dispute negotiations, the impact that emotions and psychological influences can have on the settlement process is often fairly apparent. In deal making, it may be less evident. But in both contexts, lawyers need to remain alert to these factors.

It's not just unsophisticated or first-time clients that are likely to become emotionally involved. A plaintiff who has been severely injured by the negligence of a defendant may naturally be upset at a very low settlement offer. But an experienced business seller may similarly be personally offended by a low price offered by a buyer, though less likely to admit that such an emotion plays a role in their "rational" business decision. The lawyer needs to be aware that "unreasonable" factors may be influencing a client and raise that possibility with the client.

8.2.3   Goals of the Other Side

Understanding the goals of the other side makes a lawyer a more effective negotiator. A lawyer who prepares for negotiation by focusing only on what the client wants is much less likely to be successful that a lawyer who prepares by also thinking about what the other side wants. It is easy in a negotiation to demand or offer what a client wants. It is more challenging to make a proposal that will both get what your client wants and satisfy the other side. The ultimate goal is to seek a negotiated solution that satisfies both sides.

An effective negotiator must try to see and feel the other side's goals as the other side sees and feels them. As an advocate for your client, it is all too easy to focus on your client and fail to understand (this does not mean agree with) the other side. At times, it can be difficult to understand the other side's goals. One of the best resources you can call upon to get a better understanding is your client. In many situations, your client will have had more experience dealing with the other side than you. In addition, you can talk with others who are not involved in the matter (keeping within the confidentiality rules of professional conduct, of course) until the other side's goals and position become easier to understand.

Analysis of the other side's goals is a dynamic, ongoing process because, as it's important to recognize, the other side's goals may change. It's also important to recognize that it's possible to make mistakes during this process. For a variety of reasons, the other side in a negotiation may choose to conceal their goals. You may reach a moment during a negotiation and say to yourself you cannot understand *how* the other side can seem to feel its position is so strong. This may be a signal that it's time to rethink your assessment of the other side's goals. You may be misperceiving the strengths and weaknesses of your client's position, not them.

Lastly, it may well be your ultimate challenge in a negotiation to change the goals of the other side. The opponent may need to be willing to accept a lot less money, or to pay a lot more. You'll have a better chance of changing their goals if you first understand their goals.

Think Twice

New lawyers often spend too little time analyzing the goals of the other side in a negotiation. It's easy to assume that the other side's goals are the opposite of your client's. Once that assumption is made, it gets hard to imagine what alternative goals the other side might have. Using the negotiation process to obtain more information about the other side's goals is critical. It's also important to remember that during the course of it all, every contact with the other side or the other side's lawyer is part of the negotiation. Be prepared. Stay prepared.

8.2.4   What Happens if There Is No Agreement

What a party to a negotiation wants is also influenced by what that party believes will happen if the negotiation is unsuccessful. One way of looking at negotiation is that parties will agree to a transaction or settlement because it will be better for them than not agreeing. To assess whether it is better or not, each party must assess what their alternatives are to a specific negotiated result. The key question to ask is: what will the client do, or be able to do, if the negotiation fails?

There may be very good reasons not to reach an agreement. A seller may have other buyers who will submit bids. An employee may have more than one job offer. A plaintiff can engage in further discovery believing a "smoking gun" document will turn up. A defendant can decide to go to trial expecting a defense verdict. Much of the success of a negotiated accord will depend upon the extent to which one or both parties have considered realistic alternatives to the agreement or settlement. This alternative to a successful negotiation is known as "BATNA": best alternatives to negotiated agreement.

Different types of negotiation, of course, have different BATNAs. In litigation, the parties may choose to have a judge or a jury resolve a dispute. In lease negotiations, the lessor may have other potential lessees, and the lessee may be able to lease from other lessors. In an employment setting, the availability of several potential employees will strengthen the bargaining position of the employer.

The negotiating lawyer has to prepare properly for the failure of negotiations. Part of preparation for any negotiation involves analysis of the different alternatives to negotiated agreement. A lawyer can:

- List all possible alternatives in the event negotiations fail;
- Evaluate each of the alternatives, in light of the client's immediate and overarching goals and process preferences;
- Attempt to create additional alternatives or creatively merge or modify the existing options; and,
- Have the client select the alternatives that appear to be preferable.

Failure to do this analysis may mean that a negotiated accord may be reached primarily because the attorney has not seriously considered or prepared for other options and because the client is desperate.

The alternatives to negotiated agreement available to the other side also need to be considered. Parties may not fully participate in negotiations because they believe that they have more attractive alternatives to satisfy their interests. In litigation, for example, a defendant may believe that summary judgment of a plaintiff's claims is possible (or likely) and offer less (or nothing) in settlement as a result. In a transactional negotiation, one party may simply believe a better deal is available from another potential seller or buyer. A negotiator facing these situations will need to analyze and critique the alternatives available to the other side, to explain why such options do not adequately satisfy the other side's needs, and to otherwise persuade the other party that a negotiated accord is the best possible solution.

Think Twice

It makes sense to consider alternatives to an agreement or an accord. Why can it be hard to do so? Negotiating parties don't necessarily want to focus on failure; they'd rather spend their time trying to get a deal done or a dispute resolved. Alternative options, though, may present better opportunities for the client, and ought to be thought of in that context. Rather than focus on doing a deal with one party or having to settle a dispute at an unacceptable figure, negotiators need to remain open to other choices, which may take more time and effort.

8.3 AUTHORITY TO NEGOTIATE AN ACCORD

The client makes the final decision to accept or reject a negotiated accord. A lawyer needs to discuss the range of acceptable resolutions to the negotiation with the client, and a lawyer must receive explicit authority from the client as to what will be an acceptable result before reaching an accord. Often, the lawyer and client will make a preliminary assessment, subject to revision as the lawyer and client gain information through the course of the negotiation. At times, the client may have a firm minimum need or demand that is unlikely to change. In most negotiations, it is very important to have a clear understanding of the minimum and maximum amount of money or other benefits to be received or paid by a client and the upper and lower limits of probable recovery.

It is essential to have a client clearly define the boundaries of the lawyer's authority to reach an agreement. This prevents misunderstandings between lawyer and client—misunderstandings that can have serious repercussions for both. Attorneys should not assume they have authority to get the "best" deal possible. A client may prefer no deal to the "best" deal offered, or have overarching goals that make some other alternative preferable.

A client may delegate authority to reach an accord to the lawyer. There is a broad spectrum of degrees of authority that clients may delegate to their lawyer:

Range of Authority. The client may provide the attorney with instructions that set out a range within which an attorney can accept or reject a proposition. The client may choose to give the attorney a narrow range of authority regarding major issues and more flexibility for minor issues.

Specific Authority. The client may have a particular accord in mind and give the attorney specific guidance and instructions during negotiations.

Unlimited Authority. The client may prefer or insist that the attorney make negotiation decisions. The client may give lawyer complete control over what occurs and delegate all decision-making, subject only to the final approval of the client.

No Authority. The lawyer may be involved in negotiation discussions with the permission of a client but without any authority from a client to accept an agreement or resolve a problem. The attorney will need to discuss any proposed solutions with the client before a result can be obtained.

The client may confer authority upon the attorney either in writing or orally. A written understanding is often preferable as it will help prevent future misunderstandings between lawyer and client. Oral authority can be appropriate if the client is present during the negotiations or so long as there is a clear communication between the client and attorney.

Think Twice

An obviously significant difference between your prior experience in negotiations and being a lawyer negotiating on behalf of a client is that you're not negotiating for yourself. And another difference may be that the authority a client gives you is not what you would do if it were you. You'll need to remind yourself that you are serving the interests of your client even if their approach to negotiations is different than yours.

And you'll need to continually keep in contact with your client regarding their positions. Negotiations invariably include alternative solutions to reach an accord. You'll have to obtain your client's preferences regarding various

*optional solutions, and their authority limits may often
need to be modified.*

C.   ASSESSING THE SITUATION: WHAT DO I KNOW? WHAT DO I WANT TO KNOW? WHAT DOES THE OTHER SIDE KNOW?

In negotiation, knowledge is power. Lawyers who know what
their own clients want and why have an advantage over negotiators who do not. Lawyers who know what the alternatives to
accord will be and understand the advantages and disadvantages
of those alternatives are a step ahead of lawyers without that
knowledge. A critical part of preparing for negotiation is taking
stock of what you do know and thinking about how you will
learn what you don't know.

8.4   I WISH I KNEW ...

There is no comprehensive list of everything a lawyer should
know before a negotiation begins. Each lawyer has to make that
list anew for each negotiation, customizing the list in light of the
client, the situation, and the other side. You can begin making
your list for a negotiation by asking yourself what questions
would be the most useful to have answered before beginning
negotiation. Chances are good that these two would be on the
list:

- What is the best deal for my client the other side would be
  willing to make?

- What will happen if this negotiation is unsuccessful?

Of course, you are unlikely to have either question answered
before or during negotiation. To have the first one answered, you
would need to be negotiating with an astonishingly open lawyer
in whom you had perfect trust. To have the second answered,
you would need a crystal ball.

You may, however, know or be able to learn a number of
things that give you insight into the answers to these two
questions. In fact, once we have a firm grasp of what our client's
goals and interests are, much of the knowledge we seek in
preparation for negotiation is meant to help answer, directly or
indirectly, these two questions.

8.5 BACKGROUNDS: WHAT HAVE THEY DONE? WHAT HAVE WE DONE?

History may not be destiny, but it can be a helpful predictor of what someone is likely to do. Learning what the other side or the other side's lawyer has done in similar negotiations can be extremely useful. Some negotiators have extensive track records. For example, an insurance company may have negotiated settlements in countless previous claims similar to your client's. The corporation seeking to employ your client may have hired many other people for similar positions. The lawyer negotiating for the other side may have practiced in the area for years and may be known for handling certain types of negotiations in a particular way. The time and effort spent in learning this kind of background knowledge will usually be time well spent.

8.6 BATNAS: NO DEAL, NOW WHAT?

Earlier in this chapter, you read about the importance of understanding what your client's alternatives to a negotiated agreement might be, as well as what the disadvantages and advantages associated with each of those alternatives might be. A lawyer preparing for negotiation will learn as much as possible about the client's BATNA and as much as possible about the opposing party's BATNA. Information about the alternatives to a successful negotiation gives the lawyer crucial knowledge about the appropriate evaluation of a lawsuit or transaction, about the other side's evaluation of that same lawsuit or transaction, and about the likelihood of the other side entering an agreement. As discussed in the next section, knowing your BATNA is a critical part of developing one of the most useful negotiation tools: the benchmark.

8.7 BENCHMARKS: WHAT DOES EVERYONE ELSE DO?

When you write a brief, it's important to be able to support your argument with authority. When you negotiate a transaction or settlement, it's helpful to be able to support your position with authority. Benchmarks—objective standards of valuation— are enormously useful tools during a negotiation. Quite often, lawyers will point to one benchmark or another during negotiation as authority that their demands, offers, arguments, or positions have real-world legitimacy.

The value of a transaction depends on the assessment of its utility to the parties; the value of a lawsuit depends upon the assessment of the probable outcome. Usually both of these determinations consist of a range of amounts: the buyer is willing to pay an amount between A and B; a jury is most likely to return a verdict in the range of X to Y.

8.7.1   General Evaluation of a Transaction

Evaluating a transaction includes a consideration of the following issues:

Similar Transactions. What amounts of money have been exchanged in similar transactions? Parties may be influenced by what others have done in previous transactions.

The Market. What is the market value? There may be a variety of sources of market value depending upon the type of land, goods, or services involved.

Costs. What are the total direct and indirect costs involved in the transaction? Direct expenses may be easy to determine, and indirect costs may be more difficult to ascertain but significant.

Alternative Sources. How else can this transaction be completed? There may be other businesses or individuals with whom to negotiate the same transaction.

Alternative Uses. What will happen if this transaction does not occur? What will the client do with the money not spent or with the deal not completed?

8.7.2   General Evaluation of a Lawsuit

Lawyers have developed some devices in an attempt to make the evaluation process objective:

Formula. One formula involves the selection of an average damage figure for the case multiplied by a percentage that reflects the probability of success ($100,000 average verdict times 60% chance of success equals $60,000 proposed settlement).

Multiplier. Another formula computes personal injury outcomes as an amount equal to X times the special damages with X being anywhere from three to ten in value. ($8,000 in specials times five equals a $40,000 proposed settlement amount).

Point system. Other lawyers have developed point-system formulas that assign points for various factors such as liability, injury, type of plaintiff, and type of defendant. The point total is then used as a percentage multiplier to produce a figure representing what a jury would award in a perfect case.

Verdict and settlement reports. Published reports summarizing jury verdicts and settlements may also yield comparative information. These reports may be gathered by a national firm, by a local bar or trial lawyers' association, or by governmental or judicial agencies. Verdicts or settlements involving similar cases are obtained and compared to the current case with proportionate adjustments made to reflect differences in liability, damages, and other factors.

Think Twice

These benchmarks may be based on real world objective data or may be based on factors that appear to be made up. You'll need to be careful not to become mesmerized by apparent objective information unless it's truly objective. For example, the transaction lawyer who claims to rely on market values that are not based on actual comparable deals will not be very effective. And a plaintiff's lawyer who claims five times special damages is the usual formula for settlement may not have any factual basis for that conclusion. It can take a lot of time and effort to discover specific, objective support for a position, but it can produce satisfactory negotiation success.

8.8　HOW DO I LEARN WHAT I NEED TO KNOW?

Here's the bad news: the best way to learn what you need to know to be an effective negotiator is to become an experienced negotiator in your chosen area of practice. Here's the good news: there are many substitutes for experience and many ways to borrow experience for those negotiations you will do on the road to becoming an experienced negotiator.

8.8.1 A Lifetime of Experience

Negotiation experience is derived in significant part from the life experiences of the lawyer-negotiator. In our life outside the law, negotiations occur whenever one person wants something from another. From these common, ordinary situations, individuals begin to develop their negotiating styles, learning from friends and family, from teachers in schools and religious institutions, and from bosses and co-employees on the job. That development continues throughout life, and the range of influences widens, in part because so many different disciplines touch on the skill of negotiation.

Disciplines as diverse as economics, psychology, anthropology, philosophy, and theology all have something to say about negotiation. You may find yourself negotiating with person who believes that every negotiation is a zero-sum game in which every participant's gain is offset by another's loss. You may find yourself negotiating with a person who believes that the client's social standing or economic power alone justifies a favorable deal.

And in addition, across the course of your career you are likely to be involved in negotiating with people from cultures and countries different than your own. How a negotiation is conducted, what is said and what is expected, can vary enormously from culture to culture and country to country. Understanding how those differences may influence a negotiation becomes an important part of preparation.

Think Twice

There is no reason to let the law constrain your future learning about negotiation. That liberal arts degree you worked so hard to get will come in handy in considering what you can learn from other disciplines about negotiations. It's also important to remember that not only are the people we negotiate with influenced by their background, experience, and education, so are each of us. Each of us is influenced—consciously and unconsciously—by a variety of sources, and being conscious about those sources of influence is important in preparing for and conducting negotiation.

8.8.2 A Lifetime of Legal Experience

Another primary source of experience comes from negotiating specific transactions and cases again and again. These repeated professional experiences provide knowledge, information, credibility, and confidence. This is the kind of experience that, for the reflective lawyer, will result in useful knowledge about backgrounds, BATNA's, and benchmarks. After all, it is easier to assess the likelihood of success at trial after you've tried dozens of cases. It is easier to predict how the other side will evaluate the transaction after you've negotiated scores of successful deals.

Thorough preparation and continual planning may make up for the lack of experience. The more experienced negotiator may take for granted the inexperienced negotiator or assume that experience will overcome this extra preparation. Lack of experience can be balanced by hard work and the confidence to succeed. A part of that hard work must be the willingness to do the research, investigation, and questioning necessary to obtain enough knowledge to be effective.

8.8.3 "Borrowed" Experience

If you haven't practiced for twenty years, if you haven't practiced for twenty days, how can you find out how opposing counsel negotiates? How can you learn whether lawyers in your community use a particular formula to evaluate slip and fall cases? How can you begin to guess whether the judge will grant your motion for summary judgment? Here are some sources of knowledge available to lawyers of any vintage:

Colleagues. The law *is* a helping profession and many of your colleagues will prove to be surprisingly willing to be helping professionals. If you are practicing in a firm, learn whom to ask about negotiation. If you are practicing by yourself, develop a network of mentors and advisors. For advice about backgrounds, BATNAs, and benchmarks, experienced colleagues are invaluable. Once you have developed a reputation as someone who is interested and willing to talk about negotiations, it will be a surprisingly short time before you will find yourself getting calls for advice from new lawyers.

Clients. Many new lawyers are reluctant to ask their clients questions. Part of that reluctance is no doubt borne of a fear that clients will distrust lawyers who don't know all the answers. While there are questions that might trigger that kind of response ("Will the negotiation be business casual, formal, or black tie?" comes to mind), clients are a tremendous source of knowledge about the evaluation of a transaction, recognized benchmarks in their trade or industry, or past experience dealing with the other party in the negotiation. All clients come to us with some sort of expertise. Quite often, and particularly in transactional practice, that expertise can be a useful source of knowledge for the lawyer to tap.

Public information. We live in an information age. Increasingly, records of past negotiations, benchmarks of value, and catalogs of dispute results are becoming more easily available. All it may take are keystrokes on a web search engine or a telephone call to a colleague or client. Chapter 7 contained a fuller discussion of investigation, and many of the techniques discussed there can be useful in doing a pre-negotiation investigation.

The Other Side. You want to know the opposing party's goals and interests? You want to know what this buyer has paid in similar transactions? You want to know what the other side's assessment is of the likely range of jury verdicts if negotiation of this lawsuit fails and the case goes to trial? Ask them. As discussed more fully in the next chapter, one of the most important parts of any negotiation is the exchange of information. Asking opposing counsel the answer to these questions will yield interesting and useful responses. Whether you can believe those responses and how you should use those responses is an issue dealt with in the next chapter.

Think Twice

It is easy to advise a new lawyer to ask for help from colleagues and clients, but it can be hard to do. When we begin our careers, we typically want, more than anything else, to be perceived as competent professionals. We worry that asking for help will make our client or the supervising partner think less of us. In reality, more often than not, most people are happy to be asked questions that call on them to share their individual expertise. The key to seeking help effectively is to prepare by learning what you can. For example, if you want to find out what benchmark is used to assess slip and fall cases in your jurisdiction, first research the available web and print resources. After you've done this initial work, the questions you ask your senior colleague will be better focused and more likely to elicit truly helpful responses.

D. WHAT DO I DO? SELECTING A NEGOTIATION APPROACH

In preparation for negotiation, there is much for a lawyer to learn: what are the client's goals and values? What are the other side's? Which benchmarks of value are the most commonly accepted in this type of negotiation? Negotiation results depend on a lawyer's understanding and knowledge, but those results also depend on the decisions the lawyer makes about how to approach the negotiation. An observer watching lawyers negotiate might conclude that there are as many different negotiation approaches and styles as there are lawyers. Some writers contend there are five basic negotiation styles, others claim there are more, and some insist that there is only one correct style (their own, of course). As a starting point, it is useful to analyze the negotiation process from the two most common broad perspectives: the positional bargaining model and the interest-based model.

8.9 TWO MODELS: TWO SETS OF DISADVANTAGES

The bargaining model generally involves a pattern of positions and concessions. Bargainers begin with high aspirations and opposing positions, follow with an exchange of concessions, and then reach a result at some undetermined point in the middle. Often, lawyers using the positional bargaining model will make extreme offers or demands, commit themselves to positions, argue issues, seek to persuade each other, make concessions, employ threats, and ultimately reach an agreement. Lawyers have long been engaged in this bargaining process and have achieved very acceptable agreements and satisfactory settlements for countless clients. These results contribute to the continued use and vitality of this process.

The interest-based model generally involves the parties focusing on their differing and mutual interests. These negotiators explain their client's primary interests, seek information to discover the other side's interests, attempt to establish trust, avoid asserting or inviting extreme positions, seek cooperation, explore alternative options that may benefit both sides, and ultimately reach a mutually satisfactory agreement. This process reflects a popular way to reach a negotiated accord. A growing number of negotiators use this model in place of the more traditional bargaining process.

While staunch adherents of one or the other of these models might disagree, both models have advantages and disadvantages. Subsequent sections of this chapter will discuss each model's advantages, it's useful to recognize some of the disadvantages of these models at the outset.

Disadvantages of the positional bargaining model include:

It's adversarial. Aspects of the bargaining process reflect an adversarial approach to negotiations. Whether it is a lease agreement, an employment contract, or a lawsuit settlement negotiation, many negotiators will view the other side as an "opponent" and engage in advocacy strategies, argumentative tactics, and aggressive behavior.

It's a game. Elements of the bargaining form resemble a game. Both negotiators know that each will begin with an exaggerated position, that both will assert their positions to be firm yet will soon make concessions, that both will employ tactics that attempt to persuade or manipulate the other, and that a result will be reached despite recurring threats to the contrary.

It fosters distrust. The need to establish firm positions and then later modify these positions as a negotiation progresses requires attorneys to carefully phrase disclosures. The realization by both lawyers that each is disclosing information that does not accurately reflect the true interests of a client fosters an aura of distrust between the negotiators.

It's too rigid. Various misconceptions about negotiations plague the bargaining process. Many lawyers presume that the best way to achieve success at a negotiation is to demand a lot, concede little, control what happens, and take advantage of the other side as much as possible. This viewpoint holds that effective negotiators are secretive, conniving, and ruthless—traits more useful for espionage than negotiating.

Disadvantages of the interest-based model include:

It's different. Lawyers accustomed to the traditional bargaining model may have difficulty in changing their approach. They may revert to asserting positions or making threats that destroy mutual trust. Other lawyers may have difficulty considering alternative solutions that benefit both parties because of their inclination to want to "win" the negotiation. They may prefer to be competitive instead of cooperative.

It promotes distrust. Mutual trust may be difficult to establish. Negotiators who disclose their clients' real interests may reveal too much information. As a result, an open and honest approach to a negotiation may not be reciprocated, or worse still, skeptical lawyers may view the attempt to establish trust as nothing more than a bargaining ploy. Suspicion and distrust may overcome efforts to maintain a trusting relationship.

It's too inflexible. The lawyer concerned for the other side's interest may appear too generous or flexible. The other attorney may be inclined to take advantage of this approach leading to a one sided agreement. This method may also exacerbate risks in the negotiation process. The "opposing" lawyer may exploit the cooperative nature of the other negotiator and increase demands, exaggerate differences or refuse to cooperate.

It may be inappropriate. This model may not be appropriate for all situations. A party to a potential deal may be more effective being firm and insistent. A defendant in a lawsuit who faces frivolous or weak claims may be better off adopting a principled take-it-or-leave-it position.

Which approach—or combination of approaches—works best depends upon the circumstances. Negotiators should avoid focusing on positional bargaining and concentrate on reconciling interests where best. Negotiations should also avoid the interest-based approach if the other side is unwilling to reciprocate and cooperate.

Think Twice

There are a variety of books and websites which tout various "successful" negotiation approaches. Some want you to get to yes; others to get past no. These sources are an effort to simplify the process and make it easier to understand and implement. Our advice is that you need to review all available negotiation strategies, tactics, and techniques (explained in the next chapter), and select the ones that will work best with the particular client your have and who is on the other side. This requires flexibility and an openness to new suggestions and tried and true approaches, as discussed below.

8.10   THE LAWYERS' INFLUENCE ON NEGOTIATION

Three primary factors determine how the identity of the lawyers representing the parties will influence negotiations:

- Power and how it is balanced
- The level of mutual trust
- The level of experience of the negotiators

8.10.1   Power

Power is the capacity or ability to accomplish things. The effectiveness of a lawyer as a negotiator depends upon the capacity or ability of that lawyer to achieve the desired result. A lawyer's power is derived from many sources. Money, time, needs, threats, as well as perception create power. Of course, part of a lawyer's power is also dependent on the client's circumstances. A defendant may have money to pay a settlement now, or may have more money in the future. A plaintiff may be desperate for money now, or may be willing to wait until the jury verdict. A buyer may need critical supplies immediately, or may be able to negotiate with other sources. A seller may not want to risk market fluctuation, or may threaten to sell to someone else later.

Lawyers in litigation and transactional practices may claim a substantial amount of power derived from the justice system including the reality of expenses, the time and inconvenience associated with discovery, the threat of a lawsuit trial, the willingness to walk away from a transaction, and other factors. It is important to remember that the degree of power may be largely a matter of perception. The power a lawyer is perceived to have may be the product of their assumptions regarding stereotypical negotiation situations. A lawyer who can pierce the traditional stereotype can promote their client's interests more effectively.

8.10.2 Trust

Negotiations between lawyers who trust each other may proceed differently from negotiations where distrust prevails. Lawyers who have negotiated previous agreements or who have tried many cases with each other may have developed a level of mutual trust. They may respect each other's judgment, and understand that their word is their bond. A high level of trust may permit them to arrive at a mutually satisfactory settlement without having to spend as much time negotiating as would lawyers who were strangers to each other. By the same token, lawyers who distrust each other—or the other party—will have greater difficulty communicating and negotiating. Bringing a reputation of honesty to a negotiation is an essential attribute. Lawyers, and law students, have long memories; you have already begun forming your reputation.

8.10.3 Legal Experience

As discussed earlier in the chapter, a lawyer's level of experience affects the preparation necessary for the negotiation. The level of experience of the negotiators may also affect the process. Experienced lawyers who have negotiated previous agreements or tried many cases are able to negotiate more efficiently toward results reflecting past negotiations and which will be comparable to future situations. This wealth of experience may allow them to arrive at a mutually satisfactory settlement fairly quickly.

Inexperienced lawyers may proceed differently. If both negotiators are inexperienced, they may use cumbersome or time-consuming approaches to negotiation. Their uncertainty may cause them to be overly cautious in reaching an agreement. An inexperienced negotiator who is negotiating with an experienced negotiator has some disadvantages, but also some advantages. The lack of experience may make inexperienced negotiators vulnerable to certain tactics and may cause them to miss opportunities. Some experienced lawyers may attempt to exploit inexperience by using unfamiliar tactics, being condescending, using peer pressure, and offering friendly advice. The remedy for this problem is preparation. An inexperienced negotiator who is well-prepared is going to be better able to obtain information from experienced negotiators, better able to negotiate effectively and efficiently, and better able to reach a satisfactory agreement for the client.

Think Twice

So-called "friendly" advice from experienced attorneys, offered during negotiation, can be disconcerting or aggravating to a newer lawyer. Comments such as "In twenty years of practice that position has never been taken" or "Well, I have tried this type of case thirty times and this is your first one" take their toll. Preparation is a great leveler, but there are other methods that a newer attorney can use. The novice attorney can involve the other attorney as a mentor by asking questions and appearing to use the other lawyer's experience as a resource in shaping a result. The novice lawyer can demonstrate energy and enthusiasm the more experienced lawyer may not have. One newer lawyer we know told a more seasoned opposing counsel that she planned to devote all her available time to the case, and commented, "I can't imagine anything more satisfying than winning this case with you on the other side."

8.11 TWO MODELS, ONE APPROACH

As mentioned earlier, the circumstances of each negotiation should influence the approach you take to negotiation. Your own personality and assessment of your own effectiveness will also influence your approach. So too, however, will the personality and approach of opposing counsel.

A lawyer may appropriately decide that the circumstances of the present negotiation and the lawyer's own preferences counsel approaching the negotiation using an interest-based model. At the same time, opposing counsel may have reached the conclusion that the negotiation calls for use of the positional bargaining model. What happens?

Some interest-based negotiators believe that it is possible to use interest-based negotiation even if opposing counsel is an adamant positional bargainer. That may well be true, but the question ought not be whether it is possible to use a particular negotiating model no matter what. At any given negotiation, at any given moment of any negotiation, your question should be this: what approach will best serve the goals—immediate and overarching—of my client? A believer in positional bargaining ought to prepared to use an interest-based model when that would serve the client, and vice versa. Neither model can lay claim to being the one that is always the most effective or most efficient. Ultimately, clients are more interested in their interests than in negotiation models.

You can see where this is headed. Every well-prepared negotiator needs to be prepared to switch approaches. Because of choices opposing counsel makes, it may be more practical to use the interest-based model. If trust breaks down, an interest-based approach may no longer be possible. And, in all likelihood, at some moment in the negotiation, it simply may be easier to tackle an issue using another approach. Even the most ardent interest-based negotiators often find themselves using positional bargaining to reach agreement at the last stage of negotiating a sticky issue. In short, purity of approach has to take second place to client interests. That means you need to be prepared to use a model different than the one you have chosen, and *that* means that preparing for every negotiation is twice as much work as you thought it would be.

E. ASSESSING ETHICAL CONCERNS: WHAT SHOULD I DO?

Provisions of the Rules of Professional Conduct apply to negotiations. These ethical standards require an attorney to be fully prepared for a negotiation, to accept only those negotiations that the attorney has the competency to handle, to represent a client zealously, and to be truthful in statements to others in the course of representing clients. In addition, ethical norms—whether from a divine source or otherwise—may significantly influence the negotiation process by shaping the actions of negotiating lawyers.

8.12 RULES OF PROFESSIONAL CONDUCT

Professional standards of conduct, and in some jurisdictions, state statutes govern attorney behavior. While there is some variation from jurisdiction to jurisdiction, in general, these professional standards prohibit an attorney from threatening criminal prosecution in a civil case, representing a client regarding a matter in which the attorney previously served as arbitrator or mediator, acquiring any interest in the negotiated matter, compromising a matter because of the effect it might have on the attorney's reputation, and negotiating an agreement that restricts the right to practice law. Conduct that is generally prohibited in the negotiation of contract disputes includes: conjuring up a pretended dispute, asserting an interpretation contrary to a client's understanding, falsifying information, and making harassing demands. Some jurisdictions may also impose obligations of good faith and fair dealings in certain types of negotiations.

8.13 ETHICAL NORMS

Like all of lawyering, negotiation will challenge a lawyer's morals even when the lawyer has complied with all the professional standards. What threats are acceptable, morally, personally, socially, legally? What tactics are acceptable: Scorched earth approach? Appeals to bias? Can one make a deal that one doubts the client can or will honor? Can one try to get out of a deal arguing that it's unfair after agreeing to it? If it might help the strategy to portray one's client in an unfavorable light—as having unrealistically high expectations, or being particularly bellicose or greedy or stupid—must one reveal that to the client? Good lawyers recognize these challenges, make plans for dealing with them before they occur, resolve them when they occur, and try in any event to live their lives in harmony with their personal codes of conduct. For most, it will be too high a price to sacrifice personal values for anticipated professional advancement.

The lack of accountability for statements made during negotiations explains some questionable ethical conduct. The lack of publicity surrounding negotiation discussions, the unlikelihood that a misrepresentation will be discovered, the absence of opportunity by the other side to investigate the accuracy of a representation, and the fact that an accord may be reached, all tempt some negotiators to take advantage of the situation and stretch ethical standards.

Think Twice

You bring your own moral compass with you when you become a lawyer. And that will be a primary guide for how you conduct yourself as a negotiator. Your client will have hers, his, or even its view of what's right and wrong to do during negotiations. You have the responsibility to blend your view of right and wrong and your client's view with the rules of the profession and other sources of norms and values.

8.14 THE TRUTH?

Ethical considerations surrounding truth telling in negotiations can be a quandary for lawyers. Considered opinions about the propriety of lying during negotiations range from the position that a lawyer should never resort to lies, to the position that certain situations may justify lies, to the position that a lawyer must lie in some circumstances to protect client interests.

Whether an attorney must tell the truth may depend upon the type of "lie" asserted by the lawyer, the position of the lawyer regarding the propriety of "lying," and the situation which prompts the "lie." Untruthful statements range from the very direct to the very indirect: a person may volunteer a statement that contains a blatant untruth, exaggerate some information through puffing, remain silent in a situation to avoid having to provide correct information, be asked a question and answer it evasively and incompletely, or refuse to provide any answer in response to a question. Lawyers hold a variety of views about the propriety and prevalence of dishonesty. Lawyers' decisions to be untruthful seem to depend largely on their views of such practices.

Lawyers may have a duty not to reveal certain information in negotiations and, at the same time, also have a duty not to lie. In a given situation, a lawyer may experience these obligations as conflicting, and this can complicate the process of deciding what the ethical course of action might be. If the other side has no right to the information or if the attorney has an obligation to withhold the information, some commentators say the attorney should simply remain silent. This is an inadequate answer.

The very act of silence may reveal the nature of the adverse information. It may well seem that the only way for the attorney to respond effectively will be to say something. The damage in saying something is the attorney's statement may well create a false impression. There is no easy or quick ethical resolution of these problems. It may be that in such a situation a lawyer will feel duty bound to answer in a way that seems likely to mislead the other side.

Many practitioners assert that they do not believe they engage in lying when they negotiate. Yet the nature of negotiation often seems to force lawyers to use information to mislead the other side, or to engage in other forms of misrepresentation. The following subsections describe three categories of information that produce different answers to this quandary.

8.14.1 Facts, Data, and Evidence

It is unethical and improper for a lawyer knowingly to manufacture facts, falsify data, and make up evidence. These are obvious instances of prohibited lies. It may be appropriate for a lawyer to present an exaggerated statement of facts, to interpret questionable data in a fashion favorable to the client, or to describe possible evidence that may be available. These instances reflect borderline situations of proper/improper conduct. Valid differences of opinions exist regarding what is a permissible exaggeration, what is an appropriate interpretation, and how likely it is that evidence will be available.

Considered differences of opinion also exist regarding what is and what is not a fact. Facts may be divided into past facts, present facts, and future facts. Past and present facts are actual facts, but future facts seem to be more in the nature of opinions. Many lawyers regard at least their own statements about future facts as statements of opinion. Informed differences of opinion also may exist justifying the "misrepresentation" of facts, as long as those facts are not material or relevant to the negotiation. This position mirrors contract fraud analysis that establishes fraud only if the facts involved were material to the case. It also reflects the provisions of Model Rule of Professional Conduct 4, which refers to truthful disclosures of "material" and relevant facts. These borderline decisions will be resolved differently by negotiators based upon their personal and professional ethical norms.

8.14.2   Law, Precedent, and Cases

A lawyer has an obligation to accurately disclose and present the law to a judge. A lawyer cannot knowingly falsify or make up legal precedent. A lawyer may have to disclose adverse legal precedents to a judge but not to the other negotiator during a negotiation. These duties may become confused when mixed with other obligations to interpret the law in a light that supports a client's position, to argue that legal precedent supports a certain result, and to advocate that new law should be created. These obligations of interpretation, argument, and advocacy may conflict with the duties to be accurate and complete in disclosing and presenting black and white law. Again, different lawyers will resolve these conflicts differently based on their assessment of the "grayness" of the law and their obligations to their clients.

8.14.3   Opinions, Tactics, and Positions

Our negotiation process countenances the misrepresentation of opinions and positions. An attorney may choose to deceive the other negotiator regarding these sorts of information for two possible reasons. First, an attorney may believe that this kind of misrepresentation constitutes a negotiation tactics and is therefore not a lie. Second, some lawyers believe our system permits (or even requires) them to lie in some situations. The former explanation is more palatable because the latter explanation appears to advocate that attorneys lie, a position which is ethically reprehensible to many. Model Rule of Professional Conduct 4.1 recognizes differences between misrepresentations of facts and misrepresentations of opinions. The comments to the rule explain this difference in part:

> This Rule refers to statements of fact. Whether a particular element should be regarded as one of fact can depend on the circumstances. Under generally accepted conventions in negotiation, certain types of statements ordinarily are not taken as statements of material fact. Estimates of price or value placed on the subject of a transaction and a party's intentions as to an acceptable settlement of a claim are in this category, and so is the existence of an undisclosed principal except where nondisclosure of the principal would constitute fraud.

Regardless of the explanation of this phenomenon, the reality is that some negotiators routinely mislead and deceive other negotiators concerning certain information. Examples abound in negotiations. Lawyers will:

- State an opinion about a matter that does not reflect their true opinion.

- Make an exaggerated claim that some property or injury is worth a certain value.

- Assert a threat that they or their client have no real intention to carry through.

- Present a false demand that does not reflect their client's goals or needs.

- Describe a position of their client that they have manufactured.

- Pretend to be interested in reaching an accord when their real intent is to delay or deadlock proceedings.

These and other common statements and conduct that constitute misrepresentations may at first appear to be essential to the negotiation process. But must they be? The need to rely on this kind of misrepresentation can often be eliminated if a lawyer employs different negotiation strategies and tactics. With effective preparation, a lawyer can:

- Base an opinion or evaluation not on the attorney's inflated perception of something but on a benchmark that is an objective criteria obtained from reliable, impartial sources.

- Avoid having to assert threats and instead encourage the other side to reach a negotiated accord by focusing on how negotiations can result in mutual gains for both sides.

- Delay obtaining specific authority from a client until alternative proposals have been considered and evaluated by both negotiators.

- Discuss the interests and needs of both clients instead of establishing and arguing the legitimacy of set positions.

8.15 REMAINING AN ETHICAL LAWYER AND AN ETHICAL PERSON

We believe that lawyers need not and should not lie, mislead, deceive, or otherwise misrepresent information during negotiations. Deceitful conduct is both unethical and a risky strategy. Lying may be discovered, resulting in deadlocked negotiations or providing a cause of action to set aside an agreement. Lying may also damage or destroy the reputation of attorneys, leaving them ineffective as negotiators. Lying should be avoided for professional business concerns, as well as for ethical reasons.

Think Twice

Look back over the two lists of tactics at the end of Section 8.14. The second list is of alternatives to misleading tactics and those alternatives all require more work. One major reason that lawyers engage in misleading and deceitful conduct is their failure to prepare thoroughly for a negotiation and not considering creative options and alternative solutions. Laziness and unimaginative assessments account in part for lawyers' reliance on the easier and simpler tactic of lying. While the second list of alter-

native tactics involve more work, the listed tactics are also likely to be more effective. Be prepared, and then some. And when you don't know what to do, consult with your mentor or other colleagues.

F. GETTING READY TO NEGOTIATE

8.16 A CHECKLIST: EVALUATING YOUR PREPARATION

Before beginning a negotiation, evaluate the effectiveness of your preparation and planning. The following is a checklist of factors that need to be considered:

Goals, Interests, and Needs

What are the client's immediate goals, overarching goals, and process preferences?

What other interests and needs does the client have?

How does the other side's perception of the situation differ from the client's?

What are the other side's immediate goals, overarching goals, and process preferences?

What interests and needs does the other side have?

What mutual interests do the parties have?

What will satisfy the parties?

Knowledge and Information

What information and documents should be disclosed to the other side?

What questions should be asked and information sought from the other side?

Financial concerns

What are the financial interests and needs of each party?

How are the attorneys being compensated and how much?

Negotiation approaches

What negotiation approaches should or will be used by each side?

What issues are most likely to be resolved using an alternative approach?

What experience does each party have with this type of negotiation?

How effective is each attorney as a negotiator?

Sources of satisfaction

Why does each side want to reach a negotiated accord?

Who will have the ultimate authority to reach an accord?

Will the negotiation result in an accord which matches the values of each party and negotiator?

How will the result affect the reputation of the party and the negotiators?

Relationships

How does the existence or lack of a relationship between the parties affect the negotiation, past and future?

Will the like or dislike of the negotiators for each other affect the negotiations?

How will the negotiation affect future cases or business for the parties and the lawyers?

Time

Do time considerations or a deadline affect either side?

Are the parties and negotiators available or are there conflicts with other transactions, cases, vacations?

Benchmarks

Which of the available benchmarks are most likely to support my client's interests?

Which are most likely to be cited by the other side?

Ethics

Are the strategies, tactics, and techniques suggested to be used consistent with ethical rules and professional norms?

Alternatives to Negotiation

If the negotiation fails, what will each party do?

Think Twice

Life and practice would be easier if you could read this checklist once and be done with it. However, evaluation of your preparation is something that continues throughout a negotiation. An ongoing assessment includes what is being said and what is not being said, what is being done and not being done, and predicting what will happen in the future. Negotiations vary greatly in the degree to which an attorney can predict outcomes. Some matters will be relatively easy to evaluate; many others will only permit "guesstimates."

8.17 EVALUATING YOUR OWN INTERESTS AND VALUES: WHAT ABOUT YOU?

In any negotiation, the parties' interests and values play an enormously influential role. Do a lawyer's own interests and values—as a professional, as a person—influence the negotiation? Should they? As you begin negotiating on behalf of clients, you will need to assess your past personal and professional experiences in determining how they influence your present negotiation approaches. And you will need to consider the following influences.

8.17.1 What Are Your Present Interests and Needs?

Attorneys' personal and professional needs can influence negotiations. It is important to become conscious of one's values and goals as an attorney and plan to avoid having them get in the way of a client's values and goals. For example, impressing the other side with the ability to be a patient, deliberate negotiator may not be consistent with coming to a quick agreement for a client. Or, an attorney who wants to come to an agreement quickly because of financial or time pressures may represent a client's interests as vigorously as is appropriate.

All sorts of interests may influence you. For example, settling a lawsuit may help you realize your own financial and economic goals or, it may be that *not* settling a lawsuit will help you realize those goals. Will you make more or less if an agreement is reached now? Your status as an attorney can also affect your judgment. Are you in-house counsel for a company with a larger agenda, or are you an attorney in a law firm who needs the client for continuing business? How are you being paid? Other interests of your own may include your reputation (how will an agreement or the failure to conclude a deal enhance it?) and your desire for experience (maybe you want to try a case instead of settling it). The primary way to blunt these potential conflicts of interest is to be aware of them so that you may mitigate their effects and are able to openly discuss them with the client.

8.17.2   What Are Your Values?

As we previously stated, you have developed a set of values, moral principles, norms of behavior, and ethical guidelines for both your personal and professional life. And your clients have also developed their own principles. All these factors will influence your approach to a negotiation and your client's acceptance or rejection of a result. For example, you may believe it wrong to lie about your client's interests in a negotiation, but your client may believe you should do so. You may think it appropriate to obtain as much money as possible for your client, but your client may perceive that "fairness" requires demanding less money. You need to assess your own personal and professional principles and discuss these with your client when necessary.

8.17.3   Will You Listen to Yourself?

There is a time and place to talk to yourself. Self-evaluation must be done periodically so that you can evolve and improve as an effective negotiator. Taking the time to consider the impact of values, interests, and needs and taking the time to critique actual negotiations to learn from what you did and did not do are critical to being an effective negotiator. Just make sure you listen to what you have to say.

Think Twice

That last piece of advice can be quite difficult to follow. It can be hard to listen when there are too many voices speaking, when there is too little time to reflect, and when you face conflicting financial, professional, and personal pressures. But it's imperative to take the time, find a quiet

place, and reflect on what is and will be happening so you can make sure you're following your moral compass.

8.18 THE NEXT STEP: A THEORY OF THE DEAL OR CASE

After you have done the work of preparing for the negotiation, you need to continue your planning by preparing for the negotiation process itself. Your next step should be the development of a theory for your negotiation. This "theory" is something eminently practical. "Theory," as we use it here, means nothing fancier than a short, simple, and persuasive explanation of the client's position.

A good theory of the deal or case should be persuasive to the other side, and it should also aid the attorney and client when they need to justify changes of position as the negotiation proceeds. For example, a lawyer whose client is an artist striving to license a design may have a theory that the design should be purchased because of its strong appeal to the children that the company hopes to attract to buy its product. During negotiations, the lawyer may explain a lowering of the artist's price for the license by referring to the resulting lower prices that children will pay for purchases which will in turn increase sales and profits. Developing an effective theory of the deal or case will also help focus the negotiation on the client's position.

8.19 PREPARING FOR THE NEGOTIATION PROCESS: THE BASICS

Preparation for a negotiation may include preparing written materials for use during the negotiation and rehearsing portions of the negotiation. Negotiators may mentally prepare and talk with themselves about what to say. Negotiators may also prepare with their clients, colleagues, or other team negotiators.

8.19.1 Preparing a Negotiation "Notebook"

A negotiation "notebook" (either electronic or hard copy) that contains various types of materials can be a highly useful device. What should be included depends upon the specific requirements of a negotiation. Consider using some or all of the following:

A summary of vital data, facts, events.

A list of documents or exhibits and copies or originals.

Lists of important dates, figures, and objective information.

Summaries and citations of legal authorities.

Questions to be asked of the other side.

Information and documents to be disclosed to the other side.

A summary of strong points or weak points for each side.

A description of the interests and needs of each side.

A comparison of which interests and needs are different, which conflict, and which are complementary.

An overall negotiation plan including the initial offer or demand or response, a description of subsequent positions or concessions, and final positions.

Alternative proposals and solutions.

Preparation of negotiation materials to present to the other side, such as a power point presentation or notebook containing helpful information.

A draft of written negotiation terms, provisions, and documents to finalize and formalize the negotiation.

Think Twice

This seems like a lot to do to prepare—and it is. What's the alternative? To start negotiating without being properly prepared? We are not suggesting you have to do all this for every negotiation, but you need to review the list and decide what needs to be done. And there's still more to consider.

8.19.2   Preparing an Agenda

It is always wise to prepare a negotiation agenda. Some negotiations have a defined agenda. Negotiators may submit a written agenda to the other side that lists topics for discussion and resolution. A contract or lease proposal inherently includes an agenda with its listed clauses and terms. Labor negotiations may involve a list of issues that need to be negotiated before negotiations on the merits occur.

The negotiators may initially agree on a list of all the issues to be negotiated. This single text details the matters that will be discussed and avoids problems with negotiating an unknown number of individual issues. A preliminary comprehensive agenda may operate as a device to prod both sides to engage in discussions without having to take firm positions, so that later discussions can be more productive. Negotiators working to settle cases in litigation usually do not create a set agenda, but cases in litigation have specific claims, damages, and defenses, and these can be used to define an agenda.

The lack of any agenda for negotiation creates the risk of unorganized discussion. An agenda prepared in advance permits topics and issues to be discussed in a structured, orderly manner. Organized negotiations increase the likelihood that the needs of the parties will be addressed. One clear advantage that an agenda provides is the preclusion of the later introduction of unanticipated matters. Another advantage is that an agenda prevents an attorney from refusing to discuss an issue during the late stages of a negotiation. One tactic some lawyers use is the arbitrary refusal to discuss an issue late in the negotiation simply because it was not discussed earlier. Such a refusal is often accompanied by a claim that the lawyer assumed the issue would not be pursued. The existence of an agenda helps undercut this tactic.

8.20   CONTACTING THE OTHER SIDE

Contacts between attorneys can occur through emails or letters, over the telephone, or in offices. Initial planning includes deciding which of these contacts will be made.

8.20.1   I Want to Write Them. Why?

Correspondence, either by email or letter, can be very useful in documenting positions, offers or demands. Written contacts can explain positions economically. Statements can be written in a clear and convincing manner that may avoid misunderstandings. Care should be taken to make sure electronic or telephone messages are confidential. These contacts also have some disadvantages. They provide the other attorney with time to reflect on what response should be made, and they may involve more time and expense than telephone contacts.

8.20.2 I Want to Call Them. Why?

Telephone negotiations also have advantages and disadvantages. Phone discussions tend to be shorter than face-to-face negotiations because person-to-person meetings often justify taking more time. Misunderstandings or understandings caused by facial expressions are avoided because of the lack of visual feedback. Phone conversations can be less stressful because the lack of personal contact reduces peer pressure. It is easier to say no over the phone than it is in person because phone contacts tend to be impersonal. The caller almost always has the advantage because of preparation and anticipation. The recipient may reduce this handicap by not making a decision during the initial conversation and by returning the call after planning a response. If negotiations will take place in whole or in part over the telephone, it is wise to plan to create a written memo summarizing the conversation. This written summary can be prepared after the conversation and sent to the other side.

8.20.3 I Want to Meet Face-to-Face. Why?

Many negotiations can be conducted more effectively if the negotiators meet face-to-face, either with or without their clients. These negotiation meetings may occur after emails have been exchanged and phone negotiations conducted. Which method should be used at what stage of the negotiation depends upon the assessment of what will be the most effective, efficient, and economical.

8.21 LOCATION OF IN–PERSON NEGOTIATIONS: I WANT TO NEGOTIATE HERE. NO, HERE

The decision where to negotiate usually involves choosing the office of one of the lawyers participating in the negotiation. There are advantages to using your office; there are advantages to using opposing counsel's office. It may be preferable to hold negotiations in one's own office because: it avoids the inconvenience of being removed from other obligations; it saves time and expense; it may provide the one negotiator and client with a psychological advantage over the other negotiator coming to negotiate; it is more convenient to display exhibits, use charts and arrange the room appropriately; it permits access to information and data from files; team negotiations with colleagues may be more convenient to arrange; and it may be easier to establish and maintain the proper atmosphere for the negotiation.

It may be advisable to have the negotiation discussions occur in the other side's office because: it is easier to leave; it is easier to concentrate on the negotiations without being distracted or interrupted; the other side has difficulty in refusing requests for documents and other information at hand; and information and supporting data can be selectively brought or not made available.

Other locations for meetings include a client's office or a neutral site. These alternatives may be appropriate depending upon the type of case, the kind of client, the needs of people involved, the facilities needed, the degree of comfort required, previous negotiation discussions, and the relationship between the attorneys. Settlement negotiations often occur in mediator offices and in courtroom hallways and judges' chambers. Another alternative is to use video conferencing with the negotiators being in different places. Using software that permits voice/visual calls to be made over the internet can be more effective than a phone call and provide some benefits of a personal meeting.

Seating arrangements for face to face meetings may have impact on the negotiation. For example, it may be more conducive to a cooperative relationship to have both lawyers sit on the same side of a conference table rather than across from each other, or it may make no difference. Or a seating arrangement without tables or desks may create a more conducive setting.

Think Twice

Timing and location sometimes occur without planning. The other lawyer may call you up and begin to negotiate. Or, you may meet the other lawyer in the courthouse hallways. What should you do? If you are not prepared, then you can always decline to negotiate then and there. Or, you can just listen and say you'll get back in touch. Or, you might be tempted to take advantage of the mo-

ment, and that might be a good tactic, if you are suffi-
ciently prepared.

8.22   WHO SHOULD ATTEND THE NEGOTIATION?

If more than one attorney is available to negotiate, the
choice needs to be made regarding which attorneys should negotiate. Obvious considerations are a lawyer's familiarity with the
case and with the other negotiators. A single negotiator is always
in charge of what is happening and does not have to share
decision making or implementing with anyone. The other side
does not have the opportunity to create disagreement or dissen-
sion among multiple negotiators. Depending upon the complexity
of the negotiations, negotiating alone can produce some difficulties and cause things to be missed and overlooked.

Team negotiators make it possible for the work to be divided
so that one person can concentrate on observing and listening
while another lawyer does the talking, or topics can be divided,
allowing each of the negotiators to concentrate on fewer items.
Using more than one negotiator also permits employment of
different tactics: one negotiator may take a hard line and the
other a soft line as a technique. Two people working together
may also be able to come up with more creative solutions than a
lone negotiator. But two lawyers may also have difficulty coordi-
nating their efforts.

Clients may need to or may want to be present. Many
negotiations—especially those involving transactions—require
the presence of the client to make decisions. Sometimes negotiations can begin without the client, who can then participate in
later negotiation sessions. There will be occasions when the
client's presence may not assist the negotiation because a frank
discussion may be inhibited, particularly if the conversation
involves a discussion about the client's conduct. Nevertheless, a
client can be an asset during negotiation. The client's presence
may add an appropriate dimension to the discussions, and the
client can frequently aid in obtaining information and making
decisions

Other participants besides attorneys can be present at or
participate in some negotiations. It might be helpful to have non-

lawyers attend a negotiation. An accountant may provide financial data; a real estate agent may be able to evaluate property values; a tax specialist may provide information regarding tax consequences; a soothsayer may be able to predict the future settlement. These individuals need to understand their role and how the negotiator will communicate with them.

8.23   TIMING OF THE NEGOTIATION

Time is almost always a factor in negotiations. Many negotiations include a self-contained deadline. The attorneys may have only scheduled one hour to discuss an agreement or a judge may have given litigators thirty minutes to settle a case. Even in negotiations without time limits, lawyers always have limitations placed on their availability. Their other work and their other clients require attention. Establishing time limits may be a useful tactic. These limits may or may not be revealed or discussed with the other attorney.

Negotiation discussions usually fill the amount of time available, with results reached when a deadline looms imminent. This deadline phenomenon matches other life experiences. Many attorneys complete and file briefs on the last day; many taxpayers file income tax returns near the deadline; legislatures enact many laws at the end of sessions. Time deadlines, either intentionally established or caused by the natural course of events, increase the momentum of negotiation discussions.

Negotiators who establish several periodic deadlines within an overall time frame will promote more efficient negotiations. Deadlines help impose some discipline upon the negotiating parties and may help precipitate an accord by providing a legitimate reason why a decision should be reached by a certain time. Qualified deadlines, which permit time extensions for certain conditions, provide incentives for the negotiators to reach an accord while reducing the pressures imposed by firm deadlines.

Deadlines nevertheless may cause problems. A deadline accompanied by a party's threat to do or not do something will automatically force that party to fulfill the threat or lose credibility by failing to go through with that threat, unless that party has a very good explanation why such action or inaction is appropriate. Deadlines also create pressures for the negotiators that may be unreasonable or counterproductive. The less time pressure some negotiators feel, the more relaxed, flexible, and creative they may be.

8.24 THE TIMING OF THE AGREEMENT

Outside factors involving timing often play a part in when— or whether—an agreement is reached:

Strength. Negotiators with time on their side can deal from a position of strength. A party who has time pressures, dates, or deadlines that have to be met may be at a disadvantage. The commercial tenant who has to move by a certain date may become disadvantaged the closer the negotiation discussions approach that date. The negotiator whose schedule has no available time may have a severe time conflict in postponing an agreement.

Immediate Needs. Some parties involved in negotiation discussions may have an immediate need. The stronger this interest is, the weaker a negotiation position may become. The party who needs a job to earn income will be at a growing disadvantage the longer a prospective employer continues delaying a negotiated agreement. Some parties with potential litigation claims may be at a similar disadvantage. Insurance claims adjusters often succeed with low offers made at times when a claimant needs money.

Effort and Expense. Early accords may be advantageous to one party if the other party does not want to put the necessary effort, time, and money into further discussions or litigation. Many clients will not be able to afford extensive attorney's fees, requiring a lawyer to accelerate the process of reaching an accord.

Harmful Information. Circumstances in which one party fears the other side will learn of information which would alter positions may prompt a negotiated agreement. Situations with glaring factual or legal weaknesses unknown to the other side may dictate an early settlement to avoid the discovery of such defects.

Time of Meeting. Early mornings and early afternoons will usually provide more time for protracted negotiation contacts, whereas late morning and late afternoon times may rush the negotiators into a hasty settlement or into a deadlock, to the disadvantage of one or both sides.

Client Instruction. Client needs may dictate timing. A client may instruct the attorney to resolve a matter through negotiation at a time when the client's negotiating posture is weak.

Patience. Patience is the ability to forgo immediate satisfaction in exchange for gains in the future. Parties may have many reasons for wanting to settle as soon as possible, not the least of which will be to finalize a legal agreement or end the uncertainty surrounding litigation. Some negotiators place too much emphasis on speed. They may be unable to handle anxiety and uncertainty properly or may have a psychological block about time delays. They may unreasonably fear that the other side will walk out or that some unexpected event will intervene. Patience allows a negotiator to take the time to understand the issues, weigh the risks, test the opponent's strength, appear uneager, explore alternative positions, and probe for problem-solving resolutions. A reluctance to negotiate will often strengthen a bargaining position because the negotiator does not appear anxious to resolve a matter.

Think Twice

Looking back over all of that might be done to prepare for a negotiation can be daunting. A new lawyer may well think, again: "This is too much work. Can't I cut through all of this and just wing it?" As tempting as that might be, the answer is "Not if you want to serve your client well." The best negotiators we know are the best prepared. The time spent preparing for a negotiation almost always pays dividends. Adequate preparation invariably results in better agreements for clients.

Chapter Nine

THE NEGOTIATION PROCESS: YOU TELL, I TELL AND YOUR MOVE, MY MOVE

Discourage litigation. Persuade your neighbors to compromise whenever you can. Point out to them how the nominal winner is often a real loser—in fees, expenses, and waste of time.

—Abraham Lincoln

A. THE EXCHANGE OF INFORMATION: YOU TELL, I TELL

Almost every negotiation involves two sets of exchanges: the exchange of information and the exchange of worth. Negotiators may express that worth in terms of interests or positions. In the end, however, a successful accord involves both parties providing something of worth to the other. The second section of this chapter discusses the strategies and tactics used in that exchange of worth.

The first portion of this chapter focuses on that other exchange: the exchange of information. By the time the negotiation process begins, you should have already planned to obtain information from the other side and to provide information to the other side during the negotiation. Opposing counsel has probably planned to obtain information from you. In every negotiation, you have an opportunity both to gain and give information. Always consider: What is it you want to say? What is it you want to ask?

9.1   INFORMATION YOU WANT THE OTHER SIDE TO HAVE

A negotiator not only needs to plan what information to provide to the other side, a negotiator also needs to consider how best to disclose that information. Some negotiations may involve the exchange of specific, formal documents containing information related to the negotiation. Significant business transactions typically involve a prospectus. Some of this written information may be required by the law; other information may be presented because it is meant to impress the other negotiator with the merits of the offering.

Litigators in major cases often present information to the other side using a settlement brochure. A plaintiff's settlement brochure in a personal injury lawsuit would typically include a biographical resume of the injured person, a statement of the facts surrounding the injury, a description of the medical history of the injuries, an itemization of the damages, and an explanation of the theory of liability.

Another technique for presenting information to the other side involves the use of the client or witness. Their appearance during a negotiation discussion may be an effective way to present information to the other side, and may also be satisfying to the client. You can decide what information you want to disclose and how best to communicate that information to the other side. And you should consider what the other side likely knows in determining what information to disclose.

9.2   LEGAL EFFECTS OF DISCLOSURES

Disclosure of information may have important legal effects. What an attorney or client says may constitute an "admission" that has legal consequences. In transactional work, this concern exists during negotiations. In litigation work, the common law and current evidence rules reflect a public policy that favors and encourages settlements. Typically, existing evidentiary rules make inadmissible all offers of compromise and all factual statements during settlement discussions of a disputed claim. These rules reflect a broad social policy that encourages frank negotiation discussions and attempts to resolve disputes.

9.3 PROTECTING INFORMATION FROM DISCLOSURE

An attorney must plan ahead about what information to reveal and what to withhold from the other party. Thinking carefully about what information ought not be given to the other side during negotiation helps prevent inadvertent disclosure of harmful information or the unconscious or unnecessary revelation of client confidences or secrets. Expressly planning *how* information will be guarded also helps prevent a lawyer from using unethical or ineffective techniques in an effort to prevent the other side from discovering information.

It will be a rare negotiation in which a lawyer does not have some information to protect. There are a number of ethical approaches that a lawyer can take to withhold information the other side has asked for:

- Ignore the question and shift to another topic.

- Refuse to answer and explain why.

- Admit the question deserves a response but delay the response until later.

- Answer only a part of the question.

- Provide a general and not a specific answer.

- Ask questions and refuse to answer until these questions are answered.

- Make an admission or concede a point to avoid any elaboration.

- Postpone the negotiations to obtain the information.

These techniques can also be useful when asked to respond to disclosures of surprise information by the other side. In general, the less perturbed an attorney appears in response to a difficult question, the more likely the response will be accepted by the other lawyer.

Think Twice

The disclosure of information should help the other side understand your client's situation and position. So why are some negotiators reluctant to freely provide useful information? In transactional negotiation, you may be

*dealing with a potential or existing competitor or someone
who may primarily be interested in using the negotiation
to gain information. In disputes, advocates rely on the
rules of discovery to determine what ought to be disclosed.
An essential question to ask about appropriate disclosures
is this: what will influence the other side to do what we
want them to do? The answer to that question should
prompt you to provide that information.*

9.4 OBTAINING INFORMATION FROM THE OTHER SIDE

In every negotiation, there is information the other side has
that is valuable to learn. As part of your preparation for negotiation, you should consider what information you hope to obtain
from the other side. For example:

- The goals and interests of the other side.

- The positions of the other side.

- The strong points and weak points of the other side.

- Facts and law underlying the deal or case.

- The other side's perception of your client's position.

- The other side's perception of it's own position.

- The extent of the other lawyer's preparation and available
  time.

- The other negotiator's style, experience, strengths and
  weaknesses.

- Alternatives for the other side if the deal is not made or
  the case settled.

- How the other lawyer is being paid.

- The authority limits of the negotiator for the other side.

- Time pressures or deadlines bearing on the other side.

- The interests of any third parties affected by the results.

The best way to obtain this information in most situations is
simply to ask for it. The information contained in this list is
often only available from the other side, and you'll need to go to

that source for answers to your queries. The most direct approach may well produce the most reliable information.

An efficient way to conduct the information exchange in negotiations is to conduct it as if it were an interview and combine active listening with a mix of open and closed ended questions. Negotiators who ask indirect questions may, of course, be able to mask their real motives successfully. A negotiator may mix innocuous questions with important questions. For example, apparently innocent questions about the attorney's practice, experience, or workload assist in evaluating that attorney's capabilities and time pressures.

It is useful to keep an ongoing list of information that is needed from the other side. That way, when the other side calls unexpectedly, one has a ready reference in an attempt to get information in every communication with the other side.

9.4.1 Maintaining Accountability

It is important to hold the other negotiator accountable for information revealed. Some negotiators are prone to exaggerate or misrepresent facts or the law. An effective way of holding negotiators accountable for the accuracy of statements is to ask for the source of the information, for the identity or location of documents confirming the information, for the citation to the claimed legal principle, or for the name, address, phone number, and email address of the supporting witness. Requesting sources will hold the other negotiator responsible for what is said and decrease the chances that misstatements will be made.

9.4.2 Assessing Responses

When deciding upon the accuracy of responses to questions, the reaction of the negotiator can be observed in face-to-face negotiations. Hesitations, facial reactions, gestures, and nervous movements sometimes provide a more reliable answer than the words of the response. This is why face-to-face exchanges—if they are possible—can be invaluable to negotiations. Another gauge of accuracy is to compare the response to a question with explanations or positions made before and after the response.

9.5 INFORMING AND UPDATING THE CLIENT

As discussed in Chapter 8, it is vital to keep the client fully informed about the progress, or lack of progress, of a negotiation. As negotiations progress, unanticipated information and alternatives often are discussed. As that happens, lawyers may well need to consult their clients to make sure that they are acting in accord with the authority their clients have given them.

Think Twice

What could possibly explain a failure to keep a client apprised of negotiations? Some clients may not seem to want what may be almost constant communication; and some clients will be reluctant to pay the attorney for the time regular updates take. Even in these situations, it usually will be most effective to continue to discuss the negotiation plan with the client unless the client expressly declines to have this discussion.

B. YOUR MOVE, MY MOVE: THE EXCHANGE OF WORTH

During negotiations, negotiators can discuss: the past (what has happened and why), the present (what the client wants now), and the future (what will be, will be). Negotiators can make three general types of statements about the past, present, and future. They can:

- *Make a wish.*
- *Make a persuasive statement.*
- *Make a threat.*

A *wish* is an expression of what your client wants.

A *persuasive statement* is an explanation about why the other side should engage in an exchange of worth.

A *threat* is a statement or suggestion about what may befall the other side should they fail to grant your wish or respond to your persuasive statement.

The following sections explore and discuss different kinds of wishes, persuasive statements, and threats—and the process involved in delivering them and responding to them.

Think Twice

A "wish"? Is it fair to call a demand made during a negotiation a "wish"? We think it is—if that demand isn't accompanied by a supporting persuasive statement. We've used the term as a reminder that no matter how exorbitant or forcefully delivered, an offer or demand made during negotiation isn't anything more than a wish until the lawyer justifies it.

9.6 MAKING A WISH: OFFERS AND DEMANDS, REQUESTS AND RESPONSES

Negotiators make a wish when they discuss what it is their clients want or need. Specific "making a wish" statements include offers and demands. Typically, wishes come hand-in-hand with some type of persuasive statement or threat. When to make a wish, what to say, and how to respond are discussed in this section.

9.6.1 How Should a Negotiation Begin?

How negotiations open affects how they end. The attorney deciding to initiate settlement discussions may wish to begin negotiation, but choose to justify that wish with a legitimate reason for broaching the negotiation dialogue. Examples include:

- Your client has some interests that can be met if we talk.

- We have a proposal to present to you and your client that we think you will find attractive.

- Both parties have some complementary and mutual needs that can be satisfied.

- Our firm has a policy of contacting the other side to determine whether there is any desire to resolve this matter.

- You represent the seller, so it is only appropriate that you tell me your price; or you represent the buyer, so it is only appropriate you tell me what you will offer.

- You represent the plaintiff and it is only appropriate that you tell me what you want; or you represent the defendant who is responsible for what happened and it only appropriate that you make an offer.

- Both our clients will gain by saving money if this deal gets done quickly or this case settles quickly. Matters like this may be better resolved to both sides' satisfaction if negotiations are efficient.

- We will be required to attempt to mediate this dispute. Why don't we try to settle it ourselves?

- The judge will expect us to have discussed settlement, so perhaps we should begin now to determine whether the case can be settled; or, our clients will expect us to have completed negotiations soon.

9.6.2 What Are the Advantages and Disadvantages in Making or Receiving the First Proposal?

One of the negotiators must either make the first offer or demand, or initially explain the specifics of a client's position or interest in agreement.

Going First: The Advantages

An initial proposal may set the initial tone of the negotiation or may provide the negotiator with more control of the process.

The initial offer or demand indicates to the other side the exact position of the negotiator or the interests of the client, and may strengthen that position or those interests.

In the absence of known benchmarks, the parties may not have a firm idea of the spectrum of worth the other side is willing to exchange or concede. A large demand or small offer may focus discussions at one end of that "concession spectrum" and make any responsive small offer or large demand seem unreasonable in comparison.

A position may gain credibility by being the first to be advanced and by becoming the focus of the discussion. Likewise, those interests that are first mentioned may come to seem the most significant.

The initial request may accelerate the reaching of an agreement or settlement.

Advancing the first offer or demand allows the negotiator to obtain and analyze a reaction from the other side which may help reveal the opponent's bargaining position.

Going First: The Disadvantages

The initial demand may be lower than expected or the initial offer higher than anticipated.

The opponent can more accurately assess both ends of the concession spectrum.

The other side can measure the first offer and modify a counteroffer based on that information.

An initial position may unwittingly give away too much worth if the interests of the parties significantly overlap.

It may be easier to respond and fashion a more effective negotiation approach after knowing the opposition's initial position. For example, a negotiator may have incorrectly assessed the other side's interests.

The offer or demand may be described as unreasonable.

The opponent can refuse to make a counteroffer unless the first demand is reduced or first offer increased.

Think Twice

So who should go first? Some plaintiff lawyers prefer to make the first offer to establish expectations and accelerate the settlement process; but some defense lawyers prefer to make an early first offer to set one end of a range and in an effort to minimize transaction costs. Some lawyers have preferred ways and develop a preference for always approaching the first offer during negotiation the same way. Rather than have a set way, it's better to be flexible and decide in each case whether making or waiting for an offer benefits your client.

9.6.3   How Should Offers and Demands Be Expressed?

Several considerations affect how clear and how firm an offer or demand need be. The circumstances and the issues may dictate how to describe an offer or demand. The type of negotiation, the simplicity of the issues, and the nature of the provisions all affect how resolute the position need be. It may be more effective for the lawyer to frame the initial position more generally. Available benchmarks, such as market valuation in a contract or lease situation, may support an offer or counteroffer. A range of prices or costs may be all that an attorney can propose, with a mid-range figure used as a specific amount. This range approach may also be useful in situations in which flexibility is necessary to resolve a dispute.

It may make sense to take elastic positions when the negotiators have not previously had a full discussion of their clients' interests. The major consideration in determining when to describe offers or demands as firm is, however, timing. Describing an offer or demand as "firm" too early may cause a deadlock or cause a lawyer to defend a poor position. Waiting too long to articulate a clear offer or demand may cause the other side to conclude their alternatives to agreement are preferable to continuing negotiation.

Many negotiators round off negotiation figures because it is often difficult to make a firm commitment to a specific amount, and because round numbers may seem easier to use. Other negotiators prefer to use precise amounts relating to specific factors in a case. While both of these approaches are valid, negotiators should take care to calculate the monetary impact on the client before figures are exchanged.

9.6.4   How Should Component Issues Be Discussed?

Most items involved in negotiations can be divided into components and sub-issues. An attorney representing an employee in an employment contract case can describe the amount owed to the employee in terms of a single sum of money or in terms of multiple components measured as lost wages, vacation time, savings contributions, insurance premiums, and other benefits.

When should the component approach be used? Attorneys must consider whether the component or the unit approach benefits their position and their client's interests when preparing an offer. Component demands may favor the plaintiff or seller, while lump sum, single-unit offers may favor the defendant or buyer. Positions consisting of components allow an attorney to appear to be asking for less, may lull the other attorney into perceiving that the component amounts are not that significant, and provide an agenda for discussion.

9.6.5 Responding to Wishes

How a negotiator responds to wishes—offers, demands, proposals, and other expressions of positions—has a substantial impact on the final settlement. The lawyer's reaction should be consistent with the interests and positions disclosed, and remember that both verbal and nonverbal reactions may reveal more than what the lawyer wishes to disclose. As a negotiator, you can respond to an offer or demand in a variety of ways, but will often want to begin by:

- Asking questions to clarify the position.
- Having the negotiator explain the basis of it.

After you are reasonably certain you understand the wish, you can consider:

- Searching for mutual client interests.
- Making a verbal counteroffer or concession.
- Accepting it and ending the negotiations.
- Rejecting the offer or demand and continuing negotiations.
- Rejecting it and walking out or deadlocking negotiations.
- Postponing consideration of it and discussing other matters first.
- Insisting on a larger offer or reduced demand.

Think Twice

You may be tempted to accept a proposal made early during the negotiation process that falls within the range of settlement. It's natural to feel some relief that an offer or demand has been made that would be satisfactory to your client, and you may also be happy to avoid further anxiety or tension. Before accepting the offer or demand, stop and ask yourself: Can a more favorable accord be reached? Many negotiators instinctively avoid accepting an early offer even if the demand falls within settlement range because it is early in the process and they anticipate that an exchange of counteroffers will most probably result in an even better resolution. On the other hand, if the answer to the question is that this is in all likelihood the most favorable agreement available and the timing is good for your client, accepting the terms certainly makes sense.

9.6.6 Changing Your Wish: Adjusting an Offer or Demand

Making a high demand or a low offer in a negotiation can create difficulties. Attorneys who are confident and sure about their position have little compunction in taking a firm, tactical position. However, attorneys who fail properly to evaluate a situation and vacillate in constructing a position have difficulty in expressing an extreme, but appropriate, demand or offer.

It can be difficult for a negotiator to make a proposal only to have the other lawyer react by either appearing incredulous, claiming the proposal is unreasonable or blaming the negotiator for attempting to deadlock the negotiation. Some offers and demands may genuinely appear unreasonable to the other attorney and produce such a reaction. The negotiator must be able to reasonably explain the position and provide substantial reasons to weather this reaction.

9.6.7 Focus on the Real Interests of the Party

The reasons that attorneys give to support positions often help illuminate the underlying interests of their clients. It is not unusual, however, for negotiators to include in offers and demands items that have little or no value to their clients. These negotiators mix fictitious needs with real interests, or artificially create interests and then concede the contrived interests in exchange for something that has value. This false demand tactic has substantial drawbacks. The client may have no interest in what the attorney has demanded and such an explanation of the client's needs might be an outright falsehood.

Think Twice

It's relatively easy to make an offer that appears reasonable to the other side. The challenge is to state an offer

---

that appears to be unreasonable and be able to justify it. It's the lack of justification that causes an offer to be inappropriate. You need to back up your position with good, legitimate reasons.

9.7 MAKING A PERSUASIVE STATEMENT

In life, wishes may be granted; in negotiations, they seldom will be. That is why negotiators couple wishes with persuasive statements. For example, an offer or demand will typically be accompanied by a reference to an accepted benchmark. Interests are explained; positions are justified. This process, the heart of any negotiation, involves making persuasive statements. As discussed in Chapter 8, part of preparation for negotiation is fashioning a theory of the case or theory of the deal: a short, persuasive explanation of the client's position or interests. This theory will usually accompany any initial demand or offer.

Negotiators make persuasive statements when they suggest reasons why the other side should engage in an exchange of worth. The purpose of the statement is, ultimately, to convince the other side to accept an offer or demand. Most negotiators perceive an offer or demand to be more valuable if an explanation supports that position or interest. Why? Because a demand, for example, typically consists of two parts: the extrinsic worth requested (usually money) and the intrinsic value that the negotiator attaches to the reasons or explanation for the demand. A demand that is supported by an intrinsic reason is more effective and persuasive than one from which an explanation is omitted. For example, it can be more effective for a negotiator to demand $53,400 and to explain how that demand was arrived at instead of just demanding $40,000 without any explanation.

The following sections suggest different ways to make a persuasive statement in negotiations.

9.7.1 Focus on Complementary Interests

One side may demand Y, and the other side will offer X, resulting in a substantial gap and requiring sides to make concessions. It is often presumed that, since the positions advanced by the parties conflict, their interests conflict as well.

Parties may, however, also have some related needs and wants. For example:

A consumer plaintiff who demands her money back through a breach of warranty action may want the product replaced; the defendant manufacturer may want the original product returned to determine the cause of the defect to prevent future problems.

A corporate plaintiff who demands an injunction and damages in a contract dispute may prefer re-negotiated contract terms and prices; the defendant may wish to continue the business relationship based on modified terms.

A corporate vice president may support the construction of a one-story office addition while another vice president insists on a two-story addition. These two vice presidents may discover that they have related interests if they focus on what corporate functions need how much space, instead of their set positions.

A lessor may want a six-year lease while a lessee only wants a two-year lease. Both may be interested in a four-year lease with options and liquidated damage clauses.

A landlord needs to charge market-value rent that will attract tenants who will pay regularly; a tenant may have an interest in paying market-value rent if the landlord will be able to afford to provide regular maintenance and repairs.

Parties will typically have some complementary interests and needs that can form the basis for negotiation. In sales negotiations, complementary interests exist because the buyers want the property or goods and the sellers need the money. In litigation negotiations, the plaintiffs want money and the defendants want the dispute to be over. Discussion, examination, and redefinition of interests may turn what appear to be conflicting interests into complementary ones.

Think Twice

Learning about the other side's interests continues throughout a negotiation, including during the exchange of worth. If one side makes a multi-pronged proposal during negotiation, one or more of the proposed alterna-

tives may be acceptable to the other side. When that happens, the party making the offer gains additional insight into the other side's interests. For example, an employee negotiating a restrictive covenant contract clause may present to the prospective employer three alternative provisions instead of just one provision. The employee might suggest that acceptable restrictions include (1) a three-year prohibition within a 10–mile radius, (2) a two-year prohibition within a 20–mile radius, or (3) a one-year prohibition within a 30–mile radius. An employer interested in a long-term prohibition or a broad, geographic restriction may perceive one of the alternatives to be more acceptable.

9.7.2   Use Benchmarks and Other Objective Standards or Rationales

As discussed in Chapter 8, one of the most important steps in preparation for negotiation is learning about appropriate benchmarks. These benchmarks, as well as other objective criteria, can be used to support and explain offers, demands, positions, and a client's interests or goals. This is one of the most common, and most effective, techniques for turning a wish into a persuasive statement.

Every offer, demand, or position should be supported by some explanation. It is more persuasive and efficient to gain the acceptance of the other lawyer by relying on solid, firm criteria rather than on the negotiator's own self-serving opinions and conclusions. For example, if a lessor and a lessee concern themselves with the fair market value of leased space rather than their own valuation, they will be more likely to reach a reasonable accord. Relying on objective criteria shifts the focus of the negotiation from the parties' perspectives and the lawyers' opinions to more useful matters.

Each issue in a negotiation needs to be analyzed to determine what specific, objective reasons support a client's interests or positions. The following paragraphs detail some of the more common supportive explanations.

Facts. Every situation will have some persuasive facts supporting the issues. Whether undisputed or disputed, these facts can effectively be used as reasons.

Law. Every case will have some supportive law. Every transaction will be bounded by some law or regulation, as well. This law may be employed to explain a position: "We will not pay anything for the punitive damages claims because the law does not permit such recovery," or "We included this term because the law requires us to include it in the lease."

Component Positions. The component parts of many monetary demands may be used as reasons. A consumer contract obligation will comprise X number of dollars for the amount financed, Y number of dollars for the finance charge, and Z number of dollars for other charges. Positions or concessions may be pegged to these specific amounts: "We will reduce our demand by dropping our claim for the unearned finance charge."

Setting Future Precedent. Reference to the future precedent an accord will set can provide support for counteroffers: "This case will provide our client with a legal ruling that, regardless of the decision, will clear up this problem once and for all," or "Our client refuses to include those terms for your client because then everyone else will expect the same terms."

Prior Verdicts or Decisions. Prior jury verdicts or judicial determinations in similar cases are a good source of objective criteria. These sources may be obtained from independent jury verdict research reports, from local jurisdiction records, or from the lawyer's experience.

Economic Data. The economic value of property or damages may be based upon some objective sources like market value. The more reliable the economic source, the more likely the other side will accept it as authoritative: "Valuation can be accurately determined by using the standard price list (or consumer price index) in effect at this time."

Tax Consequences. The tax consequences of an agreement or settlement may well affect the scope and terms of an agreement. The consideration of these issues may support a larger or smaller negotiable amount. For example, the lower present payout by a defendant will provide a larger settlement to the plaintiff paid over a period of years through a tax-free annuity. See section 9.7.3.

Business Practices. Existing business practices and custom and usage can justify proposals. Accounting procedures, corporate practices, industry customs, and other business concerns need to be reviewed to determine what support they provide for particular positions.

Expert Opinions. Expert judgment will often be a source of support. The more objective the data that supports the expert's opinion, the more authoritative the support will be.

Principles. Principles or moral standards may explain some positions asserted. A client may insist on a certain demand purely on principle: "Our client wants, for security reasons, to be completely protected and insists on this position," or "Our client, as a matter of principle, will not agree to an offer more than the nuisance value of this case because it gives the appearance of liability."

Fairness. Appeals to considerations of fairness can explain a compromise. For example, in a multi-party negotiation in which all parties but one have come to agreement, fairness may provide a basis for agreement by the holdout so as not to spoil the settlement reached by the other parties. "Just to be reasonable, we will offer," or "For the sake of fairness to everyone concerned, we will...."

Reciprocity. Simple reciprocity will usually produce a counteroffer in negotiations. Most attorneys expect to exchange concessions in sequence: "We have made this concession, now it's your turn."

Splitting the Difference. This reason may be effective in cases close to settlement or an agreement. It will be inappropriate if it bears no logical relationship to the positions.

Peripheral Issues. Peripheral claims will often explain away a concession without conceding much in fact. In transactions, certain language, the structure of the agreement, and its effective date may be exchanged for more valuable interests. In litigation, attorney's fees, court costs, and settlement payment schedules may be exchanged for a more valuable counteroffer from the other side: "We will drop our request for attorney's fees if you...."

Risks. Elimination of risks and costs may be alluded to as a rationale for a concession. Threats made by the negotiators, the additional time and effort necessary to close a deal with someone else or further prepare the case for trial, and future expenses will support a concession: "Your client cannot afford to lose this deal," or "Your client runs the risk of an unknown jury verdict, so...."

Public Attention. Public visibility or the lack of sufficient privacy may have an effect on one or both parties. A provision that the terms of the agreement not be made public may have significant value to a party.

Specific types of negotiations may lend themselves to additional explanations to support a position. For example, in commercial negotiations the seller may be able to explain to a prospective buyer why certain terms or a specific price is appropriate, employing such reasons as:

Identity and Reputation. The seller has created a popular and attractive reputation for the product or service which buyers identify with and which will make it easier for the wholesale buyer to sell in turn to retail buyers.

Promotion. The seller has aggressively advertised the product or service, created a market for it, and forged a highly visible position in the marketplace.

Warranties and Guarantees. The seller warrants its product or service, and will stand behind what it sells.

Good Service. The seller provides quality repair services in case any problems arise.

Credit Advantages. The seller offers favorable credit terms that make it economically more feasible for the purchaser to buy the product or services.

Think Twice

How do you know which of these factors may have a favorable impact on the other side? Making that call is part of your overall strategy and tactics. You need to decide what to say when. You may be able to predict which of these factors may be helpful, or you may be able to glean from a comment made by the other side what may influence them. Be prepared before the negotiation and be alert during the negotiation, and you'll be able to make informed judgments about what to say when.

9.7.3 Assess the Effect of Tax Considerations

Tax aspects affect the structure and provisions of nearly every negotiation transaction involving a contract or lease agreement. An attorney must be familiar with applicable laws, how those laws apply to a negotiation, what effect those laws will have upon a proposed agreement, and whether the tax consequences of an alternative proposal better serve the interests of one or both parties. For example, an attorney advising a business client regarding the purchase or lease of a $250,000 machine will need to examine the tax ramifications of alternative purchase and lease agreements and advise the client concerning feasible options. Or, a spouse involved in a divorce situation may receive tax benefits or incur tax liabilities as a result of the terms of a stipulated agreement.

Other negotiation situations highlight the importance of considering tax consequences. A client may express a desire to purchase some land, but it may be that tax considerations will influence that client to reconsider and decide that a long-term lease better serves the client's tax interests. The effect of income, sales, estate, and gift taxes may be complex, requiring the negotiating attorney to consult with tax lawyers and accountants.

Litigators must consider the tax treatment afforded by litigation settlements and must review and analyze the impact tax laws and regulations have upon a proposed settlement before finalizing an agreement. Additional factors in assessing tax consequences of a settlement agreement are the timing of signing of the agreement, the payment of the settlement, or the reporting requirement for the income from the settlement.

A structured settlement is a financial package settlement in which lump sum or periodic annuity payments are used with resulting tax benefits. Structured settlements can provide recipients with tax-free income and payers with tax gains. This settlement approach has been primarily used in personal injury litigation where a plaintiff has legitimate claims for substantial damages. The most important factor influencing courts in interpreting the nature of the settlement recovery is the payer's basic reason for making the payments. Why the payer has settled will largely determine the nature of the payments for tax purposes.

Think Twice

This is why you were smart to take that tax class. We cannot stress enough the significance that tax consequences have on many deals or disputes. And too many lawyers overlook these consequences before reaching an accord or settlement. Do your tax homework or, better yet, contact a tax lawyer who knows the consequences. Because tax laws change so frequently and affect different time periods, it's wise to make the effort and spend the money to figure out how current tax regulations can benefit your client. And it avoids a subsequently unhappy client contacting you about why you didn't think to do so.

9.7.4   Responding to Persuasive Statements: Exchanging Worth

A concession is the giving up of something of value. It may be appropriate to respond to an offer or demand with a concession anticipating this will prompt the other side to counter with an equal concession. Whether a concession should be made depends upon the negotiation approach employed and the best interests of the client. Concessions are a common technique to bridge differences in both positional bargaining negotiations and interest-based negotiations.

A goal of many negotiators will be the promotion of mutual gains for both sides. A gain is a relative proposition. It may mean that a party obtains more of something as a result of a negotiated accord. It may also mean that a party does not lose as much. When a concession is necessary, it can be made contingent upon the other side cooperating and making compromises equal in value and with the same frequency.

Most lawyers come to a negotiation prepared to make an initial offer or demand and justify it with some sort of persuasive statement. Most also come to a negotiation with some sense of the minimum amount of worth the client is willing to accept in the negotiation. Well-prepared negotiators also plan the concessions they are willing to make and think through, in advance, what might prompt them to make those concessions. The most effective negotiators do even more. The most effective negotiators prepare persuasive statements that justify their own concessions. Read back over the list of benchmarks and rationales in Section 9.7.2. Many of the examples in that section illustrate persuasive statements that can be used *in the course of making a concession.*

Think Twice

You might ask why it is worth the trouble to explain or justify concessions. A concession made without justification invites opposing counsel to make wishes and suggests that those wishes will be granted. If you make a concession without any principled explanation for doing so, opposing counsel is likely to feel no need to justify or explain future demands for concession: you have already indicated you are willing to give away worth without any good reason for doing so. Planning your concessions and tying them to persuasive statements will help prevent you dropping in free fall from your opening demand to the minimum your client will accept. The negotiators who take the time to do this sort of planning tend to be the ones who are able to negotiate agreements that are better than their clients had hoped for.

9.8 MAKING A THREAT

Negotiators can make a threat in an effort to get a result. A *threat* is an avowal to do or not do something. It may be stated as a promise ("we will withdraw an offer") or it may be stated as a conditional declaration ("bankruptcy is a probability depending upon the amount of a trial verdict"). Threats are designed to persuade the other negotiator that a failure to reach an accord will result in unpleasant consequences. Some lawyers may not negotiate unless some potential consequences exist. Threats, as we have defined them, occur in both positional bargaining and interest-based negotiations, and are often used as incentives for parties to reach an agreement or settle a case.

Threats can be used both effectively and ineffectively. To be effective, a threat must be credible, involve something of value, and be supported by the threatening party's resolve. A threat is most likely to be most effective when:

- Actions support the verbal threat.

- Reasons support the threatened action.

- The threat is effectively communicated.

- Multiple, varied, or incremental threats are made.

- The threat is substantial.

- The size of the threat is scaled to the size of the problem.

9.8.1   The Most Effective Threat

The single most powerful threat a negotiator can make involves having a very good alternative to negotiated agreement and being comfortable and willing to use it. Litigators frequently report that the best negotiators they know are the lawyers who are adept at trying cases and not afraid to do so. Having a good alternative deal waiting in the wings makes the transactional lawyer a formidable negotiator. These are lawyers with confidence in their BATNAs, and that confidence means they can be relentless in the pursuit of their clients' interests during negotiation. That is one of the reasons that, in Chapter 8, we stress the importance of understanding your client's alternatives to agreement before you begin negotiation.

9.8.2   How to Respond to Threats

A negotiator may respond in a variety of ways to a threat:

- Clarify what was said to make certain a threat was intentionally asserted.

- Be silent for a while and consider an appropriate response.

- Express disbelief or bewilderment.

- Empathize with the other side's situation.

- Explain how the threat adversely affects the threatening party.

- Seek to defer the threat and focus the discussion on another matter.

- Counter the threat with a threat.

- Call the other side on the threat and determine if they are bluffing.

- Walk out or deadlock negotiations.

While it may be appropriate to make concessions in response to credible threats, it is important to understand that making a concession in the face of a threat is likely to encourage the opposing lawyer to use more threats. In general, holding lawyers accountable for threats that are less than credible is the best way to discourage future threats. One of the best ways to hold a lawyer accountable for an ineffective threat is to discuss your own understanding of and confidence in your client's alternative to a negotiated agreement.

Think Twice

A common mistake novice negotiators make is to make a threat without being prepared to follow through. If that bluff is called, the novice lawyer often continues on as if the threat was never made. Doing this badly undermines credibility and effectiveness. Why would the other side believe any future threats made? And when you lose the ability to make an effective threat—even if you never actually make or have to make a threat—you hurt your client's position.

9.8.3   How to Resolve Problems

No matter how thorough a lawyer's planning has been, unexpected situations and problems are likely to occur during negotiations. The following techniques summarize ways to reduce problem situations that arise during negotiations:

- Recognizing that a problem exists and identifying the problem.

- Assuming appropriate responsibility for the problem and not blaming the other negotiator.

- Resisting the tendency to exaggerate a problem caused by the other side.

- Viewing the problem from the perspective of the other negotiator.

- Considering possible solutions to the problems and selecting the most mutually effective solution.

9.8.4 How to Gain the Cooperation of the Other Negotiator

During negotiations, one negotiator may refuse to engage in reasonable negotiation discussions. This refusal may occur at any stage of negotiations, and a previously cooperative negotiator may opt to take a competitive, positional approach rather than an interest-based or collaborative approach. It is critical at these stages for an attorney who believes cooperation best serves the client to attempt to make an ally of someone who prefers to act like an adversary by:

- Adopting a friendly approach and explaining why cooperation will work.

- Focusing on the parties' best interests.

- Focusing on the benefits of a negotiated resolution.

- Controlling the urge to be defensive.

- Persisting in efforts to reach an agreement.

- Avoiding gambits and ploys.

Think Twice

Persistence is often the key to a successful negotiation. Staying the course and not being overcome by the difficulties that will arise—and they will—is often the best strategy, even if there appear to be dim hopes for success. There can be a fine line between persistence and stubbornness, but refusing to quit can be an excellent negotiation trait. Mediators often succeed because they continue the negotiations in the face of difficult problems. Negotiators can use the same tactic by putting a problem aside temporarily, working on other issues in the negotiation, and returning to it later.

9.8.5 How to Respond to Gambits

Some negotiators may use gambits—divisive behavior that is meant to disconcert the other negotiator. Many of these techniques involve ploys and manipulation and most are, in essence, nothing more than a species of threat—a threat to disrupt the negotiation process. Many lawyers deplore the use of these techniques, while other attorneys endorse these ploys on the basis that the end justifies the means. It is easy to scoff at and dismiss these tactics when reading about them. It may be another thing to respond to them effectively or to avoid using them yourself during a negotiation when difficulties arise.

Examples of gambits include:

- Acting as if a position is ridiculous.
- Being condescending or rude.
- Pretending not to have sufficient authority to discuss an offer.
- Delaying negotiation talks for no apparent good reason.

Negotiators who face these ploys may be able to deflect these adverse influences effectively by:

- Recognizing the gambit,
- Informing the other negotiator that the tactic has been recognized, and
- Diplomatically requesting that the discussion shift to a more productive topic.

Some negotiators may not be aware of their gaming techniques and quickly accede to such a request. Other negotiators who have consciously tried to be manipulative may stop such attempts if they perceive such efforts to be unproductive. It may not be advisable, in some situations, to ask the other side to desist if the negotiator can effectively counter such ploys. Negotiators should not yield or accede to gambits and ploys and should make clear that they will only be influenced by legitimate justifications and objective factors.

9.8.6 How to Unlock a Deadlock

Deadlocks may occur when one or more negotiators engage in a pattern of threats, but can occur at any time during a negotiation. There are numerous alternatives to prevent dead-locks or to restart deadlocked negotiations. Negotiators may:

- Discuss the reasoning behind the position that led to the deadlock.

- Describe how the parties benefit from continued negotiations.

- Detail the practical effects of failing to settle.

- Agree to reconsider the last position if the opponent will do likewise.

- Take a short break instead of ending the negotiation.

- Seek agreement on some issue to which both sides can readily agree.

- Display some understanding and empathy with the other side's quandary.

- Concede something; make an offer; reduce a demand.

- Table the deadlocked issue.

- Change something about the negotiation process, such as its location.

- Ask: "Do we agree we should continue to talk in the future?"

- Seek assistance from a mediator.

Think Twice

Time may be of the essence in a transaction, or there may be a deadline for a dispute settlement, making some of these suggestions infeasible. Sometimes just taking a breath, stepping back for a brief moment, returning to a position that previously seemed to be acceptable, and continuing on from there may work. Deadlocks sometimes occur because the parties are unwittingly heading down the wrong path. Going back may lead to another pathway that leads to a result.

9.8.7   Whether to Use the Take–It–or–Leave–It Approach

At times, faced with demands of preparing for and conducting a negotiation, it is tempting to believe that our life as lawyers would be much easier if we could simply give the other side our best offer and have done with it. Indeed, some negotiators do make initial offers and represent that those offers are final. This firm-offer or single-demand approach is also known as the take-it-or-leave-it position. One difficulty with this tactic is that it will not work if the other side has an alternative to agreement that is preferable to the offer. Another difficulty is that many, if not most, lawyers are unlikely to believe that the first offer is actually a final offer.

More commonly, a lawyer may resort to this technique near the end of a negotiation. One attorney sets a position that must be met for settlement to occur. This tactic may be most effective when both parties are nearing settlement but for some reason are unable to reach final agreement. Many attorneys attempt to use this threat as a bluff, and making a legitimate counteroffer or demand may be an effective way to call this bluff. Other lawyers use this threat to deadlock a negotiation or as a means to refuse to negotiate in good faith. See section 9.10.1.

9.8.8　Whether to Walk Out

The tactic of walking out of a negotiation may be a planned tactic, or it may be a spontaneous, ill-advised reaction to something that has occurred during negotiation. Some negotiators will intentionally test the opponent by staging a walkout to see how the opponent reacts. These negotiators may believe that there is no need to make quick, early concessions. They prefer to be obstinate early, often hoping to disturb the opponent to see what will happen. They know that some opponents fear deadlocked situations and will be willing to make major concessions to prevent deadlocks. Some deadlocks and walkouts are precipitated by emotional interchanges and reactions. Effective negotiators stop, consider, and decide before reacting.

Think Twice

At times, using a take it or leave tactic may be effective, but since it can typically only be used once, it should be used only where appropriate. Walking out may not be the end of a negotiation because you may be able to walk back in. In transaction negotiations, the buyer or seller may

use this tactic to see if they can get a better deal. They may plan to turn around rather quickly—within minutes, hours, or days—and accept the last demand or offer from the other side, if the other side does not contact them first. This presumes the demand or offer remains available, and that is a risky presumption because the other side can easily change their position when given more time or negotiate a deal with someone else. These higher risk tactics can easily backfire, and as a lawyer you may need to obtain your client's explicit permission to use them in order to avoid a client unhappy with your efforts.

9.9 EMPLOYING CREATIVE APPROACHES

Negotiation rewards creative thinking. Effective negotiators use a blend of wishes, persuasive statements, and threats to craft creative resolutions leading to favorable agreements. Creative approaches to the formation of an agreement or the resolution of a dispute may provide both sides with mutually satisfactory results. The following examples demonstrate creative negotiation solutions.

9.9.1 The Consumer Camper Case

A consumer purchased a new, $92,000 motor home and began a one-week vacation. After driving only 550 miles, transmission problems developed and he returned to the dealer to have the transmission repaired under the warranty. The repair work took one day. He decided to shorten his trip and left again, only to encounter electrical problems about 100 miles from the dealer. Again he decided to return and have the repairs made. The dealer told him the repairs would take one day but because some of the parts were out of stock, the repairs took three days. He requested a loaner camper, but was turned down. He stayed home during the remainder of his vacation. After visiting his lawyer, he revoked acceptance of the camper, and sued, in part, for $27,000. This amount reflected lost leisure and vacation time computed at a rate of $3,000 a day. This claim represented an issue of first impression in the local courts. Liability was uncertain; damages were speculative. A main issue was how much lost vacation time was worth. The defense initially refused to offer any money for such damages; the plaintiff stood firm at $27,000. A deadlock occurred. Then the defense reviewed the interests of the plaintiff: the plaintiff wanted to recover his lost vacation time. The defense then proposed the following: that the plaintiff accept the equivalent of one week's salary ($2500) and use that money to pay for a one-week of unpaid vacation time from his job. That way, he would still get his vacation time prospectively. The plaintiff could take unpaid vacation time from his job, and after further discussions accepted $7,500 in settlement of that portion of his claim for two weeks of unpaid vacation time and for the lost week of repairs (plus a completely repaired motor home).

9.9.2 The Surviving Spouse Case

This example comes from the world of jury deliberations which, in effect, are group negotiation processes. A jury was observed on video deliberating a verdict in a civil action. In the case being tried, the defendant had negligently killed the wife of the plaintiff in an auto accident. Liability was clear; the real issue in the case concerned damages. The wrongful death statute permitted the husband to recover for loss of love and affection. During closing argument the plaintiff's attorney asked for $1,000,000 for that claim in addition to damages for other claims. During jury deliberations, five jurors were prepared to provide the plaintiff with a substantial recovery on that claim (they mentioned $250,000 to $750,000). One of the jurors resisted. He then began to negotiate with the other five jurors. He told them that if they provided the plaintiff with that amount of money they would "ruin his life!" The other jurors were so shocked by this notion that they literally laughed at him. He further explained that the plaintiff was young, handsome, likely to marry again, earned $64,000 a year, and a substantial verdict would change his life style. The lone juror then proposed that the interests of the plaintiff and the responsibility of the defendant be analyzed: the plaintiff needed some time to grieve and recover from his loss and some money to compensate for the tragedy; the defendant had the obligation to provide that opportunity and money. The juror then suggested that an award of $130,000 would be sufficient because then the plaintiff could quit work for a year, ($64,000), buy a new car ($24,000), spend the extra money on himself ($12,000), pay off his attorney (estimated $30,000), and start a new life. The other five jurors, after further discussions, agreed that $100,000 satisfied the plaintiff's interest on that claim. They were very pleased with the arrangement and believed they benefited both parties.

9.9.3 The Ski Accident

A college-age student on a skiing weekend was killed in the crash of a ski lift gondola. The ski lift operator recognized the extent of its liability and wanted to settle the case to avoid any adverse publicity. The wealthy parents of the college student brought a wrongful death case, repeatedly refused the offers of a cash settlement, and wanted to proceed with the litigation in part to hold the ski resort publicly accountable and in part to honor the memory of their son. The attorneys for the defendant began to consider alternative ways to settle the case, because no reasonable amount of money appeared to satisfy the plaintiffs. The attorneys reviewed the real interests of the parents and the needs of their client. They then prepared a professional brochure proposing a solution which required the defendant to: endow with a substantial amount of money a ski safety training program named in honor of the son, establish a college scholarship in the name of the son, publicize the availability of both, and pay litigation expenses and some damages. This proposal was modified, with the endowment and scholarship money increased, and was then accepted by the parents. They felt their interests had been recognized and they received some satisfaction plus money; and the defendant saved trial expenses, avoided the risk of a huge jury verdict, and was able to conduct an effective safety advertising campaign which promoted the name and location of the ski area.

9.9.4 Selling the Farm

A corporate farmer wanted to expand and offered an adjacent farmer $250,000 for his small farm. The farmer was not anxious to sell to someone outside his family, but was nearing the age of retirement and planned to sell sometime soon. The neighboring farmer set a firm price of $290,000 for his farm. The final purchase agreement provided: a $280,000 purchase price, payment terms of a $190,000 initial payment with six annual $15,000 installment payments, the farmer being able to live in the farmhouse for three months after the closing, the farmer retaining a right to store a camper and a boat trailer and to hunt on the land until his death, and the daughter of the farmer having the right of first refusal if the farm were resold. These provisions satisfied the interests of both parties and avoided their having to make major concessions.

C. ENDING THE NEGOTIATION

9.10 CONCLUDING A NEGOTIATION

Reaching an accord concludes many negotiations, but not all. The failure to reach an accord can result in the death of a deal or further litigation. It may also be the best thing to do.

Not all negotiations will, or should, result in an accord. Some deals should not be struck. Some cases need to be tried. The outcome of the trial may be the best alternative available to both sides because there exists no chance for compromise or no complementary, mutual interests or needs. Other negotiations may simply deadlock because both parties may evaluate the facts so differently that there is no common ground for agreement. One or both sides may need to obtain more information, verify some data, or conduct further investigation before negotiations continue. Serious negotiations may begin again after a temporary deadlock at the prompting of a negotiator, party, mediator, or judge.

9.10.1 When Is a Final Position a Final Position?

When a negotiator says "This is my last and final offer" is it? When will a "last" demand really be a final position? The best way to determine the answers to these questions is to analyze the statement's content and context.

- How did the lawyer phrase the offer or demand? Was it in absolute terms or was a condition included?

- Is the final position consistent with previous positions taken by the lawyer?

- Is the timing of the final offer or demand reasonable in light of what has occurred to date? Is it too early?

- Did the lawyer appear credible in taking such a position or did it appear to be just a tactic?

- Did the lawyer become emotionally involved and overreact by stating such a position?

- Did it appear that this tactic was planned by the negotiator? Did the demand seem intentional or inadvertent?

- How does the position reflect the real needs and interests of a party? Of both parties?

- Are there other acceptable positions that would produce mutual gains for both sides?

- How does the final position compare to alternative options to settle the case?

- Does the position appear to reflect the authority limits the client may have provided the negotiator?

Think Twice

A final position should be just that. If a negotiator asserts "This is my final offer," then negotiations should cease or the other side should accept the offer. However, final offers may not be what they seem. A negotiator may claim a position is final position as a tactic to gain more for a client. (This is similar to making a "take it or leave it" offer discussed in § 9.8.7.) Tactics like this can easily backfire. A negotiator who backs away from a final position without a legitimate reason will lose credibility. Why should the other attorney believe that negotiator the next time the negotiator says: "This is it, and this time I mean it"?

9.10.2 How Can a Negotiation Be Reconvened After a "Final Offer"?

There are some effective ways to renew discussions after one or both sides have asserted a final position that is unacceptable to the other side. One or both parties may attempt to:

- Interpret the statement in a way that makes the offer or demand firm but not final.

- Provide the negotiator with an opportunity to restate the position to soften its finality.

- Suggest a new perspective that may cause the other side to reconsider its position.

- Explain that the best interests of both parties will be served by continuing negotiations.

- Directly suggest that the negotiator reconsider the position.

- Recommend that additional authority be obtained from a client.

- Employ some tactic, like splitting the difference, if the existing gap is not large.

- Indicate that it is the other side's turn to make a concession.

- Suggest that negotiations be continued at a later date after both sides reassess their positions.

9.10.3   Has the Accord Been Reduced to Writing?

There are typically two formats for agreements memorializing the accord or settlement. The first is a concise, summary document and the other is a formal executed document or set of documents. The former needs to be done at the end of the successful negotiation; the latter will take some time to draft and execute.

Before or immediately after an agreement is reached, it is a very wise practice to prepare a concise memorandum of agreement or email or letter of understanding which informally summarizes the major negotiated terms. The purpose of these informal documents is to confirm what has been agreed upon and to provide an outline for drafting a formal agreement. At the conclusion of multiple negotiation sessions, a written summary or outline of what was agreed upon and what remains to be negotiated can be drafted.

The most effective way to conclude a negotiation is to reduce the agreement to writing formally and have it signed by the parties or the attorneys. Negotiations that create contractual relationships or that resolve litigation will typically result in a formal written agreement. Some negotiators will rely on each other's oral promise or statement regarding an agreement, but the much-preferred practice is to document final agreements in writing or to incorporate a settlement agreement in the record of the case.

Even with a summary signed agreement, negotiations will likely occur during the drafting of the final terms. There will be some issues that were unanticipated or that require additional discussions before the final, final agreement is reached. These negotiations can occasionally result in a failed negotiation because the issues cannot be easily resolved. But typically, the parties who have reached an agreement in principle on the major terms can work out whatever remaining differences exist.

There are several disadvantages in drafting negotiation agreements or settlements. Drafting will take time and cost clients money. It might be better strategically to have the other side draft tentative provisions and edit such terms. Courts usually interpret ambiguous terms of a contract against the interests of the drafter. These and other reasons may prompt a negotiator to have the other negotiator draft an accord.

On the other hand, there can be advantages in drafting the document. The words of the agreement may be susceptible of various interpretations and the drafter can employ appropriate language favoring a client's interests. There may also be an advantage in drafting a negotiation agreement when a matter arises during the drafting that the negotiators did not fully discuss. It might be best to resolve this unresolved issue as neutral or fairly as possible or to contact the other negotiator if the matter is important.

Think Twice

Put it in writing is obviously sound advice, but does it always have to be done, especially at the end of a long and tiring negotiation session? Yes, always. You want the parties to the agreement to immediately sign or initial a

memorandum summarizing the major terms of the settle-
ment. The risk is too high that one or both of them may
change their mind about something on the way home or
back to the office. Or, they may wake up at night with
remorse. Getting them to agree in writing avoids much of
this problem. Then sufficient time can be taken to negoti-
ate the specific language and terms and complete drafting
the final, final documents.

9.10.4   How Should the Attorney Draft the Accord?

The drafting of an accord may occur at various times in
negotiations. Detailed provisions for releases and stipulations in
litigation negotiations will probably be drafted after a settlement
has been finalized in oral terms. Terms and conditions of contract or lease negotiations may be drafted during the course of
negotiations. The steps in memorializing a complete, final agreement include the following steps:

- Keeping a careful and accurate record of terms agreed on
  during the negotiation

- Preparing an outline of the document

- Drafting all the terms of the accord

- Revising the initial draft

- Completing the final agreement

9.10.5   What Type of Settlement Document Should Be Used?

The contents of a negotiation agreement depend upon the
nature of the negotiation. Transaction agreements range from
simple contracts to far more complicated, lengthy documents.
Litigation settlement documents include a stipulated dismissal, a
release, or a covenant not to sue, often in some combination
form. The attorney should check the local statutes and law of the
applicable jurisdiction for specific requirements and effects of
different types of settlement. The following paragraphs explain
common litigation documents:

Stipulations. Stipulations to dismiss a case may be created
which dispose of a case with or without prejudice. A stipulation
of dismissal *without prejudice* leaves the claims and defenses

intact and permits the parties to litigate these issues in the future. A stipulation of dismissal *with prejudice* operates as a final disposition of the issues. These latter stipulations are much more common than stipulations without prejudice because their finality will meet the interests of both parties who seek to resolve a dispute once and for all. A *stipulation* is a document bearing the caption of the case with a statement similar to the following:

> The parties, through their undersigned attorneys, agree to dismiss this action with prejudice.

Releases. A *release* is the relinquishment of a claim or right to the person against whom the claim exists or against whom the right is to be enforced. It is a discharge of the claim by the voluntary agreement of the parties as opposed to by operation of law. A mutual release has the effect of both sides surrendering all claims and defenses in a compromise settlement. The provisions of a release may include statements such as:

> Plaintiff has made certain claims against Defendant, and Defendant has asserted certain defenses and counterclaims against Plaintiff, which claims, defenses, and counterclaims are in issue in a lawsuit (caption).

> Although both parties wish to pursue their claims and defenses and both deny liability, they also wish to settle their differences (reasons may be stated, e.g., in the interests of justice, to resolve a dispute, for financial reasons).

> In consideration of a dismissal of this lawsuit, mutual promises, monetary consideration, and for (additional terms), the plaintiff and the defendant release each other, their successors and assigns, from all actions, causes of action, claims, defenses, counterclaims, and judgments which the plaintiff and defendant or their heirs, executors, administrators, or assigns, ever had or now have.

Covenants Not to Sue. A *covenant not to sue* is an agreement by one who has a right of action not to sue to enforce that right. A covenant not to sue may be included as part of a release. It differs from a release in that it is not necessarily a present abandonment of a claim or right, but is instead an agreement not to sue on the existing claim, which does not extinguish the cause of action. The action is relinquished between the parties to the covenant, but is still viable as to third parties.

Other Settlement Forms. Other types of settlement devices may be available depending upon the settlement terms and the number of defendants in an action. A *confession by judgment* will be appropriate in cases in which a party is making periodic payments to the other party in satisfaction of a compromise. The default by a party of a payment will permit the other party to unilaterally seek a judgment for the unpaid balance or more, after providing the defaulting party with notice.

Another type of settlement device used when there are multiple defendants is a partial release that releases one, while retaining the right to continue litigation against the remaining defendants. In some jurisdictions this is called a *Pierringer release*. This is a release of a portion of the cause of action equal to the part attributable to the settling defendant's liability, with the case continuing against the remaining defendants and the released defendant absent from the trial.

Think Twice

Sample forms and examples of settlement documents are available from previous case or transaction files, on line from a website, or in print from a formbook. Care should be taken to tailor the documents to the specific case. It's quite all right and good practice to rely on previously used documents as long as they are legally enforceable. But take care to modify those forms as necessary. Your contract and civil procedure casebooks have examples of what happens when lawyers draft poorly worded or unenforceable agreements. You don't want your work someday to be in those books.

9.10.6 Did I Succeed?

It can be difficult to determine whether a negotiation result was a "success." This is because success means different things to different parties. Clients will have different goals and expectations, accounting for different perceptions of success.

The following criteria represent some benchmarks to determine whether a negotiation was a reasonable success.

- Did the accord meet the needs and satisfy the interests of the client at the time of the final proposal?

- Did each party achieve most of their objectives?

- Did both sides gain as a result of the negotiation?

- Did the parties through their attorneys sufficiently participate in the negotiation process?

- Did the negotiators consider alternative options to reach an accord and attempt to come up with a creative, innovative result?

- How does the final accord compare to the alternative outcomes had the negotiation failed?

- Did the parties learn something from the negotiation discussions?

- Is the accord reasonably enforceable?

Think Twice

There is an adage that after a successful negotiation the parties feel that they have both won. But the opposite reaction may also occur: both sides may feel that they have lost something. In a transaction, the buyer may feel she paid too much and the seller may believe they accepted too little. Similarly, in a dispute settlement, both parties may be somewhat dissatisfied with the results. These are common feelings, and often not only understandable, but appropriate. Because both sides started with higher expectations, the final agreement may be disappointing. The lawyer is often called on to explain to the client how the client benefits from an appropriate accord or settlement.

D. THE STAGES OF THE NEGOTIATION PROCESS

9.11 AN OVERVIEW

The negotiation process can take many forms. This is an overview of some of the common stages that occur in many negotiations. While all these stages will not occur in every negotiation, it is helpful to have an overview of them:

1. *Analyzing the Situation.* The attorney in consultation with the client analyzes the situation and determines the propriety of negotiating.

2. *Preparing for the Negotiation.* Specifics regarding alternative approaches need to be considered to create a plan for negotiations.

3. *Making Initial Contacts.* Initial contacts establish the beginning tone of the negotiation and resolve procedural matters.

4. *Establishing a Relationship.* The negotiators may spend some time becoming acquainted or renewing their relationship.

5. *Obtaining an Overview, Setting an Agenda.* The negotiators may discuss the background of the situation to obtain an overview. A formal, set agenda may be appropriate in some situations while an informal, unwritten agenda may be more suitable for other negotiations.

6. *Disclosing Information.* The negotiators disclose information to provide each other with facts, opinions, and inferences necessary to assess interests.

7. *Assessing Interests.* Disclosures concerning what the parties want and need help determine mutual and conflicting interests.

8. *Refining Issues.* After initial disclosures, the negotiators may modify the agenda and refine the issues to be negotiated.

9. *Establishing Positions.* Negotiators may communicate general or specific positions supported by reasons explaining these positions.

10. *Debating Positions.* The negotiators may engage in debate and argument in order to attack the legitimacy of the other's position or defend the client's position.

11. *Searching for Objective Criteria.* Positions based on objective factors rather than subjective impressions more often provide viable support for solutions.

12. *Exchanging Concessions.* The negotiators may make demands, offers, counteroffers, and concessions as part of the bargain and compromise pattern.

13. *Considering Alternative and Creative Solutions.* Either negotiator may suggest and consider alternative and creative solutions.

14. *Reaching Agreement.* The conclusion of a negotiation may, or may not, result in an accord.

15. *Drafting the Accord.* If a negotiation does result in an accord, the terms and provisions of the negotiated result may need to be composed and memorialized.

16. *Implementing the Accord.* The agreement or settlement may require things to be done.

17. *Celebrate.* If an agreement is reached, go out and celebrate. If an agreement is not reached, you may want to consider the services of a mediator. And then you will have another reason to read Chapter 10.

Think Twice

Of all lawyering tasks, negotiation seems to trigger the most deeply visceral, emotional responses from lawyers. New lawyers often are surprised by how emotionally raw a contentious negotiation may be. In the face of sometimes deliberate provocations from opposing counsel, it can be difficult to keep your temper. While passion has its place in our work with clients, the best negotiators we have known have tended to be fairly thick-skinned and surprisingly adept at maintaining their composure in heated situations. Not all negotiations will involve these experiences, but you should not be surprised when they occur. When all is said and done, the lawyers commonly shake hands and understand that this is all part of the business of the lawyering profession.

Chapter Ten
MEDIATION: HELP!

We need others. There is no doubt that without each other we would cease to grow, fail to develop, choose madness even death.

—*Leo Buscaglia*

Love

A. INTRODUCTION

10.1 HELP!

You have been unable to close the deal or resolve the dispute by negotiating with the other side. You know from reading Chapter Six that help is available. You and the other side can agree to mediation and have a mediator facilitate the reaching of an agreement. In some cases you may have no choice. A pre-dispute mediation clause in an agreement may require that the parties attempt to mediate a settlement before initiating an action. In many jurisdictions, the applicable rules mandate that parties mediate before trying the case.

This Chapter focuses on the mediation of legal disputes between or among disputing parties by professional mediators. There are other types of mediations used in our society and worldwide beyond the ken of this text. Community problems may be resolved by lay person mediators. Religious organizations may make available mediators to resolve differences among disputants.

10.2 PARTICIPANTS IN THE MEDIATION PROCESS

Participants in mediation include the parties, their attorneys or representatives, the mediator, and a mediation organization.

Parties. Parties need to be directly and actively involved in the mediation because they must mutually agree to any resolution. The more receptive parties are to the belief that mediation will work for them, and the more effort they are willing to invest in the process, the more successful they will be. One of the great benefits of mediation is having the parties directly involved in crafting a settlement that can best meet their needs and interests and result in an agreement that could not be achieved through litigation or arbitration.

An individual who is a party obviously has the authority to agree to a settlement. Representatives of a party must also have settlement authority. An agent or employee of a corporation or organization must obtain the authority to reach an agreement. Insurance companies that insure a party often send, or are required to send, an agent to the mediation. This agent must also have full settlement authority.

Attorneys or Representatives. The parties usually are entitled to have a lawyer or representative participate in the mediation process. A lawyer may provide helpful legal advice and counseling to the parties. Another representative may provide information or support to the parties.

The primary role of lawyers in mediations is to help the client through the process and increase the chances of a favorable settlement. Lawyers can discuss with their clients the legal issues involved and the legal ramifications of a settlement, provide the parties with alternative strategies, suggest to the mediator approaches which may help in resolving the dispute, and explain the expenses and procedures involved in arbitration and litigation, should mediation fail. The lawyer can also assist in drafting a settlement agreement.

Mediator. Mediators are selected by the parties, or appointed by an independent mediation organization, or selected by the court. These professionals need to be independent and have no real or apparent conflict of interest. Mediators also need to be experts regarding the disputed issues. The most effective mediators are usually professionals who have substantial practice experience or who understand the needs, interests, feelings, thoughts, emotions, and hopes of the parties. Mediators serve various roles during the mediation. An effective mediator should be able to do all the things explained in Section 10.6.

Mediation Organization. The mediation service is the organization used by the parties to administer the mediation. This service may appoint the mediator, assist the parties in preparing for the mediation, answer their questions, schedule the mediation, and handle any administrative matters not handled by the mediator. Parties may choose a mediator not affiliated with an organization.

Think Twice

Mediation is becoming a popular method to resolve disputes and a growing area of practice. Law students may think about becoming a mediator early in their career. As a practical matter, lawyers and clients favor mediators who have substantial practice experience and are unlikely to retain the services of a novice lawyer. When students ask how they can become a mediator, the above paragraph describing mediators explains how: become a wise person.

As a law student, you can gain valuable experience and accelerate that process by volunteering your time in a community mediation program. As a lawyer, you can work in a court sponsored mediation program. Mediation training can also be helpful, but there is no substitute for gaining practical experience in lots of negotiation and mediation situations.

B. WHY MEDIATE, OR WHY NOT

10.3 REASONS TO MEDIATE

Whether or not a case can or should be mediated depends on multiple factors. The following list details these considerations.

Party preferences. One or both parties realize they need help and may prefer or be eager to engage in mediation and should do so.

Time considerations. Mediation may be able to create an agreement or resolve a problem faster than other methods.

Cost considerations. A mediated agreement may make or save the parties money. The substantial costs of litigation and attorney's fees can be avoided in the mediation process.

The effect of no agreement. Parties may lose an opportunity to create a relationship or produce a profit if no agreement is reached, and mediation allows them to get together and achieve mutual gains.

Relief sought. A judicial or administrative decision may not provide the relief a party wants, and mediated settlement may be the only way parties can have their needs met.

Problems initiating or sustaining negotiation discussions. Neither party may want to suggest negotiation talks or negotiation efforts may have failed, and mediation may overcome the difficulties parties have negotiating on their own.

Substantially different perspectives. There may be substantial gaps between the positions asserted by the opposing sides, and the skills of a mediator are necessary to reduce these differences of perceptions.

The relationship between the parties. Opposing parties may have, or hope to have, a continuing relationship after the dispute is resolved, and mediation offers the parties an opportunity to maintain or create a relationship.

Complex problems or issues. Some matters may be very difficult, time-consuming, and expensive to litigate or otherwise resolve, and mediation provides a much more efficient and economical way to resolve problems.

The need for confidentiality. The process and results of mediation are more private and much less public than other forums, and parties who want matters to remain confidential may prefer to mediate.

The effect of obtaining a judgment. It may be best for a party to avoid the adverse effect of a judgment in a case, and mediation can avoid the permanent effect of a judgment and its precedential value for future cases.

10.4   REASONS NOT TO MEDIATE

The existence of these factors may suggest that mediation may not be especially productive.

Substantial party resistance. Mediation requires the cooperation of a party to engage in serious and good faith discussions. A party may be so opposed to mediation that it would
be useless to mediate. In a multi-party case involving significant persons not interested or available, mediation efforts
may be unsuccessful because those who are affected are not
involved. However, an effective mediator can successfully
involve stubborn parties in productive discussions.

Non-negotiable positions. If a party takes an intractable
position regarding a critical mediation issue and states that
nothing will change that position, mediation may not be
successful. But, simply stating an unyielding position does
not necessarily reflect an inflexible position. A party may
only be "posturing" and may change a position when faced
with "reality."

Sabotage. Usually, parties want a mediation to succeed.
Occasionally, a party may, however, approach mediation
with no intent or hope the mediation will succeed. This
party may attempt to sabotage the mediation process, and it
may be very difficult to attempt to mediate with a party who
operates in bad faith or is wedded to an unyielding position

Financially destitute party. Mediations involving the payment of money or distribution of assets between parties may
be unsuccessful if a party does not have the ability to make
the necessary payments or distribution. A mediation without
the potential for an agreeable result may only waste time
and energy. A settlement can include installment payments
over time to ameliorate the financial burden of a party.

Unavailable information. Mediation scheduled before investigation or discovery is completed may need to be postponed
and rescheduled if one or both parties need to obtain or
exchange information to be able to evaluate all the issues in
the case. Often, early mediation assists in resolving discovery disputes and helps the parties exchange needed information.

Think Twice

**Mediation can be a very effective way of making a lawyer
look both good and successful. If negotiations will not**

*produce the long sought after deal or the hoped for settle-
ment seems very unlikely, the lawyer can suggest to the
client and the other side a way out through the services of
a mediator. Some lawyers resist suggesting mediation because they are concerned that their clients will perceive
the notion of mediation as an admission of failure, but
proposing mediation isn't shameful.*

*Mediation presents an excellent opportunity for a deal or
resolution. As the same time, a lawyer suggesting mediation should take care not to create unrealistic client expectations. For mediation to be successful, both sides will
still have to compromise on issues in a way they have not
been able to during their own negotiations.*

C. HOW TO MEDIATE

10.5 PREPARING FOR THE MEDIATION

A mediation is an opportunity to negotiate a compromise
and so a lawyer should prepare for a mediation as if it were a
negotiation. And, because the mediation is different than parties
negotiating on their own, a lawyer also has to prepare for the
involvement of the mediator.

Planning for mediation includes:

- Objectively evaluating the case.

- Assessing what information is needed.

- Determining what negotiated results a party wants and
  needs.

- Establishing realistic mediation goals.

- Assessing the availability of insurance or other resources.

- Rehearsing being apparently nice, but not overly generous.

Objective evaluation of a case. The nature and extent of
an evaluation depends upon the circumstances of the matter
to be mediated. Each situation should be reviewed from the
perspective of the other side to obtain a balanced understanding of the strengths and weaknesses of the situation or
problem. It may be difficult to make an assessment impar-

tially, but it is essential so that the assessment of potential solutions is not overly subjective.

Exchange of information. Parties must determine whether they have sufficient information to proceed to mediation. Parties who do not believe they know enough about the facts or the law may be disinclined to agree to a resolution. The parties, prior to and during a mediation, may agree to exchange information and materials. If the parties are unable to reach a mutual agreement, the parties may present their disagreement to the mediator who may be able to assist them in assessing what information they need before proceeding to mediate the merits.

Determination of needs and interests. Parties must also determine what their interests are and what they want or need through a negotiated agreement. This determination includes an assessment of what a party will minimally accept (the bottom line), initial negotiation positions (the first offer or demand), intervening positions, and common goals and interests of the parties.

Establishing realistic expectations. The determination of what a party wants must be placed in proper perspective. Parties need to approach the mediation with realistic goals. Mediated settlements typically require the parties to compromise and accept less or give more than they prefer. A party approaching mediation should be prepared to engage in a give-and-take process.

Available Insurance. The existence of insurance in mediation may dramatically influence the outcome. A party who is insured for a claim or controversy has the resources of the insurance company available. The amount of insurance may substantially affect the mediated result. It is critical for the parties and the mediator to know whether insurance exists, the amount of coverage, and the limits of the policy. Other sources of money or remedies may also be available, and their availability needs to be considered.

Think Twice

It's critical for the lawyers, parties, and mediators to have the same goals. There are different "schools" of media-

tors. A "facilitative" mediator may assist the parties to reach their own accord. An "evaluative" mediator may offer views to the parties on what might be a reasonable settlement. A "transformative" mediator may hope to achieve goals beyond what the parties consider. The lawyers need to make sure the most effective mediator is selected who can do what the parties need to be done in reaching a deal or a resolution.

10.5.1 Assessing Factors

Lawyers preparing for mediation should consider how the mediation will proceed and what influence they want on the process. These predictions are essential to the parties obtaining a favorable settlement. Factors a party should consider include:

Questions

- What questions do I want to ask the other side?
- What questions do I want the mediator to ask the other side?

Disclosure

- What do I want to disclose to the mediator? To the other side?
- What do I want to make sure **not** to disclose to the mediator? To the other side?

ESI, Documents, and Materials

- What relevant documents, electronically stored information, or other materials exist?
- What materials do I want to provide the mediator? To the other side?
- What materials do I want to see from the other side?

Strengths and Weaknesses

- What are the strengths and weaknesses of my position?
- What are the strengths and weaknesses of the other side's position?

Time

- How much time do I want to spend in mediation?

- How do I want to spend that time in mediation?

Participants

- Whom do I want to speak? Me? The client? Another representative?

- What authority should be given to an agent or employee who will participate in the mediation on behalf of the client?

Approaches

- What strategies, tactics, and techniques will I use during mediation?

- What approaches will I suggest the mediator use during mediation?

Alternatives

- What would cause the mediation to deadlock or cause me to walk out of the mediation?

- If the mediation fails, what other dispute resolution methods are available for me to obtain what I want?

- How much will it cost me to pursue what I want through another dispute resolution method if mediation fails?

- What are my other options to get what I want?

- How can I convince the mediator my client truly deserves what we are asking for and the other side does not?

Think Twice

It would be wrong to think that little planning is needed for a mediation, however tempting that thought might be. The notion that lawyers will just react to what happens is naïve and fraught with danger. If one side prepares a mediation plan and the other side does not, who is more likely to get a better deal or resolution? And it's naïve to think that a party has less control in a mediation and so need not anticipate what will happen or what their positions should be. No agreement can be reached without that party saying yes, and that's a lot of control.

10.5.2 Preparation by Mediator

The mediator needs to become familiar with the situation or dispute before the mediation begins. Many mediators ask the parties to submit something confidential in writing. A party should comply with this request and may want to submit additional information. If a party has not been asked to make any written submissions the party should consider whether it is advantageous to submit some information and determine whether the mediator will accept or read what is voluntarily submitted. Some mediators may also do research on their own. A party should determine ahead of time what a mediator knows and how the mediator is prepared for the mediation.

Successful mediators will want to meet and/or talk with the parties and their lawyers before the mediation. They may meet with each side privately as part of their preparation. They prefer to use this time to gather information and form a judgment about how best to proceed. They understand that parties may be reluctant to put certain facts or positions in print, and they will obtain more accurate and useful information through a conversation. They may well decide not to have the parties prepare any special materials for the mediation, but limit their disclosures to materials that have already been exchanged between the parties.

Think Twice

Mediations may initially fail because they began too early, or too late, or because the parties weren't properly prepared or the mediator misunderstood their goals. The lawyers need to make sure the mediator is fully and properly prepared by providing the mediator with the information needed to make a full assessment of the case. Is this the right time? Do the parties have enough information? How should the mediation proceed? If the mediator does not consider these issues, the lawyers may be wise to raise them with the mediator.

10.6 THE MEDIATION SESSION

A mediation may begin with a joint session with all parties and their attorneys or representatives present in the same room, or a mediation may begin with the parties in separate places.

There may be no constructive reason to begin with a joint session, or it may be helpful to begin discussing common issues with everyone in the same place. Some parties may not want to be in the same room with the other party, and the mediator may initially prefer to separate the parties at the beginning, bringing them together later in the process.

Most mediators begin the mediation with an explanation of the mediation process. Typically, mediators:

- Introduce themselves.

- Commend the participants for attending.

- Describe their experience as a mediator.

- Explain their role and their neutrality and impartiality.

- Describe the mediation procedure, including caucuses.

- Explain the bounds of confidentiality.

- Describe the conference room and logistics.

- Suggest some behavioral guidelines.

- Answer questions from the parties and attorneys.

- Explain the issues the mediator believes need to be addressed.

- Ask the parties and attorneys whether additional issues need to be resolved.

- Establish a cooperative atmosphere and seek a commitment from both sides to proceed.

- Ask whether anything else needs to be discussed.

Think Twice

The lawyers will know the parties and the issues much better than the mediator, at least in the beginning. Some mediations bog down because the opening session began badly. It's critical that a lawyer or party express their view to the mediator if the mediator plans to begin in a way that may exacerbate problems rather than diffuse differences.

10.6.1   Disclosing Mediation Information

Mediators typically permit the parties during the mediation an opportunity to tell the mediator whatever it is the parties want to disclose. The parties should consider disclosing the following information:

A favorable first impression. The parties should convey an impression to the mediator that the party is prepared and open to the possibility or probability of a mediated agreement.

Theory of the deal or case. A party should concisely explain to the mediator what the party wants and why.

Issues and nature of the situation. A mediator needs to know the issues and precise nature of the situation that exists between the parties.

A summary of the important facts. The parties should make sure the mediator knows all relevant and reliable facts.

Applicable law. The mediator may or may not need to know a party's view of the law supporting the party's positions. The party should be prepared to explain the law if it will be useful or requested.

Common interests between the parties. A primary goal of the mediator will be to focus the mediation on common interests that may bridge the gap between the parties. Parties can assist in this process by suggesting mutually held perspectives on these issues.

Documents. Significant exhibits or documents that contain critical information ought to be shown to or provided to the mediator. Visual aids or presentations may be prepared which assist the mediator in understanding differences and similarities.

Status of the dispute proceeding. If a lawsuit or arbitration is being mediated, the mediator needs to know the procedural aspects of the case, including the status of pleadings, discovery, and motions.

Previous negotiation efforts and discussions. The mediator may want to know what negotiation talks have transpired, or why there have been no efforts to negotiate.

Goals. Some mediators may ask what a party hopes to accomplish during the mediation. The party should consider what mediated result will satisfy the party's needs, and what should be disclosed to the mediator.

An effective, but non-committal, answer is to say: "We're open to whatever happens. We are here in an effort to reach an agreement that meets our needs."

Results. The mediator may ask at some point during the mediation what a party hopes to achieve.

Think Twice

Mediators will have preferences on what they want to do, based on their approach and experiences. Lawyers and parties, likewise, may have their own preferences. If a mediator is not doing something you think the mediator should do, say so in a respectful way. Good mediators appreciate suggestions about strategies, tactics, and techniques and may be willing to follow your suggestions.

10.6.2   Communicating With the Other Side

A mediation session provides the parties with an opportunity to communicate with each other. A party may do so during mediation by directing statements to the other side, or may do so indirectly by asking the mediator to convey information. A party, when meeting with the mediator separately, can request that the mediator communicate information to the other side. A party may also suggest the mediator be present in the room when a party conveys information to the other side. This approach may be especially effective if the other side has refused to listen.

Equally important is to consider what parties do not want to communicate to the other side. It usually is ineffective in the presence of the other side to make negative or derogatory comments about the other party (however tempting), or to inflame inappropriate hostile emotions that exist between the parties (however cathartic). It may be very useful to explain to the mediator, in a reasonable way, the existence of hard feelings and what underlies the feelings because the mediator may need to know about these adverse attitudes.

In deal mediations, it is more likely the parties have a mutual interest in crafting an agreement. In dispute mediations, one or both of the parties may have feelings of resentment and a revengeful attitude. These may need to be privately aired at some point, preferably in the presence and with the prodding of the mediator. How open and transparent an approach to deal making and dispute resolution should be depends upon what is most reasonable.

Think Twice

However knowledgeable the mediation participants believe they are, it usually helps if they obtain additional relevant information, especially about events they don't know about or have incomplete data about. However rational participants perceive they are in a deal or dispute, it's very likely they are influenced by various emotions. Accurate and complete facts may make them more reasonable. Mediation sessions, particularly private sessions, are an excellent opportunity to provide this information and discuss these issues.

D. MEDIATION APPROACHES

10.7 MEDIATION TACTICS AND TECHNIQUES

Mediators may use a variety of effective tactics and techniques during mediation.

10.7.1 Assess the Case

Determine the needs, interests, and values of each party. A mediator must learn the actual needs and real interests of the parties and their values. The negotiation process may cause the parties to exaggerate their needs and hide their real interests from the other side. The mediator needs to probe to determine what they want and why they want it.

Identify issues. It is critical for the mediator to make a list of all the issues that need to be resolved and to have the participants agree the list is complete. The parties are unlikely to agree unless all issues, from their perspective, have been resolved.

Probe positions. Parties will take various positions during mediation. The mediator must determine how firm or soft a party is regarding a position. Certain positions may be non-negotiable, while other positions may be very malleable.

10.7.2 Communicate With the Parties

Establish an agenda. The mediator can set an agenda for the mediation or assist the parties in establishing the issues that need to be discussed and resolved.

Caucus with the parties. Caucuses are common in most mediations. Caucuses occur when a mediator meets and talks separately with a party, outside the presence of the other party. In this private setting, a party may be more forthcoming and more open and honest about real needs and interests.

Engage in "shuttle diplomacy". During mediations when the parties are in separate rooms or locations, the mediator may go back and forth between the parties. The mediator may obtain a demand from one party and visit the other party to explain the demand and then return to the first party with a counteroffer. This process works effectively where the parties need to or prefer to exchange concessions while reaching a compromise settlement.

Exchange information. The mediator may assist the parties in understanding what information is necessary to clarify inaccuracies or misimpressions. The parties may disclose to the mediator certain information that the mediator, with the permission of the parties, can communicate to the other side.

Maintain civility. The mediator can establish a productive environment for settlement by maintaining civility and order between the parties during discussions.

Encourage communication. The mediator can allow an opportunity for the parties to speak to each other or to speak privately to the mediator, encouraging full communication.

Explore feelings, hopes, and dreams. Psychological and emotional attitudes can significantly influence a party, and a mediator needs to understand, defuse, and discuss these attitudes.

Retain confidential information. Parties may and frequently should privately disclose to he mediator confidential information, which the mediator will keep confidential and only reveal to the other side if the disclosing party allows the mediator to do so.

10.7.3   Propose Alternative Resolutions

Provide a different perspective. The mediator can provide the parties with a neutral and independent perspective regarding the strengths and weaknesses of their positions, the value of their interests, and the reality of their obtaining what they want.

Suggest strategic and tactical approaches. Mediators may suggest to the parties the use of a strategy or tactic to improve the chances of settling the case. Mediators need to be cautious so that they do not appear to be taking sides by suggesting to a party what to say or do.

Explore options. One of the chief roles of mediators is to discuss with the parties various options they may or may not have considered. Mediators can brainstorm with the parties separately or together in an effort to discover and evaluate alternative solutions based on mutual needs and common interests.

Have the parties draft proposed terms. A very effective way to engage the parties and their lawyers during the mediation is to have them draft proposed settlement terms. This will help them focus on the issues that need to be addressed and will lead to a written settlement or deal document. Further, this process causes them to be more invested in the mediation increasing the chances of an accord.

Propose an innovative remedy. Mediators may suggest specific resolutions the parties have not considered or may even have previously rejected. Mediators can explain the advantages, as well as disadvantages, of the proposed solutions.

Offer opinions regarding the issues. Mediators, on their own initiative or at the suggestion of a party, may offer their opinions about a fact, legal position or issue in mediation. Mediators must be cautious when doing this, as their opinion may be perceived as favoring one party and damaging their neutrality.

Take a position. In some mediations, it may be appropriate or necessary for the mediator to assert a position. This does not mean that a mediator sides with one party as opposed to the other, but rather, that the mediator takes a reasonable position supported by the facts, circumstances, and law. It is important for the mediator to support the expressed position with a reasonable explanation and to avoid asserting a personal preference.

Suggest a non-binding solution. The parties may request, or the mediator may recommend, that the mediator make a non-binding decision regarding an issue, based upon the presentations of the parties. This resolution may effect the position and judgment of the parties and may help break an impasse.

Urge resolution. Mediators can urge the parties to reach an agreement by explaining to them the consequences of a failed mediation. The parties may not have fully considered the disadvantages of not reaching an accord, and the mediator can point out why a compromise resolution is in their best interests.

Seek joint gains. The mediator can seek joint gains for the parties by encouraging the parties to be creative in fashioning a result and by proposing creative ways to resolve an impasse.

Partially resolve a matter. A mediation may not resolve all the issues, but may still be a success. If the parties do not reach a complete agreement, they may be able to reach a partial accord on some issues, or narrow the issues for subsequent determination by an arbitrator or judge.

Think Twice

What makes one mediator better than another? It's a combination of things: the exercise of good judgment, persistence, the introduction of proposed terms at the right time, fortitude, understanding what really influences a party, more persistence, understanding what motivates the lawyers, greater fortitude, being able to predict what will work and not work, and telling the parties and lawyers something that will amaze or startle them.

You get the point about persistence and continuing the mediation even after all hope seems lost. But what about this understanding bit? It helps if the mediator can think and feel what the parties and lawyers think and feel. One way to gain that ability is to have represented clients in similar situations before. Sometimes there is no substitute for experience.

And how can the mediator amaze or startle the participants? By seemingly reading their minds and reflecting their emotions: A plaintiff may be surprised to hear the mediator suggest that the plaintiff has already "spent" the settlement money and is dreaming about taking an expensive vacation or buying a new car. And it may come something as a shock to the business executive for the mediator to challenge a take-it-or-leave-it deal breaker term as the product of ill will that executive feels towards the other side because of prior bad personal experiences. Mediators make these kinds of suggestions to acknowledge those feelings, to inject a dose of human reality into the process, and to help parties move through those emotions and reach an accord.

10.7.4   Continue or Conclude the Mediation

Schedule another session. The mediator can schedule another mediation session if appropriate or desired by the parties. If sufficient time was not allocated during an initial mediation session, a second session can be scheduled. Many deals and disputes are not going to be completed or resolved in one meeting. The parties need time and separation to reach a final accord. It's not unusual for mediations to be scheduled periodically over a week or months.

Memorialize the agreement. A written summary of the complete agreement should be recorded, and the mediator *must* make sure this occurs. Before the mediation ends, some form of signed agreement, however concise, needs to be created to reduce the chance parties will change their minds during their celebration or will have others second guess them. However anxious the parties may be to leave, particularly at the end of a lengthy and exhausting mediation, the mediator needs to insist on getting the significant terms in writing and signed by the participants.

Declare an impasse. The mediator can declare an impasse if continuing mediation discussions would be fruitless. A party can also request that an impasse be declared. The mediator can suggest the parties meet again to consider some specific issues or how they should resolve their dispute by using another method, such as arbitration.

Think Twice

No need to emphasize again that a mediator needs patience and perseverance, is there? As simple as it sounds, continuing the process even after both sides refuse to negotiate any more has resulted in many a deal and resolution. Admittedly, it's sounds and smells like being overly stubborn, but that may be an admirable trait. And it's not like the mediator is doing this to stay longer and make more money. The good ones who are willing to pursue the deal or resolution are good enough to have other mediations or other fun things to do.

10.7.5 Employ Advanced Mediation Approaches

Mediators have other techniques available. During a mediation, a deadlock or an impasse may appear imminent or actually occur. Attitudes vary among mediation professionals regarding the role of the mediator at this point in the process. It may or may not be appropriate for the mediator to become more actively involved. Some possible techniques with an explanation of philosophy follow.

Suffer/suffer. Sometimes effective mediation tactics will result in an accord satisfying everyone and creating a "win-

win" result. Many mediations, however, result in a resolution only after everyone has lost something important. Often, parties are unwilling to reach an accord unless they perceive the other side suffers as much as they do. A mediator can use this "suffer/suffer" approach, and explain to the parties that each has suffered more than their fair share.

Reality therapy. A party may not understand or perceive the advantages of a proposed agreement. The mediator can meet privately with the party and provide some "reality therapy." A party who hears this message from the mediator may reassess the situation.

Emotionally charged atmosphere. In some mediations, the parties strongly dislike each other because of prior unpleasant experiences. These hostile emotions need to be acknowledged and usually dissipated before an agreement can be reached. The mediator can caucus with both sides individually and allow each side to vent their emotions in the presence of the mediator.

The Mediator's deal or offer. Mediation may result in both sides becoming entrenched in a position and unwilling to make another offer or demand unless the other side first makes a move. At this juncture, the mediator can attempt to bridge the gap and propose settlement terms and tell both sides that if either side rejects the mediator's proposal, an impasse will be declared, but that if both sides accept, there is a final settlement.

Simultaneous exchange of a response. Parties in some mediations respond to a proposal by a mediator only after the other side responds. If both parties take this attitude, the mediation will deadlock. One way of avoiding this problem is to have the parties simultaneously and privately submit to the mediator a written or oral response to the proposal made by the mediator. In this way, neither side gains any advantage by having the other side disclose their position.

Cooling off period. Some cases require a number of mediation sessions before an agreement is reached. Instead of declaring an impasse after a mediation session, the mediator can suggest that parties have a "cooling off" period to reassess their positions and schedule another mediation session. The mediator can also suggest the parties consider some issue or do something during this time to increase the chances that the subsequent mediation session will achieve an accord.

Think Twice

If your mediator is not anxious to be persistent and persevere and is about to declare an impasse, you can suggest one or more of the above approaches. If nothing else is working, what's the harm in trying? You would be amazed how these tactics have resulted in some important deals getting done and significant cases settling.

10.8   END OF THE MEDIATION

A mediation may terminate in a number of ways:

- The parties reach an agreement.

- One or more parties decide not to participate in the mediation any longer.

- The mediator declares an impasse and the mediation ends.

10.8.1   Settlement or Deal Agreement

Before the mediation ends, some form of signed agreement, however concise, needs to be created before the parties go their separate ways, as previously explained. It's a good strategy during the mediation to have the parties begin drafting the settlement or deal terms. This helps in crafting the terms in a timely and thoughtful way.

An agreement reached by the parties during the mediation is often a binding, enforceable contract. A written agreement, even if handwritten, should be signed or initialed by the parties and attorneys before they leave. Sometimes all that can be crafted is an outline of a deal or a set of terms.

If a party later fails to or refuses to abide by the terms of the agreement, the other party may seek to enforce it. This failure or refusal may lead to a dispute, which can also be attempted to be resolved through mediation. Or, the drafted agreement can contain an arbitration clause shifting any future dispute to that forum.

Think Twice

Repeat after us: I will never leave a mediation that results in a deal or resolution until there is some signed agreement. That's always true, unless, of course, an exceptional circumstance exists. It's too easy for one or both parties to change their minds on the way back to the office or home. One of things you can do during the mediation (there will be a fair amount of down time when the mediator is with the other side), is to draft the terms of an agreement. You may gain the advantage of having favorably phrased terms, and you won't have to repeat the above adage again.

10.8.2 An Ongoing Process

A mediation that does not result in a successful resolution commonly has significant value and often has laid the foundation for a future settlement. The mediation effort may have provided the parties with a better understanding of their own interests and the needs of others and with helpful information about the facts and laws involved in the dispute. This exchange assists the parties in using arbitration or litigation to resolve their problems, or in making it easier for the parties to later reach a settlement on their own or to mediate for a second time with the same or a different mediator.

10.9 THE ROLE OF COUNSEL DURING MEDIATION

Parties have various goals and aspirations for mediation, and lawyers need to keep their plans and approaches flexible to accommodate the needs and interests of their clients and to increase the likelihood of the client succeeding at the conclusion of the mediation. Accordingly, use the following dos and don'ts as guidelines or a summary checklist of what lawyers can or should do during mediation.

Do consider communicating in an open, honest, and respectful way using neutral, non-threatening language . . .

Rather than blaming, judging, and acting in a secretive way.

Do consider encouraging your client to actively participate and supporting and assisting your client in exploring options and alternative solutions . . .

> *Rather than* speaking unnecessarily for your client or interrupting or censuring the client.

Do consider bargaining for the interests and needs of your client to meet short term and overarching goals . . .

> *Rather than* bargaining from set, inflexible positions and being unnecessarily recalcitrant or obstructionist.

Do consider clarifying issues, reviewing options, proposing solution, thinking creatively, and suggesting mutual problem solving. . .

> *Rather than* focusing on winning at all costs or ignoring the needs of the other parties.

Do consider acknowledging and reflecting the emotional and psychological aspects of the disputes . . .

> *Rather than* ignoring or belittling the obvious or underlying feelings of the parties.

Do consider being realistic and explaining to your client the costs of failing to reach an agreement and what the real alternatives are available if mediation fails . . .

> *Rather than* promoting unrealistic expectations or unlikely success in litigation, arbitration, or administrative proceedings.

Do consider what facts, positions, and settlement terms remain private and confidential . . .

> *Rather than* presuming the mediator will know what may be disclosed to other parties or the public.

Do consider participating in all phases of the mediation process and cooperating with the mediator who controls the process . . .

> *Rather than* doing little to achieve a successful result or acting in obstreperous or inappropriate ways.

Do consider all the terms of a final settlement agreement and make sure they are understandable, accurate, complete, and enforceable ...

> *Rather than* accepting a term or drafting language that is unclear or fails to reflect the final agreement.

Do consider whether the compromises that need to be reached satisfy your clients' needs and interests or whether the dispute ought to be resolved differently ...

> *Rather than* settling or compromising because that is what everyone expects ought to happen.

Think Twice

So what can really go wrong right after a mediated agreement? Here's what:

Mediator fees: If left to the very end, a party may presume the other side will pay all. Either the fees should be split or the party paying the most agrees to pay all.

Surprise issues: A party raises an issue that was ignored or forgotten, and the mediation has to reconvene until it's resolved.

Wordsmithing. When reviewing the final written agreement, a party balks at a term or word, and the mediating process resumes.

Refusal to compromise. Sometimes neither party wants to make the last concession; and the mediator needs to propose the final, final resolution.

All these can be prevented by following the advice in this chapter and planning ahead. Forewarned is forearmed. And that's what often makes the difference among differences.

Part Three
DISPUTE RESOLUTION PREPARATION

Chapter Eleven
ASSERTING CLAIMS AND DEFENSES: THE RIGHT WAY

Justice cannot be for one side alone, but must be for both.

—*Eleanor Roosevelt*

A. INTRODUCTION

Sometimes the best thing to do in a dispute is to start a lawsuit, initiate an arbitration proceeding, or file an administrative claim. Sometimes the best potential result for a client is to have the dispute resolved by an impartial judge, jury, arbitrator, or administrative judge. And, sometimes the best thing for parties is to have their dispute resolved by a neutral decision maker without them having to compromise by settlement or mediation.

Planning how best to resolve a dispute begins with an analysis of the issues discussed in Chapter Six. This chapter covers the actual process of bringing an action and responding to a claim. There are five basic parts to this process:

- Ascertaining the Right Jurisdiction
- Selecting the Right Forum for the Right reason
- Complaining the Right Way
- Drafting the Right papers
- Responding with the Right Defenses and Motions

It's critical to know about the right thing, because the wrong thing, may not just be wrong ... it may be fatal to the client's lawsuit.

11.1   ASSERTING THE RIGHT JURISDICTION

There are two essential sources of jurisdiction, which you recall from civil procedure, both of which must be present in a case: personal jurisdiction and subject matter jurisdiction.

11.1.1   Personal Jurisdiction

A forum must have jurisdiction over the defendant or respondent. The forum, as a reminder, has personal jurisdiction if:

- The defendant resides within the jurisdiction.

- The defendant is incorporated, has a place of business, does business within the forum, or is licensed by the forum.

- A defendant has substantial or significant contacts with the jurisdiction.

- The defendant has expressly consented to jurisdiction, e.g., a party agrees to arbitration.

- The defendant has impliedly consented to jurisdiction, e.g., the defendant owns property within the state.

- A long arm statute provides jurisdiction over a non-resident defendant who has sufficient contacts with the state, e.g., someone who commits a tort or executes a contract within the jurisdiction.

- A statute imposes jurisdiction over the defendant, e.g., an employer will be subject to an administrative worker's compensation claim for employees who work in a state.

- A defendant voluntarily appears in the state and is personally served with a lawsuit.

The concept of personal jurisdiction is that no forum has the power or the right to force someone to be a defendant or respondent unless it is fair to do so. A party may be subject to more than one forum; for example, several states may have personal jurisdiction over a party. And so a plaintiff may have a choice of forums where a case could be brought, as long as a forum has subject matter jurisdiction.

11.1.2   Subject Matter Jurisdiction

Subject matter jurisdiction, as you know, is the power of a forum to hear and decide the dispute. Courts derive this authority from constitutional provisions and legislative enactments. Arbitrators derive this authority from the arbitration agreement and the applicable law. Administrative judges draw this power from statutes and regulations.

State courts are courts of general jurisdiction and can hear and decide most disputes. State courts may specialize according to the subject matter of a dispute (e.g., family court, probate court, housing court) or the amount in dispute (e.g., small claims court or conciliation court). A case needs to be brought in the proper division of the state court to obtain jurisdiction.

Federal courts are courts of limited jurisdiction and only entertain certain types of lawsuits, which you may have memorized in civil procedure. Three major types of federal jurisdiction are:

- Federal law jurisdiction, which are specific types of cases required to be brought in federal court, such as patent or bankruptcy cases.

- Federal question cases, which occur when claims arise under the federal constitution, federal treaties, or federal statutes.

- Diversity jurisdiction, which exists when none of the plaintiffs are citizens (generally meaning domiciliaries) of the same state as any of the defendants and the amount of controversy involves more than $75,000.

Jurisdictions may have concurrent subject matter jurisdiction. For example, both a state and federal court (based on diversity jurisdiction) may have subject matter jurisdiction over a contract or tort case. Or, a state court judge may be able to enforce a federal statute. If, however, a dispute is subject to arbitration, because the parties have contractually agreed to arbitrate, state and federal courts may not have jurisdiction until arbitration is complete. Likewise, if an administrative agency has the statutory power to resolve a dispute, a state or federal court will typically not exercise jurisdiction until the administrative decision-making process is complete.

Think Twice

You may have spent a lot of time in your civil procedure course analyzing jurisdiction. And some day that all may be helpful. The reality is that jurisdiction is typically an easy and obvious choice. Auto accident cases are usually litigated where they happen and in state court; contract disputes are commonly litigated where the breach occurred; real estate disputes are litigated at the situs of the property also in state court. While federal court civil dockets may be crowded, the vast majority of cases are filed in state court. And most federal court cases involve uncontested jurisdictional issues. Difficulties will arise when there are multiple potential forums or multiple parties.

B.   SELECTING THE RIGHT FORUM FOR THE RIGHT REASON

11.2   HOW TO SELECT A JURISDICTION

When you have a choice among judicial forums, you need to consider the differences:

Judicial appointment system. Federal judges are appointed for life; state court judges are appointed for a set term and/or periodically elected.

Civil procedure rules. Discovery and motion practice may be more advantageous or disadvantageous depending on the jurisdiction. Federal discovery rules may be more—or less— liberal than some state procedural rules.

The decision maker. Federal and state courts allow jury trials in similar cases, but the pool of available jurors may differ significantly, with federal districts often drawing from a larger geographic area.

Rules of evidence. Some jurisdictions have different rules, for example, about expert testimony or the admissibility of subsequent remedial measures.

Precedent. Specific state laws create liability or allow generous damages, or federal laws may be preferable that favor one party over another.

Appellate options. It may be preferable to have the opportunity for appeal before a federal circuit or a state supreme court.

Think Twice

Because lawyers specialize, there are advocates who exclusively practice in federal courts, and there are many more attorneys who appear only in state courts. In determining whether to go to state or federal court when there is a choice, these lawyers will have strong preferences based on their experiences. Advocates need to consider where it's best for a client to be and not be swayed by their biases. That may mean referring the case to another lawyer.

11.3   WHERE CAN RELIEF BE OBTAINED?

Venue determines the specific location where the hearing or trial is conducted. In litigation, the city or county where a trial is held is usually where the defendant resides, where the cause of action arose, where the defendant is doing business or has an office, or where the plaintiff resides. Similarly in administrative proceedings, venue is where the defendant is or where the claim arose. In arbitration, the place of the arbitration hearing is determined by the written agreement between the parties (a reasonably convenient location) or the rules of the arbitration organization (the place where the respondent resides or does business).

Think Twice

So what can go wrong with jurisdictional and venue choices? It's not likely that the attorney is trying to get into the wrong court or courthouse, but it may well be that counsel failed to consider other forums that are available. Lawyers, like everyone else, want to stay in their zones of comfort. That means we like to stay home and advocate in our own community. We are more familiar with the applicable procedures and law and often know or know about the decision maker. It would take more of an effort to

consider whether the substantive laws of another avail-
able forum would provide stronger claims and potentially
better results. And it would likely mean that the lawyer
would have to seek co-counsel in another city to bring or
help the case, diminishing the fee prospects for the origi-
nal lawyer.

C.   COMPLAINING THE RIGHT WAY

11.4   HOW TO BRING A LITIGATION CLAIM

A complaint to initiate a lawsuit commonly requires the
plaintiff to put the defendant on notice of the facts, the claims,
and the relief sought. Federal courts and most state courts
subscribe to the theory of "notice pleading." So long as a
complaint generally informs a defendant of the nature of the
allegations and claims, this minimal information is usually
enough to make the complaint acceptable and to defeat a motion
to dismiss by the defendant.

Federal court rules specifically require the content of a
complaint to include a short and plain statement of facts, a legal
claim, and a statement of the relief sought. While the federal
standards have grown somewhat more strict since 2007, essentially, the facts can be stated as a summary conclusion; the legal
claim must reflect a recognized cause of action; and the relief
sought can be generally stated. The Appendix of Forms to the
Federal Rules of Civil Procedure includes examples of complaints
that are quite short.

Discovery and motions are then used to uncover the bases of
the complaint and to challenge allegations and causes of action.
In practice, many lawyers prefer to draft more detailed complaints to present a stronger case, withstand dismissal motions,
and better define the scope of discovery. Statements made in a
complaint are usually deemed judicial admissions and bind the
plaintiff to those statements.

State court rules vary the level of detail required. Approxi-
mately half the states follow the federal rules, and the remaining
states typically require more factual detail and a more explicit
exposition of the legal right to relief. This usually involves
pleading more facts and the elements of the cause of action. For

example, an auto accident complaint in some state courts would allege that defendant owed plaintiff a duty of careful driving, that defendant breached this duty through speeding and inattentiveness, and that as a result plaintiff suffered specific damages. A federal complaint, by contrast, would be sufficient if plaintiff alleged that defendant negligently caused the plaintiff's injuries and resultant damages.

11.5 WHAT ARE THE COMPONENTS OF A COMPLAINT?

There are four major parts of a complaint:

- The caption
- The contents
- The request for relief
- The signature

11.5.1 Caption

The caption includes the name of the court, the applicable division within a district, the names (and addresses in some jurisdictions) of the parties, the civil action number of the case, the word complaint, and any labeling required by the rules (e.g., contract case). Local custom often dictates the arrangements of these various parts.

11.5.2 Contents

The contents contain the legal and factual information discussed in the previous section. The averments of the complaint should be set forth in separate paragraphs, with each paragraph limited to a single set of circumstances. Each paragraph should be numbered, with Arabic numerals preferred. Exhibits may be attached to the complaint and adopted by reference in an allegation. Multiple causes of action may be stated as separate counts with preceding paragraphs incorporated by reference, sometimes designated with Roman numerals.

There are decisions to be made regarding the number of causes of actions to bring. The "kitchen sink" approach is to include everything that reasonably can be fit in the complaint. The selective approach suggests only strong claims be made. The answer to which approach to use depends upon the circumstances. There must always be a good faith basis to bring a claim as explained in Section 11.5.4.

There may also be decisions to be made regarding who the defendant(s) should be. The general rule is that the plaintiff is the master of the case and gets to pick whom to sue. Not all potential defendants need to be included. The reality is that the plaintiff wants to ensure that the defendant(s) has the resources and money to pay any potential judgment. Plaintiffs need to match their rights with the remedies that a defendant can provide. As we said previously, the initial inquiry a plaintiff must consider is: can the defendant ultimately pay what they owe or provide the relief the plaintiff wants.

Some causes of action may be unavailable against certain defendants. Frequently, lawyers will plead claims in the alternative in hopes of recovering money. For example, many defendants have liability insurance that may not cover a policyholder's intentionally caused injuries. A complaint that includes negligence causes of action in addition to intentional tort claims may increase the opportunity to recover. This alternative type of pleading is permitted in almost all jurisdictions and forums.

A well-drafted complaint usually includes the following:

- A statement of jurisdiction (required in federal court complaints).

- A description of the parties.

- A summary of relevant events.

- A specific reference to a legal cause of action (e.g., statutory cite).

- A statement of the injury suffered or damages sought.

- Averments of specialized matter when required, e.g. actions for fraud.

- A statement of relief.

A complaint may look something like this:

STATE OF MITCHELL
COUNTY OF SUMMIT
DISTRICT COURT

Northstar Oil Company,

    Plaintiff

        v.

Southstar Oil Corporation,

    Defendant

COMPLAINT

Civil Action No. _____

Jury Trial Demanded

For its Complaint, Plaintiff Northstar Oil Company ("North-star") states:

1.   Northstar is a corporation organized under the laws of Mitchell with its principal place of business in Summit, Mitchell.

2.   Defendant Southstar Oil Corporation ("Southstar") is a corporation organized under the laws of Grand, with its principal place of business in Lexington, Grand.

3.   On January 2, 2010, Southstar offered to sell Plaintiff fuel oil at $75.00 per barrel.

4.   On January 3, 2010, Northstar accepted Southstar's offer and ordered 30,000 barrels of fuel oil at the $75.00 per barrel price.

5.   Southstar failed to deliver fuel and in a January 10 email informed Northstar that it would not perform the contract.

6.   As a result of Southstar's failure to deliver, Northstar was forced to purchase 30,000 barrels of fuel oil at $90.00 per barrel.

7.   As a result of Southstar's breach of its agreement with Northstar, Plaintiff Northstar has suffered damages of four hundred fifty thousand dollars ($450,000.00).

WHEREFORE, Plaintiff Northstar requests Judgment as follows:

1.   Judgment in favor of Plaintiff Northstar and against Defendant Southstar in the amount of four hundred fifty thou-

sand dollars ($450,000.00) plus interest and costs to the extent recoverable by law.

2.   Such other relief as the interests of justice may require.

Dated: May 1, 2010.

———

Cara Commercial
Laissez & Faire
123 Commodity Place
Commercetown, New York
11111
(123) 999–9999

Attorney No. 45678
Counsel for Plaintiff
Northstar Oil Company

This same complaint reduced to its bare minimum might look like this:

In January 2010, Defendant breached a contract with Plaintiff to sell 30,000 barrels of oil at $75.00 a barrel, causing plaintiff damages in excess of $50,000.

11.5.3   Request for Relief

We already covered this in Section 6.4, which you can happily review.

11.5.4   Signature

The lawyer representing the plaintiff must sign the complaint, include an address, phone and fax numbers, email address, and an attorney registration number. This signature in federal court and most state jurisdictions constitutes a certification that counsel has read the pleading, that there is evidentiary support for the facts, that the legal contentions are warranted by law or a good faith extension or modification of the law, and that the pleading is not interposed for harassment or delay. Sanctions for violation of this signature may be available under Federal Rule 11 or similar state rules.

You should not draft and serve a pleading unless you are reasonably sure that such a claim is valid. This will require you to make a reasonable investigation to support your client's factual position and to conduct reasonable legal research to determine whether such a cause of action exists in the jurisdiction or should exist.

11.6   HOW TO BRING AN ARBITRATION CLAIM

The document initiating an arbitration proceeding is usually called a claim and not a complaint. There are two basic types of arbitration claim forms, a short one and a detailed one. The rules of the arbitration organization specify which is required. The short version may be submitted by completing a form available from the arbitration organization. The detailed arbitration claim may explain the details of the dispute, the supporting facts and law, and the specific relief sought. The advantages of the short form are that it is quick and efficient. The advantages of the longer form are that it requires the claimant to prepare a case, it more thoroughly advises the respondent of the details of the claim, and it reduces the assertion of frivolous claims.

11.7   HOW TO INITIATE AN ADMINISTRATIVE ACTION

The initiation of a proceeding in administrative cases is usually called a claim, although it may also be called a complaint or a petition. The statutory provision or rules of the administrative agency determine what is required. The document may be short or lengthy, or may be something as simple as a form document that the claimant completes on-line.

11.8   IS THAT ALL THERE IS?

Pleadings are important not only for their formal aspects but also because they reflect counsel's strategic and tactical objectives. For example, a summons and complaint not only initiates a lawsuit and satisfies the statute of limitations, it also reveals what is at issue in a lawsuit. Consequently, it defines what is relevant in a case for purposes of disclosure and discovery. In addition, the allegations of the complaint may foreclose or invite certain claims, defenses, and responses. Similarly the complaint also determines the forum, and this can affect other aspects of litigation. This analysis applies also to arbitration and administrative proceedings. Whatever happens in the beginning of a case has an influence on the middle and end of a case, as we shall discuss.

D.   DRAFTING THE RIGHT PAPERS

11.9   HOW TO DRAFT

Drafting a complaint, claim, or petition, involves consideration of the following drafting techniques:

Mimicry. There are various sources that can produce sample and example complaints. A few keystrokes and a search engine, a perusal of form books, a phone call or email to a colleague, and you can readily locate pleadings in similar or virtually identical cases. Many of these may have the advantage of already surviving and succeeding in other cases. You'll need to review, pick and choose, and modify what you need. And do change the names in the caption.

Clarity. Pleadings should, somewhat ironically, avoid legalese. Plain, simple language is usually preferred to legal jargon, such as: on or about, at all times material and relevant, hereinafter, and aforesaid.

Brevity. Whether the pleading is short or detailed, you should strive to be concise. Say what you mean, and nothing more.

Documents. Pleadings can and should be supported by relevant, attached documents. The document can generally be incorporated in the complaint by reference to avoid having to repeat the contents of the document in the body of the pleading.

Structure. Pleadings should be structured so that they are easily understandable. Pleadings that contain multiple causes of actions can be structured with headings such as: "First cause of action" or "Second claim for relief." Specific items of relief can be structured in a list rather than in a one sentence conclusory statement.

Realistic request for relief. Demands for billions of dollars or for an order requiring defendant to read this book do little to enhance a plaintiff's case. Grossly inflated claims have little utility and may be counter-productive. Some judicial jurisdictions prohibit a plaintiff from stating a specific amount of the damages sought and require. Instead, the request for damages might be a more general statement such as "damages in excess of $50,000." The request for money damages in arbitration claims may be pragmatically limited because the amount of the filing fee often depends upon the amount of damages requested. Small claims may have a filing fee of $50; a million dollar claim may have a filing fee of $10,000. The relief sought in an administrative petition may be specifically limited by statute or rule.

Reviewing the complaint. After drafting a proposed complaint, claim, or petition it is useful to review to see if it is understandable and to attempt to answer it as if you were the opposing party. This approach usually reveals deficiencies that may be alleviated with proper redrafting.

Think Twice

Problems with complaints may start with a client who wants you to sue for fire and brimstone when all that may be available are smoldering ashes. Some clients will be quite certain about their facts and quite convinced that there must be better causes of action out there, and expect you to deliver the right result immediately if not sooner. Your obligation to ascertain all the facts and search for evidentiary support may appear to your clients that you don't believe them or in them.

The pressure you feel to do something now can translate into taking precipitous action by not completing your duties and fully researching the law. Explaining your professional responsibility obligations to your client will help them understand that you will be both a zealous and responsible advocate. And taking the requisite time to be sure you satisfy those duties is often the best thing you can do for your client and your career.

Then there are the form pleadings. It can be tempting to simply copy other complaints. And that may actually be okay if that earlier case is identical to yours. You still need to ask: what do I need to include and to state in a complaint? The precedent established by other successful

cases can provide you with the right pleading, but it is more likely that you will still need to invest your time and attention to modify that earlier complaint to meet the specific needs and interests of your client.

E. RESPONDING WITH THE RIGHT DEFENSES AND MOTIONS

If your client is a defendant or respondent, you need to determine how to raise appropriate defenses and counterclaims. Once the dispute-resolution process is underway, you may need to bring a motion to resolve or limit that process. If you bring a motion, you may have an opportunity to present an oral argument to the decision-maker. Section 11.10 reviews defenses and counterclaims; section 11.11 discusses motion practice; section 11.12 offers suggestions about effective motion argument.

11.10 HOW TO RESPOND

In litigation, a defendant serves an answer. In arbitration and administrative proceedings, a respondent usually serves a response. The contents of this answer or response commonly consist of admissions and denials and affirmative defenses, and may include a counterclaim, third party claim, or cross-claim. Alternatively, a motion to dismiss or related motion may be brought.

11.10.1 Admissions and Denials

A party must respond to each of the numbered paragraphs in a petition or complaint by: admitting the numbered allegation, denying it entirely, admitting or denying it in part, or stating that the defendant/respondent is without knowledge or information sufficient to form a belief about the truth or falsity of the allegation. In other words, you have to admit what is true, deny what is untrue, or state that you cannot admit or deny because you don't reasonably know.

11.10.2 Affirmative Defenses

An affirmative defense may need to be explicitly stated to provide notice to the plaintiff/claimant about a defense that exists. An affirmative defense alleges that the defendant/respondent is not legally liable. Examples of affirmative defenses include statute of limitations, statute of frauds, accord and satisfaction, payment, contributory negligence, and fraud. If an affirmative defense is not pleaded, it may not be used as a defense. If in doubt, assert the defense so everyone has notice of your position.

11.10.3 Counterclaims

An answer may also include counterclaims, which are claims made by the defendant/respondent against the plaintiff/claimant. A compulsory counterclaim arises out of the same transaction or occurrence that is the subject matter of the complaint and must be asserted or it is barred from a subsequent case. A permissive counterclaim is one involving any dispute between the plaintiff/claimant and the defendant/respondent. The judge/arbitrator has discretion to refuse to hear a permissive counterclaim if it is too remote from the main action. Prior considerations described in drafting a complaint apply to the drafting of a counterclaim. It is a truism that that a good defense includes a good offense, and asserting a valid counterclaim is a good way to try and balance the case and provide greater opportunities to compromise in a subsequent settlement.

11.10.4 Defensive Motions

A defendant/respondent may respond with a motion instead of an answer. The dismissal motion attacks the pleadings and seeks to dismiss all or part of the complaint. Federal Rule 12 and similar state rules list available grounds for dismissal motions. Section 11.11 explains the purpose and usefulness of these motions. It is critical to remember that these grounds for dismissal need to appear in either the answer or the motion to avoid a party waiving these remedies.

11.10.5 Other Claims and Defense

Other claims and defenses may be brought by a party including:

Cross-claims. Cross-claims are claims between co-parties and differ from counterclaims, which involve parties on opposite sides of a case. A plaintiff may bring a cross-claim against another plaintiff; a defendant may bring a cross-claim against another defendant.

Third party claims. A defendant may bring in another party as a third party defendant in limited situations. In litigation, a defendant may file a claim against a third party who is derivatively liable to the defendant if the defendant is liable to the plaintiff. A third party claim states that if the defendant is found liable, the third party defendant should pay (indemnify) the original defendant because of the third party defendant's legal obligation owed to the defendant. This process is known as impleader.

The third party action does not assert that the original defendant is blameless and the third party defendant is the one at fault or that the plaintiff sued the wrong defendant. The defendant cannot bring in any potential defendant, that is the prerogative only of the plaintiff who has decided whom to sue and whom not to sue. A common example is a products liability case in which the plaintiff sues only the retailer who can implead the manufacturer who made the product because there is an indemnity agreement between the two that requires the manufacturer to reimburse the retailer for any product liability damages.

The third party defendant answers the third party complaint just as a defendant answers a complaint. In arbitration, a respondent may be able to bring a claim against a party who has also signed an arbitration agreement to arbitrate the dispute. In administrative proceedings, a respondent may be able to bring in a third party with the permission of the administrative judge.

Reply. A plaintiff must respond to counterclaims. This response is known as a reply, and is drafted like an answer

Amending pleadings. Any of the pleadings discussed above can be amended. Amendments are usually allowed with the consent of all the parties or by leave of the judge or arbitrator provided that the amendment is timely, promotes fairness, and does not prejudice other parties. The applicable rules may establish deadlines for the bringing of an amendment. The latest deadline is usually a reasonable time before a trial or a date after which a party becomes unfairly prejudiced. Fairness is promoted if justice will be advanced by an amendment. Courts tend to grant motions to amend in order to bring together all the disputed issues in one lawsuit, unless that would cause undue prejudice to a party.

Related procedures. There are other procedures involving the addition of claims and parties. Joinder rules provide standards for the inclusion of additional parties and causes of action. Other rules regarding severance and separation provide ways for causes of action and parties to be removed from a case and actions tried independently. Intervention is the request by someone who is not a party to become a party in a case because of a specific interest in a case. We leave the details of these, less common, proceedings to civil procedure and your late nighttime reading.

Think Twice

Defending a case can be difficult with a client who believes they did no wrong and that it's our unfair civil justice system that allows anybody to sue anyone for anything. It is certainly understandable that defendants feel aggrieved that a plaintiff alleges they are irresponsible rascals, when, from their perspective, the plaintiff is the real culprit. Plus, defendants are being dragged into a dispute that will cost them a lot of time, money, and aggravation. It's no wonder they are ... well, you can imagine.

Your task is to guide your clients who have been sued through this process, assure them you will do the best you can to defend them, make every effort to maintain reasonable fees and costs, and help them ultimately resolve the dispute in a way that meets their needs and interests. Defendants have rights too, and they need to understand you understand that.

11.11   BRINGING THE RIGHT MOTION

Proceeding with and defending a case often involves the use of motions to get some things done. The best approach, required in many jurisdictions, is to discuss with opposing counsel what you want and why. These opportunities to meet and confer are an excellent way to resolve a procedural dispute if your opponent is somewhat reasonable and you are willing to compromise. You may be able to reach a stipulated accord with opposing counsel by email or phone, or both. It will save your client money and you aggravation, unless you really enjoy walking, riding, or flying to the courthouse.

Attorneys may or should bring the following motions when they answer any of the following questions affirmatively (rule references are to the Federal Rules of Civil Procedure):

11.11.1   Motion to Dismiss

Do I want all or part of a case to be over? If the answer is yes, the motion that may be brought is a Rule 12 Motion to Dismiss. The grounds for this motion seek to dismiss a complaint because:

> *Service of the complaint is improper.* Service may be insufficient because the summons is inadequate or, more commonly, the service of process defective. The most common defects are that the service did not comply with the required service rules (e.g., required personal service was not made) or the wrong person was served (e.g., an employee not able or authorized to receive service was served).

> *There is no personal or subject matter jurisdiction.* Section 11.1 explained the need to have both valid personal jurisdiction and valid subject matter jurisdiction. This motion tests the existence of valid jurisdiction.

> *The pleading is deficient.* The complaint may be deficient because it does not include required information (See section 11.5), or because a cause of action is only possible and not plausible, or because it does not include enough specificity required with certain claims (e.g., fraud and others listed in Rule 8).

> *The claim or defense is legally inadequate.* Rule 12(b)(6) permits the dismissal of a complaint that fails to state a claim upon which relief can be granted. A complaint must be based upon a legally cognizable cause of action. In federal cases, the asserted facts need to support a plausible claim, and not just a possible claim. If the jurisdiction does not

recognize the asserted claim, this motion will cause the complaint to be dismissed.

Procedurally, in considering whether to grant or deny a Rule 12 motion, the judge or arbitrator can only review the pleadings. If matters outside the pleadings need to be considered, the proper motion to be brought is the following motion.

11.11.2   Motion for Summary Judgment

Do I want all or part of this case to be really over? The grounds for a Rule 56 motion are that no genuine issues of disputed material facts exist and that the movant is entitled to a judgment as a matter of law. This motion permits a judge to review the undisputed material facts of a case and determine which party should prevail. Because there are no disputed material facts, there is no need for a trial and the judge can apply the law to the uncontested facts and decide the case summarily.

This motion needs to be supported by affidavits or discovery responses that establish the facts and the absence of any material dispute. This motion may be brought at anytime but is typically brought after facts have been disclosed or discovery completed. Rule 56 explains the procedures to be followed in successfully bringing and defending this motion. Strategic and tactical decisions about whether, why, and when to assert this motion are left to other texts and courses.

11.11.3   Other Motions

Do I want to change, add, or delete some issues or parties? A motion to amend or supplement a pleading permits changes to be made pursuant to Federal Rule 15. A motion to include or exclude issues (allowed by Rule 20) or parties (allowed by Rule 14 and 22) may also be brought to change the shape and scope of a case.

Do I want to do something procedurally the other side does not want me to do? If you want to obtain more time to do something or delay something from happening, you can bring a motion under an applicable rule.

Do I need something from the other side or want to have them sanctioned? The most common situations involve discovery disputes. If the other side does not comply with your proper discovery request you can move to require them to respond or seek sanctions for their refusal pursuant to Rule 37.

Do I need some immediate relief? Your client may need urgent injunctive relief, and you can bring a Rule 65 motion; or your client may need to seek relief from a default judgment, and you can bring a Rule 60 motion to vacate that judgment.

There are many other reasons to bring motions. The number of different motions is only limited by the number of different needs lawyers have for some form of relief. If you need something, you can probably find a rule, statute, or court decision permitting a motion to be brought seeking the needed relief. Whether you get it or not, of course, depends upon whether the judge thinks you are right and deserving of it.

11.11.4   Reasons Not to Bring a Motion

There are also reasons not to bring motions. You don't want to:

Ask for something you don't really need or want.

Ask for something you can't get.

Bring a motion you have no support for.

Bring a motion primarily to retaliate against the other side.

Unnecessarily bother a judge or arbitrator or appear to be a whining, desperate lawyer.

11.11.5   Motion Documents

The bringing of a motion ordinarily requires the submission of supporting documents including a written motion, a notice for the hearing of the motion, an affidavit(s)or declaration, a memorandum of law, and a proposed order. The motion hearing often requires the preparation and presentation of an oral argument, although many motions may be decided without oral argument. The same sources that provide sample and example pleadings can provide you with all the form documents you need. Your client's story told by them or a witness can provide the supportive facts. Thorough legal research and your exemplary writing skills will yield the brief that will persuade the judge of the righteousness of your client's position. And you may want to begin your drafting with the proposed order so you focus on the remedy being sought as you prepare the other documents.

Think Twice

The good news is that available motions are plentiful. The bad news is that motions are costly, time consuming, and a chore. Spending time on trivial or needless motions creates unnecessary suffering. Your client suffers the most, financially, and you lose whatever momentum you have built in the case. Of course, it is possible that legitimate delay and expenses may favor your client because they have the resources and you have a strategy that time rewards.

That being said, it appears that many lawyers love motions. That may at least explain why there are so many. Peruse F.3d, F. Supp., and sources entirely made up of motion decisions (F.R.D.) and then review the state court decisions, and you'll realize motion practice is a staple of our litigation profession. The danger with all this is that lawyers reflexively bring motions because that is what we do, or are supposed to do. It takes a very good advocate to stop and say no: "No motion this time. I'll work out this procedural dilemma with opposing counsel. That is the best thing I can for my client."

Figuring out when to bring a motion, and if necessary, what motion to bring can also be difficult. What to bring when for what reason? What motion now may trigger another motion in the future? How will a motion really help the end result in a case? The right answer, as it is so often in law school, is that it depends. The right answer doesn't depend on what lawyers usually do or what you yourself did in your last case. It depends on your considered judgment about what is right for this client and this client's case.

11.12   THE MOTION ARGUMENT

Depending on the forum for dispute resolution and the type of motion, you may have an opportunity to present oral argument to the decision maker. Oral argument on a motion is often available in a district court proceeding, occasionally available in an administrative proceeding, and less often available in arbitration. Oral argument is most often available on motions that completely resolve a proceeding, such as summary judgment motions, and least often available on motions that are purely procedural, such as motions to amend.

There is a trend in state courts not to allow oral argument unless a party makes a request and there is a good reason to do so. And federal judges are likely to limit the time available to present an argument. Arguments may also be presented over a telephone conference call or by video web conferencing.

11.12.1   A Place to Start

Ask a trial court judge to list a courtroom skill that civil litigators need to sharpen and chances are excellent that motion argument will make the list. Part of the reason is that most of the energy and thought devoted to motion practice goes into the drafting of the written motion; and the argument, all too often, receives whatever time and thought can be spared at the end of the process. It is also true that many judges view civil motion practice as one of the principal burrs under the saddle of the judiciary and oral argument of civil motions as the sharpest thorn on that burr.

Is there something that can be done to make argument of a civil motion more effective? While it is difficult to generalize about an area of practice as varied as all civil motions, there certainly are some basic guidelines that should help keep the judge from visibly wincing the next time you stand up to argue a motion.

First, just as we suggested it was important to have a theory of the case, it is also important to *have a theory of the motion* before you stand and deliver your argument. This theory needs to explain, simply and persuasively, why the court ought to issue the order you are asking for. In essence, the theory of the motion should tell the judge the critical facts and law that entitle your client to the ruling you seek—and do it as succinctly as possible. If you begin your argument with a statement of your theory of the motion, the judge will have a helpful overview of your argument.

Second, be clear, *be very clear*, about what it is that you want the judge to do. It's frustrating for a judge to listen to an attorney cite case law and deposition excerpts, chapter and verse, before the attorney has explained what the judge is supposed to do with all this authority. Judges report that this is nonetheless a common frustration. All too often, lawyers bring a motion to put an end to something the other side in the litigation is doing. It is all fine and good to ask the judge, "Make them stop!" It is certainly fair, however, for the judge to respond, "How?" The answer to that question should, of course, be spelled out in the proposed order filed with the motion papers and explained at the beginning of oral argument.

Third, *organize your argument* to the judge around two or three of the most important points that justify granting your position—not several or a dozen supportive points. Judges frequently complain that lawyers arguing motions are long-winded and slow to come to the point. A litany of factual complaints, string cites of cases, and lengthy recitation of affidavit statements will only make the advocate that less effective. A few well-chosen points are far more useful than a barrage of rhetoric. Typically, a strong organizational structure—whether thematic, topical, or chronological—will make your argument more cogent and, in turn, more persuasive. You ought to begin your argument by summarizing those points so the judge knows what grounds you have to support your position.

11.12.2   Why Am I Here?

If you follow the three guidelines set out in the preceding section, your oral argument will become part of your overall plan of advocacy. Ideally, your motion argument should add something to your position in a way the motion brief does not or cannot provide. As you think strategically about how to use your time in front of the judge, ask yourself: What can I do in this argument that I haven't already done in the motion papers or brief I have filed? If you're stuck for an answer, consider the following suggestions.

Crystallize. Your memorandum in support of your motion tells the judge everything needed to rule in your favor. The last thing a judge needs or wants to hear is you recite your brief. Instead, your argument is your chance to focus on what is really critical and tell the judge the few things that the judge needs to remember no matter what. Often, as lawyers, we are loathe to shorten our list of arguments for fear that what we leave out will prove to have been the one point that might have been the most persuasive. A motion argument in front of a busy judge is no time to indulge this sort of worry. The argument is the time to think about what primary factor(s) might be used to fill in the blanks in these sentences:

"Your honor, the law supports you granting my motion because _____."

"_____ prevents you from ruling in opposing counsel's favor."

This is a helpful exercise in defining the essence of your position. In the course of pondering this question, you may learn that your already potent theory of the motion can be distilled to an even stronger proof.

Truth, justice, and the American way. Judges care about justice—and that is something we often forget is true. Judges want to rule in ways that comport with their values, with their beliefs in what is right, with their visions of justice—even when ruling on something as mundane as a motion. Part of your challenge as an advocate is finding the justice in your client's position. Once you have done that, expressing that justice in a way that comports with the judge's values may well prove to be something that is more readily done at the argument.

For one thing, the judge is present and free to ask questions. Consequently, it is possible to engage the judge in a conversation about why it is that ruling in your client's favor is the just thing to do. Argument may also be the appropriate venue for voicing the depth of feeling you have about the merit of your position. Expressing passion about the justice of your position is something that may be easier and more believable to do orally than in print. Passion is strong stuff, however, so be careful about the dose. Opposing summary judgment and arguing passionately for your client's right to have a jury hear his case may be plausible. Arguing passionately for a discovery extension may be laughable.

Welcome questions. When a judge asks a question during argument it is not an interruption, it is an opportunity. Take a moment to do this thought experiment: If you could read minds, what would you be looking for in the judge's mind during oral argument? The answer surely must be that you would be looking for points of doubt, disbelief, and skepticism about your argument. By finding these areas of concern, you could address those doubts and thereby strengthen your argument and make decision in your client's favor more likely.

A question from the judge is nothing less than a wonderful opportunity to respond to concerns the judge has. When that opportunity comes, by all means seize it. Indeed, you should invite and welcome questions from the judge because these questions give you the chance to overcome the obstacles the judge has seen that stand between you and a favorable ruling. Successful advocates suggest that early in an argument you ask: "Judge, what questions do you have that I can try to answer about this motion?" And, may be wise to follow up a sharply worded question or puzzled look on the judge's face with: "Have I addressed your concerns, Judge?"

11.12.3 Choices, Choices, Choices

Here is a checklist of choices for oral argument of a motion. Some of the choices we invite you to consider; others we advise you to avoid.

Condense your argument to its essence and emphasize those central points, *rather* than attempting to deal with every issue and argument raised in the motion papers.

Focus the judge's attention on two or three pieces of critical authority, *rather* than referring vaguely to "the law" or reciting sections of a variety of different opinions. If there is critical language in a statute, read it; if there is an authoritative decision, quote it. Then move on.

Edit your argument with an eye toward time limitations, *rather* than assuming that the judge will give you enough time to make whatever argument you choose to make. In years of practice, we have yet to hear a judge say, "Counsel, I am sorry your argument didn't last longer."

Illustrate your argument with visual presentations *rather* than simply talking, talking, talking. Charts, graphs, enlarged exhibits, concise power point presentations, and other visual displays that illustrate your argument can be very persuasive.

Address the court when responding to points raised by the other side, *rather* than speaking to opposing counsel. Motion argument is the venue in which it is easiest to fall into the behavior of talking directly to opposing counsel, rather than the judge. Many judges view this behavior as not only annoying, but deeply disrespectful.

Answer questions directly and be willing to say "yes" or "no," *rather* than trying to sidestep a difficult issue or finesse a troubling question. Judges ask lawyers questions all day long, and they have no difficulty identifying evasion. Your honest answer to a difficult question is likely to be more helpful to your client than the assumptions the judge will make about the answer if your response is less than forthright.

Admit to the weak points in your argument and be willing to talk about them, *rather* than attempting to hide them from the judge. It is hard to hide weakness from a judge who has spent a career finding the soft spots in lawyers' arguments. And, even if the judge doesn't find the hole in your argument, opposing counsel likely will.

Ask for what you want but be willing to compromise if compromise seems warranted, *rather* than insisting your position is intractable. There are times that motion practice involves "all or nothing" issues, but usually some sort of middle ground is not only possible, but the probable outcome. A willingness to accept and suggest compromise makes the middle ground you identify the more likely resolution.

11.13   MORE ON MOTION PRACTICE

If you want to know yet even more about motion practice, you may refer to any number of authoritative sources, including those listed in the Epilogue.

Chapter Twelve
DISCLOSURE AND DISCOVERY: WHAT DO YOU KNOW?

If you're going to play the game properly you'd better know every rule.

—Barbara Jordan

A. INTRODUCTION

What and when information needs to be disclosed depends upon the type of transaction or case. Transactional work usually involves the disclosure of information during the negotiating and drafting segments of the transaction. Chapter 5 discussed disclosure of information during these stages. Dispute resolution work involves the disclosure and discovery of information during the pendency of the dispute. The exchange of information permits lawyers to know as much about a matter as necessary and allows them to review and probe the good, the bad, and the unknown in order to evaluate a transaction or case.

12.1 PURPOSES OF DISCLOSURE AND DISCOVERY

Disclosure and discovery—known as discovery—serve many functions in a dispute resolution proceeding, including the exchange of relevant information explaining a party's claim or defense and supporting information. This information exchange:

- Promotes negotiated settlements.

- Explores the other side's case to understand their positions.

- Equalizes resources on both sides without allowing one side to take undue advantage of the other.

- Obtains information to support or oppose a motion, such as for summary judgment.

- Provides information for a hearing or trial.

- Fosters a final decision based on shared information.

"Disclosure" requires parties to provide information that supports their case to another party. Disclosure rules require a party to provide information without the need for a request from the other side. Discovery is a process of one side asking for information and the other side responding to these discovery requests. Discovery rules allow a party to search for information and obtain data the other side may not want to disclose. Federal Rule of Civil Procedure 26 and similar state rules govern the scope of disclosure and discovery.

12.1.1   Early Disclosure

Parties to a dispute may voluntarily exchange information to each other before the formal initiation of a proceeding or during its pendency. Information may be provided before a claim is filed in an effort to resolve the dispute quickly. Information that supports a party's position may be exchanged along with information that weakens or rebuts an opposing party's position. Lawyers make this information available by:

- Providing fact summaries.

- Disclosing original documents and ESI (Electronically Stored Information) or providing the other side with copies of originals or reproductions.

- Submitting a draft of a complaint to the other side, called a courtesy complaint.

- Preparing a settlement brochure and other documents to encourage a negotiated result.

- Discussing their positions and evaluations of the case.

12.1.2   Disclosure During a Proceeding

Arbitration, administrative, and judicial forums may require the disclosure of certain information when initiating a proceeding.

Arbitration. A detailed arbitration claim by its nature includes specific information and documents that support the claim. The procedural rules of the arbitration organization may require the following specific information and documents:

- The claim setting forth in plain language the nature of the dispute, the specific grounds supporting the claim, the amount of any money requested, the computation of the amount sought and the reasons for the various amounts requested, other relief sought, and any other relevant and reliable information supporting the claim.

- A legible, authentic copy of the arbitration agreement signed by the parties.

- A legible, authentic copy of any documents supporting the claim.

- An affidavit or declaration establishing the authenticity of the arbitration agreement and supporting documents.

The purpose of this detailed information is to provide the responding party with information supporting a claim so the party understands the claim and is better able to respond and engage in settlement discussions. Similarly, the party responding to the claim must usually include specific detailed information and documents, so that all parties to the arbitration understand each other's positions.

Administrative proceedings. The type of administrative proceeding determines the extent of required initial disclosures. Some administrative proceedings are initiated by the completion of a form that includes very little information about a claim. Other administrative proceedings are initiated by a petition that includes very detailed and specific information and supporting documents. The applicable statute or rules determine the scope of this disclosed information.

Litigation. The initiation of a lawsuit may include the disclosure of very little information or significant information. At present, most state court jurisdictions require only notice pleading in drafting a complaint, as explained in Section 11.4. The information disclosed may be cursory and need not be supported by documents. Federal courts and a growing number of state courts require the disclosure of specific information in addition to the pleadings filed.

Federal Rule 26, in operation in most federal cases, requires initial disclosures of the following specific information that *supports* a party's case: the identity (name, address, and phone number) of each person likely to have relevant information, a brief summary of what witnesses know, and a copy of or description of relevant documents, electronically stored information, and tangible things. Rule 26 also requires a party seeking damages to disclose the computation of the damages and documentary information supporting the computation. Further, this Federal Rule requires a disclosing party to provide any insurance agreement that may satisfy part or all of a judgment. The parties are not required to disclose information that *does not support* a case. Federal Rule 26 also requires the disclosure of information later in a case regarding experts and expert testimony and evidence to be offered at trial.

The parties are obligated under the federal rules to meet and discuss issues surrounding the scope of these disclosures. These discussions provide both sides with a better understanding of each other's case, help promote early settlement, and can result in a stipulated discovery plan that a court may review and approve. A defendant has the same disclosure obligations as a plaintiff.

Think Twice

A lot of information is obtained and exchanged by disputing parties before litigation, arbitration, or an administrative proceeding. Before evaluating a case, a lawyer will gather information from as many sources as possible, as described in Chapter 7 on Investigations. In preparing to negotiate an early resolution, the attorneys will exchange factual and legal information about the strengths, as well as the weaknesses, of their case. Advocates will use a variety of investigative tools and approaches to obtain even more information and documents about a potential case. And litigators have a obligation to make reasonable efforts to gather evidence and conduct legal research before initiating a lawsuit. All these efforts accumulate a lot of relevant and reliable information before formal discovery and, accordingly, ought to help reduce the need for extensive additional discovery.

12.2   METHODS OF DISCOVERY

There are five major discovery methods a party may use to demand information:

Depositions (Federal Rules 28, 30, 32). Depositions require deponents to testify to what they know. A deponent answers questions under oath asked by a deposing attorney, with other attorneys in attendance. The questions and answers are recorded and may later be transcribed.

Production of documents and electronically stored information (ESI) (Federal Rule 34). One party may require another party to provide documents, ESI, and tangible things for inspection, copying, or reproduction or to permit entry onto land or access to other property for inspection, testing, or sampling. A party may be able to obtain the same access to documents, ESI, tangible things, and land from a non-party through a subpoena (Federal Rule 45).

Interrogatories (Federal Rule 33). Written interrogatories are written questions submitted to a party to be answered in writing under oath. This device can be useful in obtaining information involving specific factual data and the existence of information.

Request for admissions (Federal Rule 36). Responses to requests for admission help determine the truth of specific matters and the genuineness of documents and ESI. This device primarily resolves or identifies disputed issues for trial and may also discover useful information.

Physical or mental examinations (Federal Rule 35). A party may be able to obtain a physical or mental examination of another party if the condition of that person is in controversy and if there exists good cause for an examination. These types of examinations usually occur in personal injury litigation.

Depositions are discussed in greater detail in Chapter 13. The other discovery methods are discussed in greater detail in Chapter 14.

12.2.1 Availability of Discovery Methods

Litigation. These five methods are generally available in judicial disputes. Federal Rules of Civil Procedure 26 through 37 and similar state rules authorize and govern these devices. The availability of liberal discovery permitting extensive searches for information and requiring the exchange of lots of information is a reason why parties choose litigation to resolve certain types of disputes.

Arbitration. The extent of available discovery in arbitration depends upon the rules of the arbitration organization and the agreement of the parties. An arbitration code of procedure ordinarily allows requests for the production and exchange of relevant documents, ESI, and things, the use of a reasonable number of depositions, a limited number of interrogatories, and reasonable requests for examinations and admissions. The rules of some arbitration providers or an individual arbitrator may limit available discovery. The parties in arbitration may agree to expand or reasonably restrict discovery.

Administrative proceedings. The extent of discovery in administrative proceedings varies depending on the type of proceeding. All five discovery devices may be available, or parties may only be able to demand the production of documents and written information. The rules and statutes governing the administrative proceeding determine the availability of discovery. Informal administrative proceedings usually allow only very limited discovery, but formal administrative proceedings may allow fuller discovery.

Think Twice

Discovery, certainly in its current extensive and broad coverage, is a relatively recent phenomenon, especially if you are our age. And it's largely an American way of preparing cases for hearings and trial. Similar to motion practice, discovery practice has developed a life of its own, often times causing parties substantial cost, enormous waste of time, and a lot of aggravation.

There are so many ways to obtain so much information that discovery can be staggering to a client. We lawyers become numb to discovery's inconvenience for our clients and its intrusiveness into their lives and businesses. It is easy for us to take discovery as a given, when we should question whether we really need to ask for something. That danger is compounded when our income directly benefits from taking or responding to discovery. We need to sit back, recognize the potential economic conflict, and make sure we're using the most efficient and affordable discovery methods—and if we're not, consider whether what we are doing in a case is really necessary.

B. SCOPE OF DISCOVERY

12.3   RELEVANT INFORMATION AND DOCUMENTS

Relevance usually determines the scope of discovery, and information that is relevant is usually discoverable. The general rule is that the extent of relevance in litigation is broad, in arbitration reasonably broad, and in administrative proceedings more restrictive. In litigation and arbitration, parties may be able to obtain information regarding any matter relevant to a claim or defense and to the subject matter if good cause exists. Relevance in some cases may also encompass information that could reasonably be calculated to lead to the discovery of relevant information. See Federal Rule 26(b)(2). The scope of discoverable information includes oral and written facts, lay and expert opinions, legal contentions and conclusions, and documents and electronically stored information.

The litigation standard of relevance is not limited by the evidentiary standard of relevance. The standard for litigation is much broader in scope and encompasses information that relates to the claims or defenses regardless of admissibility at trial. It includes information exclusively within the knowledge or possession of the other side and information already known to the discovering party, as well as data equally available to the parties. This standard has been liberally interpreted by judges and arbitrators creating a relatively broad scope of discoverable information.

12.3.1 Litigation

Trial practice has evolved the following general approaches to discovery:

Ask for everything you want to discover, whether you firmly believe it to be discoverable or not. The broad discovery standards result in wide divergence of opinions regarding the discoverability of various types of information. What one lawyer or judge thinks is not discoverable, another attorney or judge may believe is always discoverable.

Ask only for relevant information you have the time and finances to pursue. The theoretical scope of relevant discovery will be limited by your client's resources and your strategies. There will be financial restrictions on the number of depositions or interrogatories available, and you will need to use reasonable discretion in discovering information. This is especially true regarding the discovery of ESI, which in even routine cases may be astonishingly extensive and difficult to locate and reproduce.

Ask for information you can obtain through compromise and agreement. Disputes regarding the discoverability of information can often be fairly resolved through mutual agreement, a stipulation. Both sides may agree to seek less than what they want and reveal more in order to reach an accord that saves everyone time, money, and further litigation.

Ask for information you intend to obtain through a court order, if your request is refused by the opponent. If an opposing party refuses to provide information, you can seek a court order requiring them to produce the requested information. The interest of one party may outweigh the discovery interest of another party, especially when the use of the discoverable information is questionable or marginally relevant.

12.3.2 Arbitration Proceedings

The standard and practice of discovery in arbitration is either similar to litigation or, in some situations, more limited and restricted. The applicable rules of the arbitration organization or arbitration agreement will determine the extent and availability of discovery. Relevance in arbitration may refer to matters directly relevant to the issues in the case and may not include potential information likely to lead to new issues. Arbitration practice encourages parties and lawyers to exchange information voluntarily, may require them to meet and confer on their own or with the arbitrator to resolve discovery differences, and often has a shorter permissible discovery period.

12.3.3   Administrative Proceedings

The standard of relevance in administrative proceedings once again depends upon the type of administrative proceeding and applicable rules and statutes. All five discovery devices may be available as they are in litigation, or discovery may be more akin to arbitration, or more limited with only document and electronically stored information discoverable.

Think Twice

There are, without exaggeration, hundreds of thousands of judicial decisions dealing with discovery and relevance issues. Many cases are reported, many more are not. Common sense is frequently the best standard in determining whether a particular piece of information or document ought to be sought. Perhaps the rule for discovery in litigation should read: relevant information is information that will help a party win a case or reduce the chance the case will be lost. Admittedly, that is too subjective of a standard for a judge to try to apply. But, it is a useful way for a lawyer to think about whether certain information should be gathered and how much time and money should be spent on the effort.

12.4   DISCOVERY RESTRICTIONS

All discovery requests regardless of the forum—judicial, arbitration, or administrative—have restrictions placed on their scope. The three major restricted areas are:

- Privileges

- Work product, including trial and case preparation materials

- Attorney mental impressions

In some jurisdictions, all these categories are lumped together under the rubric of work product. It's easier, however, to better understand them as separate categories.

12.4.1 Privileges

The general rule is that privileged matters are non-discoverable. The law has established specific privileges that allow the parties to withhold information in certain circumstances. What is and what is not privileged for discovery purposes is defined by constitutional provisions, statutes, evidentiary rules, and judicial opinions. Common privileges allowing a party to refuse to provide information in discovery include: the attorney/client privilege, marital spousal privilege, business privileges, physician/patient privilege, government privileges, and the fifth amendment privilege. Other privileges may exist, such as clergy, parent/child, political vote, reporter, peer review, deliberative processes; and these depend upon the law of the applicable jurisdiction.

In determining whether an existing privilege should restrict discovery requests, courts apply balancing tests that include the following factors:

The scope of the invasion of privacy. The broader the breach of confidentiality sought by discovery, the less likely discovery will be permitted.

The needs of the party for the information. The more essential the information is, the more likely it will be obtainable.

The availability of the information. If there is no other way a party may obtain critical information, the balance may swing in favor of discovery.

The status of the person claiming the privilege. If the person claiming the privilege is a party, it is more likely discovery will be allowed.

The specific kind of privacy invaded. The more critical or essential the right protected by the privilege is, the less likely it will be revealed.

The interests of society. If the greater interests of society are better served by disclosure, it will more often be allowed.

12.4.2   Work Product (Trial and Case Preparation Materials)

Work product consists of materials that parties and lawyers prepare or complete in anticipation of a trial or hearing. See Federal Rule 26(b)(3). Lawyers are not allowed to use discovery to obtain this work product, which includes written trial or case preparation materials of an opponent. This information is protected because attorneys should be encouraged to prepare a case thoroughly without concern about having to turn over their work to an opponent.

Four primary factors determine the practical application of work product restrictions:

Who assembled the materials? Materials prepared by or with the involvement or assistance of an attorney are usually protected. The involvement of a lawyer advocate usually means a dispute exists and litigation or arbitration is anticipated.

When were the materials gathered? Materials gathered or created immediately before an action or during its pendency will ordinarily be protected. Materials existing before a claim arises or before a proceeding begins will often not be protected. Timing is often critical to determining whether materials are protected.

Why were the materials prepared? If the materials were prepared primarily as trial or hearing preparation materials, they will be protected. If the materials were assembled because of governmental or public law requirements or in the ordinary course of business, they will not be protected. For example, if emails are written and sent by party employees at the request of a lawyer investigating a case, these materials would be protected. If written materials are routine business reports or reports prepared pursuant to government regulations, they would be discoverable.

Is the document a witness statement? Discoverable documents include certain types of witness statements. A witness statement is defined as a written statement signed or approved by a witness or a recording of a witness interview. A party can obtain a witness statement that the party made which is in the possession of the other side, and a witness can obtain a copy of a statement the witness made from any party. Witness information that does not fall within this definition is ordinarily non-discoverable. For example, notes made by an investigator during a witness interview not signed or approved by the witness will usually be considered work product and not discoverable.

Work product and trial and hearing preparation materials are not absolutely protected. A party may obtain these materials from an opposing party if they can make a showing of substantial need and undue hardship. Substantial need is demonstrated by showing that the materials are critically important to a case, and undue hardship is established by showing that the substantial equivalent of the materials sought cannot be obtained from any other source. Judges, arbitrators, and administrative judges are usually reluctant to permit the discovery of work product and trial preparation materials, and consequently, these standards are strictly applied.

Some forums differentiate between two types of work product: fact work product and opinion work product. When these terms are used, fact work product is the type of work product described in this subsection. Opinion work product is used to refer to work such as attorney mental impressions, described next.

12.4.3 Attorney Mental Processes

Attorney mental impressions, conclusions, opinions, legal theories, strategies, or tactics concerning a case are protected from discovery. See Federal Rule 26(b)(3). This protection prohibits one party from inquiring into the thoughts, ideas, and strategies of another party. Our judicial, arbitration, and administrative law systems permit attorneys to say or compose their theories, opinions, conclusions, and impressions about a case free from concern that this information will be discovered, and this information is absolutely protected.

Think Twice

You could spend the flower of your youth trying to figure out the nuances of these various discovery doctrines, and it might be worth the effort. Litigators have to know the ins and outs of fact and opinion work product in their jurisdiction in order to avoid committing malpractice. An effective way to understand it all is to understand the reasons why the rules are what they are.

We don't want our adversary poking around our office files or accessing our computer system to learn our side of the case. We don't want them listening in on our conversations with our clients or reading our emails to those clients. And we want the freedom to think about a case and preserve any ideas we have, however fanciful, from the prying eyes of others, especially opponents. Understanding these and other reasons underlying the rules is one step on your way to becoming an effective litigator.

12.5 DISCLOSURE AND DISCOVERY OF EXPERT INFORMATION

Experts are an essential part of many court, arbitration, and administrative cases. An expert can provide information about medical, scientific, psychological, engineering, economic, and technical matters. Experts include medical doctors, scientists, psychologists, engineers, economists, and anyone who has specialized information helpful to an attorney, party, and decision maker. Experts assist lawyers in preparing a case and testify at hearings and trials.

The disclosure and discovery of expert information depends upon the use an attorney makes of an expert during a case. See Federal Rule 26(b)(4). Advocates typically employ experts as trial or hearing experts, specially retained or employee experts, and informally consulted experts.

12.5.1 Trial and Hearing Experts

A trial or hearing expert is an individual who will testify during the case or who is identified by a party as likely to testify. A party must disclose the identities of these experts and their experience, opinions, bases of opinions, and reports they have prepared for the case. Many cases involve the "battle of the experts" and parties have a right to know which experts will testify, what they will say, and what they will rely on to support their opinions. The opposing party can usually obtain this information through interrogatories, document production requests, and depositions.

12.5.2   Retained or Employee Experts

This type of expert is an individual who is specially retained for a case or is an employee of a party involved with the case. It is common for an attorney to retain an expert to assist in investigating or preparing a case who will not testify at trial. It is also common that a corporation may make available experts who are in their employ to assist its attorney. The general rule is that discovery of information about the opinions of this type of expert is limited. A party may be able to obtain some basic information about the expert, but may not be able to use interrogatories or depositions to obtain more detailed information absent exceptional circumstances.

12.5.3   Informally Consulted Experts

This type of expert is one who has been approached by a party for some information or an initial opinion but who will not testify at trial and who has not been specially retained and is not an employee of the party. The general rule is that nothing is discoverable from or about an informally consulted expert. One reason for protecting this information is that this permits an attorney to search for an expert who has a favorable opinion without a concern for having to reveal the steps of that search or the information learned during that search. An expert who is initially contacted may later be specially retained or be designated as a trial expert and then the previously described disclosure and discovery rules would apply.

Think Twice

Lawyers joke, with more rue than humor, that you now have to be a legal expert in order to figure out what needs to be disclosed and is discoverable about an expert. As experts have become more commonplace in cases, the rules have evolved to ensure that parties learn what they need

to know about expert opinions and reports. A simplistic view of what ought to be disclosed or what needs to be revealed is this: if you are going to rely on what the expert will say, then you have to disgorge it. You don't want to be surprised or unable to rebut what an opposing expert says, and so you should do what you would expect the other lawyer to do. Reveal what will become evidence.

12.6   SUPPLEMENTAL DISCLOSURE AND DISCOVERY

A party is usually under a continuing duty to supplement disclosures and discovery responses. See Federal Rule 26(e). This duty extends to all types of discovery. A party is typically required to supplement previously revealed information that is incomplete or incorrect in some material respect. A party has to disclose this new information within a reasonable time after learning about it or at some appropriate stage of the proceeding. If a party does not supplement or is not obligated to supplement information, a discovering party can request a supplementation through interrogatories or a request for production of additional documents or electronically stored information.

Think Twice

Here's a thought about what might happen if you don't supplement discovery responses: the judge may very well prevent you from introducing that undisclosed information into evidence. That sanction alone ought to encourage lawyers to make sure the other side has updated knowledge about previously disclosed material information.

C.   PLANNING

12.7   DISCLOSURE AND DISCOVERY PLANNING

It is axiomatic that advocates need to plan for the disclosure and discovery of information. The rules of the forum will determine applicable disclosure requirements and allowable discovery requests. An advocate planning a disclosure/discovery plan should consider the following issues:

INFORMATION: THE WHAT

Types/Sources of Information	What Must I Disclose	What Must The Other Side Disclose
Witnesses		
Documents		
ESI		
Insurance		
Claims		
Remedies		
Damages		
Defenses		

METHODS: THE HOW

Types/ Sources of Information	Depositions	Production of Documents	Interrog- atories	Request For Admissions	Physical/ Mental Examinations	Other
Witnesses						
Documents						
ESI						
Insurance						
Claims						
Remedies						
Damages						
Defenses						

Disclosure and discovery plans can and, in many cases, must be developed in other ways. Advocates may confer voluntarily or meet pursuant to a court rule or order. Cases involving little or limited discovery, including arbitration and administrative cases, may require less planning. Litigation cases involving significant discovery will usually involve more planning and preparation. Court rules may require the attorneys to meet on their own to agree on a discovery plan, or may require the attorneys to attend a discovery plan conference with a judge, magistrate, or special master who will issue a discovery scheduling order, or both procedures may be used. See section 12.9.

12.8   DISCLOSURE AND DISCOVERY BY AGREEMENT

A substantial amount of information is exchanged by agreement of the attorneys. Federal Rule 29 and similar state rules and arbitration rules encourage such oral and written agreements. For example, attorneys may agree to schedule more depositions than provided by a rule, to exchange documents without formal requests, or to answer more interrogatories than allowed. The attorneys cannot vary any time deadlines for discovery imposed by a court without obtaining the court's approval.

Attorneys may agree to certain procedures by a written stipulation containing the agreement and signed by the parties or the attorneys. Stipulations may be formalized in a written agreement or be contained in a confirming email or letter from one attorney to another. A sample stipulation may read: [Plaintiff] and [Defendant] stipulate that (explain agreement) (signatures). It's as simple as that. A court may issue an order upon the filing of a stipulation without any notice or hearing.

12.9   CASE PLAN AND ORDER

Federal Rule 26(f) and similar state rules require parties to confer and develop a case plan. This plan is to contain a mutual agreement by the parties or their separate, different views concerning: what disclosures will be made, the timing and scope of these disclosures, what discovery requests will be served, when responses will be due, when discovery should be completed, what changes will be made in any of the applicable discovery rules, what additional pleadings may be served, and what motions may be brought.

The report may contain legitimate disagreements the parties have or alternative suggestions to the court regarding a plan. An agreed upon plan may be submitted to the court and become the basis for a scheduling order issued by the court. If the parties have disagreements or if the court rules do not require the parties confer and prepare a plan, a discovery conference can be scheduled with the judge to discuss these issues after which an order will be issued. In some jurisdictions, these conferences are known as pretrial conferences. As the case approaches to trial, changes may be made by agreement of the parties or by the court in the discovery scheduling order or the final pretrial order.

12.10   DISCLOSURE/DISCOVERY ORDERS

Parties may seek an order from a judge, arbitrator or administrative judge regarding disclosure and discovery. There are two basic types of orders. One is a *protective order* seeking to limit discovery or protect a party from unnecessary discovery, initiated by a motion or request for such an order. The second is an *order enforcing a discovery request* and requiring a party to provide information, initiated by a motion to compel discovery or for sanctions.

Think Twice

The vast majority of discovery requests and responses are dealt with by lawyers freely and fully. Actually, out of the billions and billions of discovery requests, not that many discovery disputes go to court or lead to published opinions. That's because good lawyers understand what is and what is not likely discoverable and appreciate the importance of working cooperatively with each other. Sure, there will be differences, but good lawyers work out their disagreements without seeking help from a judge, magistrate or judicial master.

12.10.1 Protective Orders

A party faced with disclosure or discovery problems may seek a protective order requesting any of the following relief (Federal Rule 26(c)):

- Discovery not proceed: for example, because it is not authorized by rule or is untimely.

- Discovery be permitted on specific conditions: for example, documents be disclosed before the taking of a deposition or a deposition be limited in time or scope.

- The scope of discovery be limited: for example, prohibiting the disclosure of irrelevant or privileged information or attorney mental impressions.

- Selected individuals not have access to revealed information: for example, only attorneys or named representatives of a party have access to confidential information.

- Trade secret or other confidential information be sealed and not made public: for example, the disclosure of such information may place a party at a significant disadvantage with competitors.

- Discovery requests or responses be exchanged simultaneously: for example, to avoid parties from being influenced by what they request or exchange.

- For any other reason which justice requires: for example, whatever else your client needs that you as an advocate can justify.

Protective orders will more likely be granted if the harm caused by the disclosure is not substantial or serious, the request for the relief is narrow and appropriate, and there is no alternative way of protecting the interests of the parties. Protective orders may also be modified after being initially granted depending upon the type of information disclosed and the circumstances of the particular case.

Think Twice

Many cases involve protective orders. Both sides often want their discoverable information to remain private, and certainly the defense usually does. That's why stipulated protective provisions are routinely agreed to by lawyers and submitted to the judge to be approved in an order. There will be fights over what should be covered and who has access to what, but reasonable heads will reach an accord. Previously agreed upon orders are excellent sources of exemplary protective orders.

12.10.2   Enforcement Orders

Parties may disagree about what is to be disclosed or discovered. Legitimate attempts to obtain information may be met with unsatisfactory or dilatory responses or objections, or even silence or threats. A party can enforce its disclosure and discovery rights in two primary ways. First, a party can attempt to resolve the dispute with the opposing party through discussions and negotiations. A party may revise a discovery request to satisfy the concerns of the other side. The responding party may be willing to disclose most but not all of the requested information. These informal efforts of enforcement should first be made before attempting the second enforcement method: an order.

Federal Rule 37 and similar state rules provide methods for obtaining judicial assistance in enforcing disclosure and discovery rights. Arbitration and administrative rules authorize similar enforcement. The typical relief is an order requiring the other side to respond to the discovery requests or to complete incomplete disclosures: for example, to appear for a deposition, to answer all interrogatories, or to provide relevant documents. A party may also seek the award of attorney's fees and other expenses if the motion is granted, and the judge or arbitrator may impose these costs on the non-responsive party if the reasons for being recalcitrant are unreasonable.

The rules of particular forums may also provide for other sanctions that may be imposed for failure to comply with a discovery request and with an order for discovery, such as:

- Discovery the offending party wants may be restricted.

- Fees and costs may be awarded against the offending party.

- Facts may be deemed established against the party.

- Evidence may be barred in a hearing or trial.

- Pleadings may be stricken, eliminating a party's claim or defense.

- Part or all of case may be dismissed or a default judgment entered (only in egregious situations).

- A party may be found in contempt (in even more egregious situations).

Think Twice

The day of a Rule 37 sanction hearing ought to be a sad day. It should not have to come to that. Sure, some disputes are so contentious or the law is so unclear that a judge is required to figure it out. But far too many Rule 37 motions are brought, only to have the recalcitrant side finally disclose the information on the eve of the hearing. Fortunately, having read this chapter, you shouldn't be the lawyer doing that.

Chapter Thirteen
DEPOSITIONS: GETTING TO KNOW YOU

Any fact is better established by two or three good testimonies than by a thousand arguments.

—Nathaniel Eramens

A. THE WHY

13.1 WHY SHOULD I TAKE A DEPOSITION?

During a deposition, you can question a witness under oath, in real time, in the presence of the opposing lawyer and a court reporter. You should take depositions to:

- Determine what a deponent knows and does not know.
- Obtain information through prepared and spontaneous follow-up questions.
- Assess the demeanor and credibility of a witness.
- Probe for weaknesses in a case or confront a deponent with damaging information.
- Obtain admissions or impeachment evidence.
- Obtain information in support of or in opposition to a motion.
- Preserve direct and cross examination testimony from a witness who will be unavailable for a hearing or trial.
- Obtain useful information to support a successful negotiation or mediation.

That's why. Federal Rules of Civil Procedure 28, 30, and 32 and similar state rules govern depositions. Arbitration codes of procedure and administrative regulations govern depositions in those dispute-resolution forums.

B.   THE HOW

13.2   WHOM SHOULD I DEPOSE?

You should depose anyone who has information that can help you accomplish the purposes described in the previous paragraph. You can depose any party or any witness who has information relevant to the case. Usually depositions are taken of adverse parties, their agents and employees, and witnesses who know about the claims or defenses or who are unwilling to talk with you. You may also take a deposition to preserve testimony of a favorable witness who will be unavailable to testify at trial.

If you are uncertain who from a corporation or organization knows specific information, you can submit a deposition notice describing the information you seek and the other side must select a person or persons who have knowledge of that information for you to depose. The corporation or organization must also prepare the witness for the deposition.

13.3   WHEN CAN OR SHOULD I DEPOSE?

You can ordinarily schedule depositions shortly after a case has begun. See Federal Rule of Civil Procedure 26(f). You may depose after pleadings have been served or the discovery plan has been established, depending upon the rules of the forum. You may be able to schedule a deposition earlier if you have good reason and can convince a judge or arbitrator of your urgent need.

You should depose when you are prepared to depose and when it is strategically best to do so. You may want to take a deposition of an adverse party as soon as possible. You may want to delay a deposition until after you have reviewed documents and electronically stored information. If there are a number of important witnesses to be deposed, you may want to schedule them in a specific sequence.

13.4   HOW OFTEN CAN I DEPOSE?

You can usually depose a person only once, unless the initial deposition has been continued or good reason exists for a second deposition. Some jurisdictions place limits on the total number of depositions to be taken in a case. Federal Rule of Civil Procedure 30(a)(2) limits the number of depositions to ten and permits more to be taken only if a judge or the opposing party approves. State court jurisdictions and arbitration forums often place more stringent limits on the number of depositions, typically permitting from three to ten, with court or party approval needed to take more depositions. You should take the number of depositions necessary to reasonably obtain the information you need.

13.5 WHERE SHOULD I DEPOSE?

You can specify the location of the deposition, within reason. See Federal Rule 30 (b)(1). Plaintiffs can be required to attend depositions in the district or county where the action is pending. Defendants may be deposed where they do business or have their residence, or where the case is venued. Attorneys usually will mutually agree to a reasonably convenient and economical place.

Depositions can be held in your office, the court reporter's office, the opposing attorney's office, the deponent's office, or in a courthouse. Holding a deposition in your office is convenient. Holding a deposition in the office of the deponent may make it more convenient for you to inspect and copy documents and electronically stored information in the possession of the deponent.

13.6 HOW LONG CAN I DEPOSE?

A deposition lasts for as long as it reasonably takes to obtain the information and complete the deposition. Many depositions take half a day, some take a day or more, and others take only an hour. The parties may agree or the rules of some jurisdictions may limit the number of hours of a deposition. Federal Rule of Civil Procedure 30(d)(2) restricts a deposition to seven hours in one day. Lawyers can agree to vary this or other rules. An attorney facing an unnecessarily lengthy deposition may seek a court order establishing a time limit or controlling the opposing attorney. Sanctions, including reasonable costs and attorney fees, may be imposed upon any person responsible for impeding or delaying a deposition.

13.7 HOW DO I NOTICE A DEPOSITION?

You notice a deposition of a party by serving the deponent and all attorneys by mail with a deposition notice that states the date, time, and location of the deposition:

Please take notice that the deposition of _____ will be taken by oral examination pursuant to the _____ Rules of _____ Procedure before (name of court reporter) at (location) on (date) at (time). The method of recording this type of deposition will be [specify: stenographic/audio/video]. The deposition will continue until completed. You may appear and examine the witness.

That's it. If you want the deponent to bring documents and electronically stored information (ESI), including emails, files, and other records, you may serve on the party a request for production of documents and ESI. This request directs the deponent to bring the materials to the deposition for inspection and copying or reproduction. It is ordinarily a better idea to obtain these materials before the deposition so you can review them and be better prepared to ask questions about those materials at the deposition.

You take the deposition of a non-party by personally serving them with a subpoena stating the time, date, and location of the deposition, along with a check for the witness fee established by statute or rule. See Federal Rules of Civil Procedure 30 and 45. If you want the deponent to bring documents and ESI, you must also serve them with a Rule 45 subpoena identifying the materials to be brought. Some jurisdictions require that before you can compel a non-party to produce materials you must make arrangements to compensate them for the time it takes to compile and produce the materials.

13.8   WHEN SHOULD I SCHEDULE THE DEPOSITION?

Depositions can be scheduled anytime during regular business hours, and at other hours for very good reasons. Brief recesses are permitted for rest and recuperation. Adjournments may be necessary if the deponent needs time to search for more information or if some other reason exists. You should discuss deposition format and the timing of breaks and lunch with the other attorney.

13.9   WHO IS PRESENT AT A DEPOSITION?

The following people are usually present at the deposition:

The deponent. All persons who have information relevant to the case may be deposed. This includes parties, witnesses, and experts who will testify at trial. In some cases, you may not know exactly whom you want to depose, and court rules permit you to describe the information you seek and require the opposing party to produce someone who can provide that information.

Attorneys. The attorney taking the deposition will, of course, be present at the deposition, as will be the attorneys representing the other parties and the attorney representing the deponent. All parties in the case have a right to have their respective attorneys present, even though those attorneys may not represent the deponent. The deponent, whether a party or non-party witness, has a right to have an attorney present.

The person who administers the oath and who records the testimony. The person who records the deposition is usually an independent court reporter hired by the deposing attorney. This person administers an oath to the deponent and records the deposition. This person can also have an assistant present, for instance, to operate a digital recorder or video camera. See Federal Rules of Civil Procedure 28(a) and (c).

Parties. All parties have a right to attend all depositions. Individual parties can attend; a corporate party may have a representative appear. It is a more common practice for parties not to attend depositions other than their own. If there are good reasons to have them attend, however, parties should be there. For example, their presence may help them prepare for their own deposition or may assist in obtaining complete and accurate testimony from the deponent. It is possible, although highly unusual, to obtain a court order excluding a party. You need better than a very good reason.

Witnesses. It is not common for witnesses to attend depositions. The applicable laws may allow witnesses and potential deponents to attend depositions unless they are excluded by agreement of the parties or by a court order; and, the parties or a judge or arbitrator may readily exclude them. There may be a good reason for witnesses to attend. For example, they may learn more about the case or what another witness knows. Some jurisdictions allow the exclusion of witnesses at the request of one party.

Assistants. A lawyer can have an assistant present during the deposition to help the lawyer. For example, an expert can attend a deposition and assist the lawyer by suggesting lines of questioning or questions to ask.

Third persons. Can third persons (interested persons, reporters, or just plain members of the public) attend a deposition? Is a deposition a public hearing? The rules of the forum determine these answers. Depositions are usually private and not public proceedings. Third persons typically have no interest in attending a deposition. If they want to appear, and one or more of the parties excludes them, they will need to seek a court or arbitrator order to attend.

13.10   DO I HAVE TO ATTEND?

Obviously, if the deponent has an attorney, that lawyer will attend. If a deposing attorney fails to appear at a scheduled deposition, expenses may be assessed and additional sanctions may be imposed. Lawyers who represent other parties commonly do attend to protect their clients' interests and ask some questions, although they are not required to attend.

13.11   HOW IS THE DEPOSITION RECORDED?

The party who notices the deposition chooses the method of recording. The three most common methods are: stenographic (a reporter uses a machine or computer), audio recording, and a video recording. See Federal Rule of Civil Procedure 30. An audio or video recorded deposition may be supplemented by a stenographic record. Audio recordings are handy if no transcript is immediately required or to supplement the stenographic method.

Video recordings are becoming more common as they are the most effective way to capture and retain what is said and how it is said. The rules of the jurisdiction typically have specific procedures to be observed when taking video or audio recordings of the deposition. For example, it is common for rules to require that everything that is said during the deposition must appear on the recording, and the deposition must be indexed by a digital time generator or another method.

Depositions may also be taken by telephone and remote electronic means. See Federal Rule of Civil Procedure 30(b)(7). Telephone depositions take place as conference calls, and satellite, cable, or web-based transmissions may be used with video monitors. These methods permit the deposition participants to be in different cities making travel unnecessary. Documents and written information may be exchanged through fax or email transmissions. A disadvantage to these methods is that it may be more difficult to assess the demeanor and credibility of the deponent.

13.12   WHEN IS A TRANSCRIPT NEEDED?

Depositions are transcribed to provide the parties with a printed version of the deposition testimony. See Federal Rule of Civil Procedure 32(c). Transcripts help in reviewing what a witness said, in supporting a motion, and in preparing for trial.

13.13   HOW MUCH DO DEPOSITIONS COST?

Deposition costs (excluding the fees for the lawyers) include the hourly fee for the court reporter, the cost of any audio or video equipment, and the cost of transcribing the deposition (if done). Whatever the total is, your client may think it is too much, and there are ways to reduce the cost. If no transcript is necessary, costs are substantially reduced. In many jurisdictions, the parties may agree not to have an independent reporter appear but to record the deposition by audio or video recording.

Think Twice

So what are common problems that occur with depositions that, with some forethought, could be avoided?

- *Deposing an unprepared deponent. Ordinarily, parties have a vested interest in making sure the deponents who represent them are well prepared. And if not, the deposing lawyer can take advantage of this miscue by using their lack of preparation to the lawyers advantage.*

- *Not showing up. Since there are at least four people who need to be present for a deposition to be held, there is some chance one of them will not show. Advance and repeated notices help remind all about the date.*

- *Disagreeing over a location. The parties may complain about an inconvenient location. The lawyers know the options and should be able to reach agreement on a site that both meets the legal criteria and satisfies the parties.*

- *Not bringing the right stuff. If a deponent was told to bring certain documents or materials and fails to so, the deposition can be adjourned and reconvened when those materials are available.*

- *Taking too long. A deposing lawyer who questions a deponent at length runs the risk of exceeding the permissible time (i.e. seven hours in federal cases) or running out of time (the deponent falls asleep after dinner). Pacing the deposition and focusing on critical information are the keys to timeliness.*

- *Someone uninvited shows up. The lawyers can avoid this problem by communicating with each other whom they plan to bring to the deposition.*

- *The recording equipment breaks down. Modern recording equipment seldom causes this problem as the machines are very reliable.*

C. THE PLANNING

13.14 DEPOSITION PREPARATION

You know from your first law school exam that you had to prepare thoroughly for questions and the answers in order to do well. The same is true of a deposition.

Preparation of a case requires familiarity with sources of factual information, legal claims and defenses, and overall discovery strategies. You need to be familiar with the subject matter of the deposition and what the deponent might or might not know. If the deponent is an eyewitness to an accident, you should be familiar with the location, circumstances, and other matters relating to the accident. [Depending on the location, internet search engines (e.g. Google Earth) may be a reasonable substitute for an in-person visit.] If the deponent is an expert engineer, then you need to be versed in whatever specialized engineering areas the deposition will cover. Your expert can help prepare you.

Thorough preparation also requires a determination of the purpose or purposes of the deposition. Why are you taking this deposition? Do you want to obtain information, search for documents, obtain admissions for a summary judgment motion, or do all those things?

The rules of evidence applicable to the ultimate hearing or trial should not unduly influence your preparation for the deposition. You should seek everything the witness knows, from whatever source, whether hearsay or documentary. Unless you are taking the deposition to preserve the witness's testimony for trial, it is usually best to probe for the best and the worst of what the witness knows. This helps you evaluate the case and prevents surprises at trial.

You will need to prepare a written outline and questions. Make a list of what you want to know and the areas you want to explore. Organize the outline in some logical sequence, such as chronological or topical (by issues, claims, defenses). After you organize and prepare your outline, check it twice to make sure it is complete. Organizing your notes and questions in an electronic or paper folder or a three ring binder may be of great assistance.

You may need or prefer to compose specific questions. How many questions you prepare depends upon your level of experience, your confidence in your ability, and your goals for the deposition. The less experience you have the more preparation you are likely to need. Preparing too few questions may make it difficult for you to be thorough during the deposition. If you are seeking vital admissions or detailed foundation or answers related to a particular legal standard, prepared questions may help you obtain this information during the deposition. On the other hand, having too many prepared questions may reduce your flexibility during the deposition or make you too dependent on the prepared questions.

A deposition taken to preserve the testimony of a witness for a later use at a hearing or trial needs to be especially carefully prepared. You will need to prepare specific direct or cross-examination questions that will be admitted as evidence at the hearing or trial. Your preparation for this type of deposition will be similar to your preparation for the hearing or trial. If the deposition is stenographically recorded, the written transcript of the deponent will be read to or by the fact finder. If the deposition is electronically recorded, the fact finder can see or hear the testimony.

Think Twice

If the deposition is an opportunity to question someone you haven't talked to before, why spend so much time preparing? Why not conduct sort of an interview? You may think you need not prepare much, but thorough preparation leads to a more thorough deposition, and that's what your client has retained you to do.

If experienced lawyers don't need to prepare as much and just ask whatever they want, why not me? Those highly experienced lawyers know what they want to ask and have spent years or decades learning how to depose. We know plenty of seasoned lawyers who still prepare extensively for every deposition they take. Once you have a substantial amount of experience, you can decide which approach works best for you and your clients. In the meantime, extensive and robust preparation makes up for the lack of experience.

D.   THE TAKING

13.15   HOW IS THE DEPOSITION ROOM ARRANGED?

The typical deposition room is a conference room with a large table in a law office. The opposing attorney sits across from or at an angle to the deponent. The deponent's attorney sits next to the deponent. The reporter is in a position to see and hear the attorneys and the deponent. Other attorneys sit around or near

---

the table. If the deposition is video recorded, the camera will be placed to focus primarily on the deponent.

13.16 HOW DOES THE DEPOSITION BEGIN?

The attorneys provide the court reporter with their professional information and the names of the deponent and other attendees. There may be some discussion about who will sit where, if there is a disagreement. The reporter notes the caption of the case, the appearances of attorneys, and the persons present, and administers an oath or affirmation to the deponent.

13.17 HOW DO I BEGIN THE DEPOSITION?

You may begin by discussing procedural matters with the other attorney, by providing the deponent with some directions or by asking questions of the deponent.

Procedures. You should make sure that the record contains the preliminary information mentioned in the previous section and that the oath or affirmation has been properly administered. You or the other attorney may suggest some stipulations. Whatever stipulations are made should be specific and understood by all. It is unwise to agree to "usual stipulations" if you do not know what they include. There may be no need to state that the deposition shall proceed under the applicable rules or that all objections shall be preserved according to the applicable rules, because the applicable rules will apply. It may be useful to suggest some stipulated procedures, such as:

> In a non-party deposition, it is useful to determine who, if anyone, is representing the deponent. That attorney will be the one who can counsel and instruct the deponent during the deposition.
>
> In multi-party cases, it may be useful to suggest that an objection by one attorney will be considered an objection by all attorneys to avoid repetitive objections.
>
> If the deposition is proceeding differently than required by the rules, a stipulation concerning those differences should be confirmed on the record to avoid objections being raised later.

If the deposition has not been properly started, correct any deficiencies unless it is to your advantage to either object to these deficiencies or not do anything to correct them.

Directions and Questions. It is common for the deposing attorney to explain to the deponent common deposition procedures to ensure the deposition will proceed efficiently, such as:

> *Mr. Hatfield, I represent Ms. McCoy in this lawsuit. We appreciate your attending this deposition. I am going to ask you a series of questions about this case, and the reporter will record your answers. If at any time you don't understand any question, please tell me and I will repeat or rephrase the question. Is this understood and acceptable to you? (The witness will invariably say yes.)*

> *Everything needs to be recorded accurately and completely. Please state your answers to the questions and do not merely nod your head or make a gesture. We all need to speak one at a time, so please wait until I complete my question before answering. Is this understood and acceptable to you? (The witness will invariably say yes.)*

Additional explanations may be useful depending upon the approach you wish to take during the deposition:

You may want to make certain the deponent understands what is happening:

> *Do you now understand what a deposition is? (or, Has your attorney explained to you what a deposition is?)* (If no, explain in more detail.)

You may want to emphasize the witness's obligation to tell the truth:

> *Your testimony will be under oath, as if you were in a court of law. You have sworn to tell the truth, and if you fail to do so, adverse consequences may result. Do you understand this?*

You may want to explain to the witness what will happen if they give incorrect or inconsistent answers in the future:

> *Everything that is said here today will be recorded. At the trial, we will have the testimony available you give today. If I ask you the same questions at trial that I ask you today, and*

> *if your answers differ then from the answers you give today,
> you will be held accountable for the difference in your an-
> swers. Do you understand this?*

You may want to create a cooperative atmosphere:

> *We are here to find out what you know to help us evaluate
> this case. We ask that you tell us all you know. If at any time
> you need a break, please tell us. We will be taking a break
> within a reasonable time.*

Think Twice

**There ordinarily is no duty under an applicable rule to
begin the deposition with these statements. Sometimes it is
done to make sure the witness understands what is about
to happen and to avoid later misunderstandings. Sometimes it's also done to create a constructive atmosphere
for the deposition to encourage the deponent to tell all.
And often it is done because the lawyer doing it has
always done it that way. It need not be so. If there is a
good reason to do something different, do it. You could
begin by asking relevant questions, which could be the
easiest or toughest questions.**

13.18   WHAT SHOULD MY DEMEANOR BE?

Two principal factors affect your demeanor and conduct. The
first is your obligation to conduct yourself during a deposition
professionally as if you were at trial. The rules and court
decisions prohibit you from conducting an examination by being
unreasonable, harassing the deponent or attorney, or acting in
bad faith. You need to—and should want to—act responsibly and
civilly.

The second factor influencing your demeanor is your strategic and tactical approach to the deposition. Strategically, your
approach should depend on how this deposition fits in with your
case theory and your overall goals for the case. Tactically, your
approach will depend upon the type of witness you have. Will the
witness be favorable or unfavorable? Cooperative or uncooperative? What is the most effective approach you can use? A friendly, empathetic approach? A firm, persistent approach? A cooperative, informal approach? An assertive, confrontational approach?

What approach will best create a constructive atmosphere? Should one approach be used at the beginning of the deposition and a different one later?

How you conduct yourself during this deposition may be as important as the questions asked. An approach that is perceived by the deponent to be reasonable and fair will generally produce a fuller, more cooperative story, and a more stern approach will produce a more restrictive story. A calm approach may be more effective with some deponents, and a more spirited approach may be more useful with others. Your tactical demeanor should be designed to meet the goals you have in taking the deposition.

Think Twice

It may be reasonable to think, "My client may expect me to ask mean questions or to be belligerent because they think the deponent deserves this treatment. Why not do this?" The answer is that it's usually the wrong strategy. That approach is apt to upset deponents and make it unlikely they will say much in response to many of your questions. Your client may want the deponent to become very uncomfortable by having you use such techniques. Being a reasonable person may be the better tactic to find out information that helps your client's case and hurts the other side.

13.19   WHAT SHOULD I ASK?

You are already prepared to ask questions. Review Section 13.14.

You could decide to submit written deposition questions instead of taking an oral examination. See Federal Rule of Civil Procedure 31. This method is seldom used in practice. It can be a less costly way to obtain information from a witness who lives some distance from the lawsuit and who has useful, objective, and non-critical information. Prepared questions are submitted to the deponent by an officer, and the deponent answers them in writing. The attorneys need not be present during this process.

13.20   HOW DO I EFFECTIVELY ASK QUESTIONS?

Your goal is to achieve completion, clarity, and closure. You can do all this by asking:

Anything and everything reasonable. Ask what you want to know. Search for supportive and helpful information and also search for harmful and negative information. You need to learn about the weaknesses as well as the strengths of your case.

Who, what, when, where, and how. These questions will help produce a narrative of the story the deponent knows.

Why. Why? To learn about what motivated the actors in that story.

Facts and opinions. Learn what happened and what the deponent believes or perceives what happened.

Feelings, emotions, attitudes, and thoughts. These questions often produce useful fact and opinion information. Remember to ask for the basis of the opinion. "You said Mr. Hatfield was angry. How did you know?"

The source of the information. Determine whether the information is based upon personal observation or knowledge, hearsay, inference, or assumption.

Comparison stories. Ask why the deponent may have a different story than another witness or a document.

Clarifying questions. If the deponent doesn't provide information about details, ask for it. "You say 'fast,' how fast?" "Many people were there? How many?"

Closure questions. Make certain you know everything the witness knows by periodically asking "Do you know anything more about ..." or "Have you told us everything you know about...."

13.21   HOW DO I EFFECTIVELY PROBE?

Insist on responsive answers. Have your specific questions answered completely. Follow up with certain responses:

If they say "I don't know," ask why they don't know.

If they say "I don't know for sure," ask for their opinion or estimate.

If they say "I think so" or "I believe so," you may want to insist on a more specific answer or you may be satisfied with this response because it is sufficiently favorable.

If they say "I don't remember" or "I don't recall," attempt to refresh their recollection by asking what will help them remember or by asking leading questions.

Encourage deponents to talk and talk. Ask them to tell you more about what they know, unless they are rambling or providing irrelevant information. Encourage witnesses to talk by asking them questions that will require sentences or paragraphs of response, not one or two words.

Explain what you want and why. They may be able to provide more information if they understand what you want and why. Or, you may prefer not to disclose this to them.

Help witnesses recall. If they are uncertain, ask questions that place them at the event, hopefully prompting their memory. If they look confused, ask them what they do not understand. If they are tired, take a recess.

Search for details and more details. Deponents may answer with generalities or summaries. Pursue details. If they are describing an event, ask them questions about different times or different views of the event. If they are restating a conversation, ask who said what first, then who spoke what next, and who said what last. Determine whether an answer is a summary, an impression, a close approximation, an exact detail, or some other recollection.

Repeat unanswered questions. Repeat questions. You may not want to use the same words. Instead, you can ask a differently phrased question that serves the same purpose, until the deponent answers fully.

13.22   HOW SHOULD I ASK QUESTIONS?

Use a structured approach. An effective technique may be to ask general, open-ended questions, followed by clarification questions, concluding with very specific questions.

Take notes. These notes will allow you to pursue topics you needed to skip, reconfirm what the witness previously said, or search for inconsistencies. You can record them on your laptop or on a legal pad. Or, you can have an assistant take notes while you concentrate on asking questions.

Pace the deposition. A reasonable pace may keep everyone focused and alert. A fast pace may provide less time for reflection and listening. Too slow a pace may remind you of some of your law school classes, but hopefully not this course.

Lead the witness to specific admissions. You may know what you want the witness to say about a specific issue to support your theory of the case. For example, if you want to establish that the deponent has a poor grasp of the circumstances of an auto accident, you could ask leading questions such as: "This accident happened very quickly. This was a frightening experience for you. You became tense anticipating the crash. You were moving at the time of the collision." If you want to establish that the deponent had a good grasp of what happened, you could ask: "You have a good memory of this event. You were especially alert because of the potential danger. You had a clear view of the scene. You were paying a lot of attention to what was happening."

Ask about other witnesses. Who else might know what they know or what they don't know? Take names and where they can be found.

Change the format of your questioning approach if what you are doing isn't working. Shift from an orderly approach to a seemingly more haphazard approach. Skip around, and return to topics previously covered to obtain more information, although this could be confusing to you as well as the deponent.

Think Twice

"Whoa. That's a lot to digest. With so many possible areas of inquiry, it all seems overly complicated." These lists present choices, and you can decide what to do in a particular deposition. And that's why we earlier stressed you need to prepare quite thoroughly for the deposition because it's so hard to do spontaneously. And there's still more to consider.

13.23   WHAT DO I DO ABOUT DOCUMENTS AND ELEC-TRONICALLY STORED INFORMATION (ESI)?

You can bring with materials the deponent knows or should know about. You can review materials the party deponent brought to the deposition at your request. Section 14.2 explains this procedure.

During the deposition, you can:

Ask questions of the deponent about all or part of the materials. Have the deponent read aloud or to themselves, or read to the deponent the relevant portion on the record. Have the deponent authenticate or explain the materials.

Ask the deponent how materials were disclosed and produced. Ask how deponents searched for documents and ESI in their possession, custody, or control.

Ask about materials not produced that should have or could have existed. Ask whether specific materials were created, maintained, misplaced, or lost, and how.

Ask about destroyed materials. Determine whether any documents or ESI were destroyed or deleted before or during the case.

Create an exhibit. Have deponents draw a diagram to help tell their story.

Review written and printed materials. Review pleadings, discovery disclosures and responses, and other file materials with the deponent. The witness may be able to explain and elaborate pleading responses, answers to interrogatories, and other information.

Seek an agreement to produce documents and ESI during the deposition. If you discover the existence of relevant materials during the deposition, you may ask the deponent to allow you to inspect or copy them or to provide you with a reproduction of them without the need for a formal production request. This stipulation should be reflected on the record with a description of the materials to be provided and a deadline for this disclosure. If you are the attorney asked to produce such materials, you should decline to do so until you have had a chance to review them to determine their relevancy and discoverability.

Search for materials used by the deponent to refresh recollec-tion. You are usually allowed to obtain documents, ESI, and other materials which the deponent read or reviewed before the deposition and which helped refresh their recollection for the deposition. See Federal Rule of Evidence 612. Ask the deponent: "Did you review any materials before this deposition? Did they help refresh your memory?" If the answer to these two questions is yes, say to the opposing lawyer, "Counsel, please have these materials produced now or before the end of this deposition so I can review and determine whether I wish to have them intro-duced as exhibits." If counsel refuses, you may compromise by asking them to provide the materials at a later date when the deposition will be resumed. Or you may serve them with a formal request for production and wait until they respond.

Think Twice

Remember, you may have to take the deposition of a non-party to obtain documents and ESI from a non-party witness in state court cases. Absent voluntary cooperation from the witness, the only way to obtain these materials from a third person not a party to a case may be to schedule their deposition and serve them with a subpoena requiring them to produce the materials at the deposition.

13.24   HOW CAN I HANDLE EXHIBITS EFFECTIVELY?

Exhibits may be marked before or during the deposition by the reporter with a designated letter or number. Having them marked ahead of time saves time. Having them marked during the deposition may be necessary to surprise the deponent:

Please mark as Plaintiff's Exhibit Number 1 this three page will, dated October 1, 2009, signed by Mr. Potter and wit-nessed by Mr. Weasley and Mr. Granger.

You can and should ask the deponent questions you need to about the exhibit to authenticate or explain it. Ask two basic questions and then follow-up questions: Ask *"what is it"* and *"how do you know?"*

Q: I hand you Plaintiffs Exhibit Number 2. Do you recog-nize it?

A: Yes.

Q: *What is it?*

A: This is an email that I wrote and sent.

Q: *How do you know* that is an email you wrote?

A: It has the company information on it along with my name. It looks like the email I composed.

Q: Is this your X on the electronic signature line?

A: Yes, I signed it with my distinctive electronic X mark.

Your follow-up questions should be designed to make certain there is a sufficiently complete foundation for the authentication and identification of the exhibit.

With exhibits, you can approach examination of the deponent in at least two different ways:

Ask about the content of the document or ESI before showing it to the witness. If you want to inquire about the deponent's understanding or recollection of an ESI or document, ask about it before showing it to the deponent.

Show the deponent the materials first before asking any questions. If you prefer to have the deponent review the materials before answering questions, do so. When you first show it, the deponent has a right to review it before being asked questions.

Whatever your choice, you should provide a copy of the exhibit to opposing attorney. It is a professional courtesy and may be an efficient use of time to provide opposing counsel with a copy of the exhibit. It usually is more productive to have multiple copies of the exhibit available for the attorneys present while the deponent reviews the exhibit. A short exhibit may be able to be reviewed simultaneously by the deponent and attorney.

13.25   WHAT DO I DO WITH THE EXHIBIT?

You need not and should not offer the exhibit into evidence. There is no reason to offer an exhibit on the record at a deposition because the process is not a trial and there is no judge to receive the evidence. It becomes part of the deposition after it is marked, and it or a duplicate copy is usually attached as an exhibit to the transcript.

You should make sure the exhibit is preserved, however. A copy of the original exhibit used during the deposition is usually made available to the reporter for inclusion as part of the transcript. See Federal Rule of Civil Procedure 30(b)(1). The original exhibits used during the deposition are returned to the party who provided them and must be retained by this party for future use. In some cases, it may be necessary to secure the originals in a neutral location. Administrators and court clerks usually do not accept these exhibits because they do not have sufficient storage space.

13.26   WHAT ABOUT CONFIDENTIAL INFORMATION?

You already know the law protects specific types of information from discovery, based on irrelevancy, work product, privileges, attorney mental impressions, and trade secrets. Some attorneys make it a practice to claim general privacy or broad confidentiality protections afforded to information and materials. The law may not recognize these claims.

You may inquire into areas that the opposing lawyer claims are private, confidential, or non-discoverable. You can offer to stipulate on the record at the deposition that you and a designated client representative will be the only ones to hear or see the information. If this stipulation is refused, you can agree to stipulate on the record that the other side does not waive any objections or rights applicable under the law to the protected status of this information. If this fails, you should ask detailed questions about the basis of the claimed protection and the existence of the information or documents without inquiring into the content.

If you foresee these issues arising during a deposition, you can discuss them with the opposing attorney ahead of time (or in the deposition) to reach an agreement about the disclosure of this information. It is common for the attorneys to enter into confidentiality agreements or stipulated protective orders that allow the disclosure of protected information to specific individuals. If these discussions fail, you may seek an order from the judge or arbitrator allowing the disclosure of this information under restricted conditions. You may ask the judge or arbitrator to review the information or materials *in camera* (that is, alone) to determine if there is a basis for the protection claimed.

13.27   HOW DO I DEPOSE AN EXPERT?

The previous suggestions about how and why to ask questions apply to all deponents, including lay and expert witnesses. In addition, there are some specific areas to explore with experts, including:

- Their qualifications.
- Their opinions.
- The bases of their opinions.
- The sources of information relied upon in forming their opinions.
- Information, tests, or sources of information they do not know or did not perform.
- Possible causes or explanations contrary to their opinion.
- Their familiarity with treatises which contain contrary opinions.
- How and why they differ with opinions held by your experts.
- Their fees and whether they expect to testify for the party in the future.
- The number of times they have testified for plaintiffs and defendants in previous cases.

13.28   WHAT SHOULDN'T I SAY OR DO DURING THE DEPOSITION?

Here is a list of the most common mistakes made while taking a deposition. Avoid making these mistakes:

Don't listen to the deponent's responses. If you don't pay close attention or ask obvious follow-up questions, you will miss critical information, although you certainly will speed up the deposition.

Don't observe the witness. Witnesses may react in the most telling ways to certain questions with facial expressions and body postures revealing their uncertainty or anxiety. If you don't watch the witness, you don't have to worry about what these reactions mean.

Fail to be curious. If you don't understand something or are unsure about a response, keep your puzzlement to yourself. You will have enough to do already, so don't bother asking even more questions.

Assume everything is in your best interests. Guess what happened rather than asking detailed questions to determine whether you are right or wrong.

Insist on generalizations and not specific responses. It takes an effort to ask "How do you know that?" and "What facts do you have to support that position?" Be content with incomplete information.

React visibly to damaging information. As your case disintegrates before your eyes, make sure the opposing lawyer and the deponent know how weak you believe your case to be.

Avoid asking follow-up questions about damaging information. Instead of learning more about problem areas with your case, wait until trial for more damaging surprises.

Ask complex and unclear answers, chock full of legalese. If you ask these kinds of questions, they may think you are a law professor.

13.29   HOW SHOULD I REACT TO OBJECTIONS?

Your opponent has the right to make proper and limited objections during a deposition, even though no one is there who is authorized to rule on the objections at that time. See section 13.32.2. Ordinarily, your reaction is to insist on an answer to the question, which is your right. See Federal Rule of Civil Procedure 30(c). If your opponent does not specify grounds to support an objection or suggests an inappropriate ground, insist on a response from the deponent. If there may be some merit to the objection, you may want to do something about your question or the anticipated response:

- If an objection to the form of the question is raised (vague or multiple question), you should decide whether your

question is appropriate and insist on an answer or whether you should rephrase the question.

- If the objection is lack of foundation, you may want to establish more foundation by asking additional questions.

- If an objection is based on relevance, you may insist on an answer if your question is relevant, or you may cure the objection by rephrasing it or focusing on more relevant information.

- If an objection is based on any other ground (e.g. hearsay), you can ignore the objection and insist on an answer from the deponent.

- If the attorney objects and properly instructs the deponent not to answer, you will find it impossible to extract an answer. Your recourse is to seek an order compelling an answer. Section 13.32.3 explains the proper use of instructions not to answer.

Reacting to objections should not include arguing with the deponent or other attorney about the correctness or appropriateness of the objection. If an attorney insists on making frequent objections, there are several ways to control the situation:

You may suggest that the record reflect a continuing objection to all or certain of your questions to avoid the other attorney constantly interrupting you.

You may tactfully remind the other attorney that nearly all objections are preserved for trial or hearing, and there is no need for these objections.

You may advise the other attorney that such unnecessary objections unduly interfere with the deposition and that such conduct is improper.

You can seek a protective order or a sanction order against the attorney if the behavior is especially egregious.

13.30   HOW DO I CONTROL INTERFERENCE DURING A DEPOSITION?

Rules of civil procedure and court decisions prohibit an attorney from unnecessarily interfering with the deposition, but these restrictions do not deter some attorneys from attempting to interfere. You may counter interfering tactics with the following approaches:

Insist the rules be followed. Remind the attorney of these rules and that their breach will not be tolerated. Hand the attorney a copy of Federal Rule 30 or its state court or arbitration code equivalent.

Insist that court decisions regulating deposition practice be followed. Advise the lawyer, or better yet, provide the lawyer with a copy of a decision (be sure to bring one along) sanctioning attorneys for engaging in obstructive behavior during depositions.

Record everything that occurs, especially non-verbal conduct by the opposing attorney, whether it involves passing a note to the witness, whispering in the deponent's ear, signaling the witness, conferring with the client, or other interfering conduct. You can record the behavior simply be describing out loud what is happening. The court recorder should transcribe what you say.

Refuse to take unnecessary breaks. Insist on continuing with the deposition and note on the record the frequency and duration of these breaks unilaterally taken by the other lawyer and deponent.

Insist that the deponent respond to your questions and advise the opposing counsel not to testify.

Admonish an attorney from unnecessarily conferring with the deponent. If the deponent is unrepresented, another lawyer at the deposition should not advise them. If the deponent is represented, and if you are in a jurisdiction that prohibits a lawyer from counseling the client during a deposition, so advise the attorney.

Advise the opposing attorney you will telephone or text a judge or arbitrator to seek a ruling regarding the improper behavior, who, hopefully, will be available for a conference call.

Advise the opposing attorney you will adjourn the deposition if the misconduct continues and seek a protective order with sanctions against the attorney.

Reschedule the deposition. In unusual cases in which the opposing attorney is uncontrollable, conduct the remainder of the deposition in a courthouse or before an arbitrator, referee, or magistrate judge who can control the situation.

Think Twice

"Now you're making this stuff up. Why would advocates do such things?" Some do and they do it because they think it will be an effective strategy, because they have not sufficiently prepared the deponent, or because they are testing you to see if you know how to combat those tactics. Those are some of the reasons why. It can be tough to battle through a deposition when opposing counsel acts inappropriately. You'll need to attempt to stop and correct such behavior to protect your client's case and your own sanity.

13.31   HOW DO I CONCLUDE THE DEPOSITION?

Before concluding the deposition, you should take a moment and review your prepared topics and questions to determine whether you asked everything you needed and whether the deponent provided you with any information you need to explore further. You may consider asking broad questions to make clear the witness has both understood everything and has told all. Questions such as "Have you understood all the questions you answered?" or "Did you answer all the questions truthfully and completely?" may produce something, or may produce only an affirmative response "to the best of my recollection." You may also want to advise deponents that they have an obligation to provide supplementary answers to the deposition questions if they recall any additional information after the deposition or if they need to update answers.

After you are done asking your questions, the attorney for the deponent and other attorneys involved in the case have an opportunity to ask questions of the deponent. Typically, these attorneys ask a reasonable number of questions for rehabilitation purposes or to clarify or supplement areas you explored. After they are done, you have an opportunity to ask follow-up questions of the deponent if you deem it necessary. Additional considerations concerning the end of the deposition are explained in section 13.34.

E. THE DEPONENT

13.32 DEFENDING THE DEPONENT

Attorneys defending client-deponents have three primary responsibilities:

- Preparing the deponent.

- Making objections during the deposition.

- Protecting the deponent.

13.32.1 Preparing Your Client to Be the Deponent

Your preparation of your client for the deposition should include a thorough explanation of the general procedures of the deposition and the specific elements of the case. You can provide deponents with a set of general deposition instructions to educate them, and you can also have them observe a video of a simulated or real deposition. When the deponent is a witness you represent, your specific preparation about a case should include the following elements:

Explain what the case is all about to the witness. You ought to make certain the witness understands not only what is happening but why it is happening.

Review all the facts and documents they may be asked about. Prepared deponents make more effective and credible witnesses.

Explain conflicting stories. Deponents need to understand that their story will differ from the stories of other parties or witnesses to the case and that this is to be expected and is normal.

Be the devil's advocate. Explain the type and scope of questions the deposing attorney will probably ask, and the approach the attorney may take with the deponent.

Rehearse the deponent. Ask the deponent questions, listen to the answers, and suggest accurate, truthful, alternative ways to answer the question if the witness's answer is problematic.

These preparation suggestions apply to deponents who are clients. You can meet and assist non-client deponents for an upcoming deposition, but, because they are not your client, you cannot provide them with legal advice or otherwise counsel them, and what you discuss with them will not be protected by the attorney/client privilege.

13.32.2   Making Objections During the Deposition

You have a right to make limited objections to questions asked of the deponent, including client and non-client deponents. See Federal Rule of Civil Procedure 30(c). If a question is asked that is objectionable, you can say "Objection" followed by a one or two word or brief statement of the grounds in support of the objection. Whether your objection is correct or not, the examining attorney still has a right to insist on an answer, unless you have a right to instruct the client deponent not to answer (soon to be explained). No judge or other person is present at the deposition to rule on the appropriateness of any objection or disagreement between the attorneys.

The vast majority of depositions are conducted without many objections being made, because there is no need for them. With only few exceptions, objections that could have been made at a deposition are preserved for trial. A lawyer who believes that a question calls for hearsay, for example, need not object at the deposition. If the witness testifies at trial or the deposition testimony is offered at trial, the lawyer can object at trial. The deposing lawyer who understands the rules and goals of a deposition typically asks non-objectionable questions. Defending lawyers understand that there are few legitimate grounds to support objections.

Some attorneys may attempt to make many objections, either because they misunderstand the rules, or because they are trying to prevent the examining attorney from discovering weaknesses in the case, or because they are want to obstruct the deposition. This conduct is improper. Illegitimate objections should never be made.

Appropriate and inappropriate objections made during a deposition include the following (Federal Rule of Civil Procedure 32(d)):

Objections to errors or irregularities in the deposition notice or in the initial deposition procedures must be made on the record at the beginning of the deposition, otherwise they will be waived. Examples include a defective deposition notice and a failure to place the deponent under oath or affirmation.

Improper questions by the examining attorney that can be corrected at the deposition must be objected to in order to preserve the objection for trial. For example, objections to the form of the question (vague, ambiguous, complex, multiple, and argumentative questions) should be made. You may also object if a deponent's response is inappropriate because it is non-responsive or rambling.

Objections to the substance of the response need not and usually should not be made. These objections are not waived and can be made at trial. Objections such as irrelevant, improper opinion, and hearsay will be preserved even if not made during the deposition. The liberal scope of discovery allows a broad examination into these areas, unless, for example, obviously irrelevant information is sought.

Objections based on grounds of privilege or similar rules should be made to prevent an inquiry about the privileged matter. In fact, these objections must be made. If information is privileged, it can be protected from disclosure during the deposition. If the examining attorney insists on an answer, an instruction not to answer can be interposed, otherwise the objection may be waived.

13.32.3 Instructing the Deponent Not to Answer

An attorney can instruct a client deponent not to answer only in very limited circumstances. An instruction not to answer occurs when the attorney representing the deponent advises the deponent not to answer a question that is objectionable.

An attorney usually may instruct a deponent to refuse to answer only in three limited situations: to preserve a privilege, to protect a deponent from harassment, or to enforce a protective order. See Federal Rule of Civil Procedure 30(d). If there is no legitimate reason supporting an instruction not to answer, the attorney has acted improperly and is subject to sanctions. An attorney not representing a deponent cannot instruct that deponent not to answer.

13.32.4   Protecting the Deponent

There are some things a defending attorney can legitimately do during a deposition to protect a deponent, as explained above. But there is much that cannot be done. An attorney cannot interrupt proper questions, testify instead of the deponent, or demand frequent breaks to consult with a client. Some jurisdictions go so far as to prohibit an attorney from counseling a client at any time during the deposition.

The following situations reflect what can and cannot be done:

If you do not hear a question, you can ask the court reporter to read the question back.

If you do not understand the question, you can object if the deponent does not understand either.

If the deponent becomes visibly fatigued, you can insist on a brief recess.

If the deponent has difficulty remembering, you cannot interrupt and volunteer the information. The examining attorney has a right to determine what the deponent knows and not what you know.

If the deponent has answered a question and begins to ramble, you can object on the ground that the deponent has answered a question and is being non-responsive.

If a deponent has difficulty providing an answer that is contained in a document, it is usually inappropriate for you to show the deponent the document to provide the answer. The examining attorney has a right to assess the memory of the witness without reference to a document.

If the deponent is shown a document by the examining attorney during the deposition, you and the deponent have a right to review the document before any further questions are asked.

If the deponent has incorrectly answered a question, you cannot interrupt and testify to a correct response. You may object on the ground the deponent did not understand the question if it appears so; you may be able to discuss the issue with the deponent during a break; and you may ask questions at the end of the deposition to correct or clarify the deponent's answers.

It is improper during the deposition to signal deponents with some gesture or facial expression, or whisper an answer in their ear, or otherwise interfere with the deposition.

If you and your client deponent wish to consult during the deposition, you usually are able to do so, within reason. A few jurisdictions prohibit an attorney from consulting with a client during a deposition, and a few prohibit consultation even during recesses of the deposition. These jurisdictions hope to encourage lawyers to prepare deponents properly before a deposition and prevent undue influence during a deposition. Jurisdictions which permit consultation during a deposition generally permit only infrequent and short discussions to avoid unnecessary interference and overly long depositions.

An examining attorney facing situations of improper behavior can do what was suggested in Section 13.30, or become a transaction lawyer.

13.33   QUESTIONING THE DEPONENT

You can ask questions of the deponent after the examining attorney is done. There may have been responses that need correction or clarification, or there may be some relevant areas you want to cover. You may not want to or need to ask any questions. You may not want to give the examining attorney another opportunity to ask questions. If the deposition is being taken to preserve testimony because the deponent will not be available to testify at a later hearing or trial, you will want to ask questions and obtain information that supports your case.

Think Twice

If it appears that courts favor lawyers who are taking the deposition and restrict attorneys who are defending the deponent, that appearance would be correct. Courts, reflecting the goals of the civil discovery rules, want the inquiring lawyer to learn as much as reasonably possible from a deponent without interruptions and interference.

You may perceive that this increases the chances that the deponent will say things that will hurt the case. You would be correct. That, in fact, is one of the primary goals of the deposition. Our system wants both good and bad news to come from a deposition. The defending lawyer cannot muzzle the deponent and prevent the deponent from saying what happened if that presents bad news.

F.   THE END

13.34   CONCLUDING THE DEPOSITION

After all the questioning has been completed, there are a number of concluding matters that may need to be addressed.

13.34.1   Review of the Deposition by the Deponent

The deponent has a right to review the deposition after it is completed. See Federal Rule of Civil Procedure 30. The deponent may read a transcript of the deposition or review the recording. Most jurisdictions require that the deponent review a transcript or recording within 30 days after receiving a copy or after being notified of its availability. An attorney representing a party other than the deponent may request that the deponent review the deposition. If the deponent fails to review the deposition within the time permitted, the deponent waives any right to later review the deposition.

It is usually a wise practice to have the deponent review the deposition. It is critical that testimony be accurate and complete, and a review of the deposition will help assure this. The reporter may have misunderstood the deponent; there may have been some malfunction in the recording system causing an incomplete or inaccurate transcript; the deponent may have inadvertently misspoken and this may not be apparent until the deposition is reviewed; or, the deponent may want to change an answer.

A deponent has a right to make changes to answers. See Federal Rule of Civil Procedure 30. Most courts permit a deponent to make any change for any reason. The deponent may correct typographical errors, misunderstood questions, and wrong answers. The deponent must usually explain the reason for the change. Other courts restrict the changes a deponent can make and no not permit a deponent to change a substantive answer.

The typical manner of making changes is by the witness completing a separate written statement identifying the changes and stating the reasons. The original deposition transcript or recording and any changes are available to be used at a later hearing or trial.

Tactical considerations should discourage making several changes throughout the transcript. Reasonable inferences may be drawn from making changes in the deponent's testimony. These inferences may not be favorable to the deponent because the changes may appear to be alterations of relevant responses or inconsistent testimony. Substantive changes in the record make a deposition incomplete and allow the examining attorney to reopen the deposition for further questioning.

While it is generally a good idea to do so, there are reasons not to review a deposition. If the deponent is satisfied with the responses, there may be no need to take the time and incur the additional expenses. The attorney representing the deponent may not want the deposition to be reviewed, which may help the deponent avoid impeachment attempts at trial. The attorney taking the deposition may want the record to remain unchanged and not want the deponent to review the transcript.

13.34.2 Signing the Deposition

A deponent may have a right or obligation to sign a deposition transcript or recording. Some jurisdictions require deponents to do so, and others provide deponents with an opportunity to do so which they may decline. If changes are made to a deposition, the deponent will need to sign the changes. Deponents often do not sign because there is no advantage to do so. A disadvantage is that they can be more effectively impeached at trial. Whether a deposition is signed or unsigned does not affect its use for a motion, hearing, or trial.

13.34.3   Filing the Deposition

After being completed by the officer taking the deposition, the deposition transcript or record is usually delivered to the attorney who noticed the deposition. (Alternatively, the transcript might be filed with the court, in those few jurisdictions that still require filing.) Either the officer or noticing attorney must advise all parties of the completion and filing of the deposition. It is critical that a deposition be stored in a safe place for later use. It is common for other parties to request a copy of the transcript or recording from the officer or from the custodial attorney.

13.34.4   Stipulations

Attorneys at the deposition may stipulate on the record concerning the review, signing, and filing procedures. These agreements make clear what happens after the deposition is concluded. "Usual stipulations" suggested by an attorney should only be agreed to if everyone understands what is included in the stipulations. If in doubt, specific agreements should be stated on the record.

Think Twice

Your work with the client does not end with the end of the deposition. You will want to review the transcript and determine what next needs to be done. You'll need to decide whether and when to have the deponent read the transcript, to suggest any changes that could be made, to have any changes made, and to follow up with any signing or filing matters. It's never over until the case is over.

G.   THE FUTURE

13.35   USE OF THE DEPOSITION

Deposition testimony may be used for any purpose permitted by the rules or law and is typically used (Federal Rule of Civil Procedure 32):

- In support of or in opposition to a motion for summary judgment.

- As evidence at a hearing or trial.

- As admissions. Statements made by a deponent party may be offered against that party as party admissions.

- As testimony. The deposition may be introduced as evidence in lieu of the live testimony of the deponent who is unavailable as a trial witness.

- For cross-examination purposes. The deponent may be impeached with prior inconsistent deposition testimony. See Federal Rule of Evidence 613.

- To refresh the recollection of a witness. Witnesses who do not recall something may have their memories refreshed with the use of their deposition testimony.

Think Twice

Another significant use of a deposition is its effect on the merits of the case and likely settlement demands and offers. A key deponent who does poorly at the deposition may significantly weaken a case; conversely, an important witness whose testimony is strengthened by a deposition will also strengthen a case. While many depositions will not provide numerous, if any, surprises, there are some that have a significant impact on the outcome of the case. And that's why we spend so much time harping on preparing and planning. But, we're done, for now.

Chapter Fourteen
DISCOVERY METHODS: IS THAT ALL THERE IS?

You can't always get what you want, But if you try sometime, you just might find, you get what you need.

—The Rolling Stones

A. INTRODUCTION

14.1 MORE DISCOVERY METHODS

In addition to asking questions and seeking information at depositions, advocates can get:

- Documents and electronically stored information.
- Interrogatory answers.
- Admissions.
- Physical and mental examinations (not for us).

How this is done is the subject of this chapter.

B. GETTING DOCUMENTS AND ELECTRONI-CALLY STORED INFORMATION (ESI)

14.2 HOW DO I OBTAIN THESE MATERIALS?

You can obtain documents, records, and electronically stored information that the other side has not voluntarily disclosed by asking for them or demanding them pursuant to a procedural rule.

You can ask for these materials by saying please and requesting voluntary production. You can describe what you want, and ask the other side to provide you with the originals for inspection and reproduction or for an identical copy of the original. It is usually best to make this request in print through an email or a letter or formal request, but you may also do so orally. If the other side concurs with your request, you have what you want. If they do not, you'll have to demand the documents in accordance with the applicable procedural rule. Federal Rule of Civil Procedure 26 and similar rules from other forums provide that any party may serve any other party with a demand to produce original materials for inspection or copying, to produce tangible things, or to permit entry onto land or other property.

14.2.1   Whom Can I Ask?

You can ask anyone who has what you want. If they are a party, you can usually submit a written demand. If they are a non-party, you usually have to serve a subpoena to produce the documents or schedule a deposition for them to appear and produce the materials. See section 14.11.

14.2.2   What Can I Demand From Parties?

You can request any document, record, memo, email, social network communication, other electronically stored information, tangible thing, or property in the possession, custody, or control of the party that is relevant as discoverable information. Possession and custody includes both actual and constructive possession, and control means a party has a legal right to obtain the documents. The broad scope of discovery provides for reasonable access to all sorts of materials, things, and property.

Think Twice

The scope and extent of these potentially discoverable materials and information can be so broad, you'll need to remind yourself that you should only seek what you really need and what your client can afford to pursue. You could well imagine that there exists out there some piece of information that would devastate your opponent and win the case for you. And perhaps there is. But keep your imagination in reasonable check and pursue the more probable and likely available information.

14.3   WHEN CAN I MAKE A DEMAND?

You can usually make a demand when you need the documents. If the applicable rules require voluntary disclosures, you usually have to wait until these disclosures have or have not been made before making a demand. Practically, you may have to wait until the litigation pleadings, arbitration claim and response, or administrative petition and answer have been exchanged. Tactically, you may want the documents early in the case in order to evaluate the case, decide how you want to proceed, and prepare for depositions or a hearing.

14.4   HOW DO I MAKE A DEMAND?

The written demand typically describes the documents and electronically stored information to be produced and specifies the reasonable time, place, and manner for making the inspection or producing copies. A production of materials request under Federal Rule of Civil Procedure 34 provides:

The plaintiff _name_ requests that the defendant _name_ respond within _____ days to the following requests:

1. That defendant produce and permit the plaintiff to inspect and to copy each of the following documents, including electronically stored information:

    [Describe the document and the electronically stored information individually or by category,]

    [State the time, place, and manner of the inspection and any related acts.]

2. That defendant produce and permit the plaintiff to inspect and to copy, test, or sample each of the following objects:

    [Describe each thing, either individually or by category,]

    [State the time, place, and manner of the inspection and any related acts.]

3. That defendant permit the plaintiff to enter [describe property] and to inspect and to photograph, test, or sample [describe the real or personal property].

    [State the time, place, and manner of the inspection and any related acts.]

Dated and Signature

14.4.1   How Do the Documents and ESI Need to Be Described?

According to applicable rules, typically the description must be in writing and set forth with "reasonable particularity." The description should be sufficient to allow a person of ordinary intelligence to say "I know what they want," and to permit a judge or arbitrator to determine whether all the materials have been produced.

14.4.2   How Do I Draft These Descriptions?

You want to draft with sufficient specificity to make certain you obtain the documents and ESI you want and to avoid allowing the other side to withhold documents. You also want to draft with sufficient breadth to make certain that no existing relevant materials escape your attention. Three drafting techniques that help produce these results are: use *definitions* of important words, draft *requests* seeking both specifically designated items and generally described items, and include *instructions* to the other side.

An example of a *definition* is:

The term documents means all writings and electronically stored information and printed materials of any kind, including the originals and all non-identical copies, including without limitation, correspondence, memoranda, notes, email, social network communications, text messages, diaries, blog entries, list serve messages, statistics, letters, telegrams, minutes, contracts, reports, studies, checks, statements, receipts, returns, summaries, pamphlets, books, interoffice and intra-office communications, notations of any sort of conversations, telephone calls, voicemail files, bulletins, printed matter, computer printouts, telefax, invoices, worksheets, drafts, alterations, modifications, changes and amendments of any of the foregoing, graphic or oral records or representations of any kind (including, without limitation, photographs, charts, graphs, microfiche, microfilm, video recordings, recordings, motion pictures, digital images), and any computer, electronic, mechanical, or electric records or representations of any kind (including, without limitation, tapes, cassettes, discs, recordings, hard drives, and computer storage and electronically stored information devices).

An example of a *request* is:

Provide all documents and electronically stored information concerning any contractual breach by defendant alleged in Paragraph Two of the Complaint including but not limited to:

The original and all copies or reproductions of each document and electronically stored information exchanged between the plaintiff and defendant beginning on May 1, 2010 and ending on August 1, 2010.

All documents and electronically stored information submitted by the plaintiff to the Banking Commissioner which contain the name of the defendant.

Examples of *instructions* are:

If you refuse to disclose some of the documents and electronically stored information in existence, specifically identify these materials and state their location and explain your objections in detail.

If your response is that the documents are not in your possession or custody, describe in detail the unsuccessful efforts you made to locate the materials.

If your response is that the documents and electronically stored information are not in your control, identify who has control and the location of the materials.

Think Twice

There are a variety of internet and print sources and colleagues that can provide you with forms and lengthy or brief descriptions of what you seek. As with other samples and examples of discovery requests, you'll need to customize them for each of your cases.

14.5 HOW, WHEN, AND WHERE CAN I OBTAIN THE DOCUMENTS?

The demand states a time, place, and manner for production. The date is typically scheduled at least 30 days after service of the request. The hour is usually during business hours. The place is the office of the requesting attorney where copying and reproduction equipment is available, or the location of the documents. The manner depends upon the kinds of items requested.

14.6   HOW CAN I OBTAIN ELECTRONICALLY STORED INFORMATION?

Modern discovery rules generally permit the discovery of any "data or data compilations stored in any medium from which information can be obtained—translated, if necessary, by the respondent into reasonable usable form." Jurisdictions may allow ESI to be disclosed in its native format, and without having to be reformatted. This is reasonable when the native format is one that can be recognized without undue burden and excessive costs.

The use of computer and electronic databases may make materials available as electronic documents or paperless files. Duplicate copies can be transferred through computer programs or email attachments. There may be a need to verify the contents with the originals of the documents. The accessibility of ESI affects its discoverability, and the type of media storage determines the degree of accessibility.

Metadata may be discoverable if it is readily accessible. Metadata is secondary information that describes the characteristics, origins, and usage of an electronic document. This information cannot be seen on the face of the document. There are various types of metadata including substantive, systems, and embedded metadata.

The party who seeks the ESI needs to establish its relevance and specify how it can effectively be translated or transferred. The party from whom the discovery is sought has the burden to establish undue burden, excessive cost, and inaccessibility if the party is going to refuse to produce the ESI as requested. A judge can use cost shifting to allocate the financial burdens on the parties proportional to their resources.

14.6.1   Scope and Extent of ESI

The existence of electronically stored information raises several issues relevant to what is practically discoverable. While there may be a galaxy of potential ESI information floating in the ether world, practical issues affect what can be and is obtainable for the asking.

There is the issue of volume. You can imagine in routine cases there could be hundreds if not tens of thousands of communications that may have some relevance to the dispute. And you can imagine that in more complex or multi-party cases there could be millions of ESI documents.

There is the issue of cost. Who pays for the discovery time and efforts to obtain this information? Who bears the cost of translating ESI into readily understandable formats? Who pays for the expert technicians needed to assist lawyers in these endeavors?

There is the issue of accessibility. What is reasonably accessible? How do the parties compromise on accessibility? How does the judge gain enough information and expertise to resolve accessibility issues?

There is the issue of proportionality. It makes sense that because of the enormous volume, excessive costs, and accessibility difficulties, discovery should only be allowed if the time and costs are reasonably proportional to what is at stake in the case and what the parties can afford. Parties with limited resources involved in $50,000 disputes ought to be treated differently than parties with significant resources in million dollar disputes.

Think Twice

You'd be right to ask, "What does this really mean?" Relevant electronically stored information—including website content, email messages and attachments, social network communications like Facebook, electronic tweets on Twitter, blog entries, list serve messages—are now apparently all discoverable. Plus, the underlying metadata revealing who created them, who received them, and what has happened to them is also discoverable. ESI raises a whole new world of discovery issues that are still in the process of being sorted out.

The current discovery rules were primarily crafted to deal with writings and paper documents. Recent revisions deal-

ing with ESI are a patchwork solution grafted onto these rules. Judges struggle with how best to handle ESI discovery issues and disputes. It will be up to your generation of lawyers to eventually deal with these and future issues created by ESI and as yet unknown technologies.

14.7   HOW MAY THE OTHER SIDE RESPOND?

The party receiving the demand may within the allowable time:

Abracadabra! Produce the requested documents or reproductions of the ESI materials according to the suggested time, place, and manner. It is common practice for a party to provide the requesting party with copies of the originals. This may be the most efficient and inexpensive method of responding, especially if the documents and ESI are not numerous. Or the producing party may incur the cost of reproducing them and provide printed copies, or may insist under the rules that the demanding party pay reasonable reproduction costs. The party producing documents usually has to produce them as they are kept in the ordinary course of business or organize them and label them to correspond with the categories in the request. ESI may be provided in its native format via computer transmissions or may need to be translated into a different format in order to be revealed. These matters are often discussed and mutually agreed upon by the attorneys. If a party requests many documents which would take a substantial amount of time to organize, the responding party may make them available for the requesting party to search through and reproduce.

Provide copies or disclose the requested documents, ESI, or materials at another time, place, and manner agreeable to the requesting attorney, or serve a written response upon the requesting party stating that the production will be permitted at another time, place, and manner agreeable to the requesting party.

Seek a protective order to prevent or safeguard the disclosure of certain items. It may be necessary to obtain an order from a judge or arbitrator restricting or modifying the request: (1)

If a party believes the request to be improper or burdensome, or (2) if the request seeks privileged or confidential information, or (3) if the ESI is not readily accessible and the costs are not proportional to the disputed issues and resources of the parties.

Serve a written response objecting to all or part of the request. The response may indicate which materials will be produced and which will not with the objections explaining the grounds for the refusal.

14.8 HOW DO I KNOW I GOT EVERYTHING?

Your inspection and approval of the requested items should include several considerations: Has everything you requested been turned over? Too little? Too much? Do the records or deposition or interrogatory answers indicate other relevant documents? You can seek assistance from your law firm IT staff or a retained computer expert.

You should maintain some means of listing and identifying the materials and things examined, which will help you organize the production and prevent later confusion about what was produced when. Exchanging copies of computer documents may not cost you anything. Photocopying or printing documents is usually done at your own expense. You can arrange to use another's copying equipment and reimburse those costs. The lawyers usually work out these details.

Think Twice

Much of discovery is self-regulating, including responses to discovery requests. Professional and ethical lawyers routinely comply with reasonable requests and disclose information however harmful or helpful. That's their obligation. They do so because that's what they expect the other side to do as well. And they do so because it's always the right thing to do.

14.9 HOW DO I TEST AN OBJECT?

You may have a right to test relevant objects in certain cases. The decision to test turns on a number of considerations: Is the test likely to do more good or more harm due to the destruction or material alteration of the evidence? Will the test produce supportive information, or may it help the other side? Will the results of the proposed tests be admissible at a hearing or trial?

Whatever testing is done must be done with the full knowledge of the other side. Your request for testing should spell out in detail what and how you intend to test. It is wise to seek a written stipulation or order detailing the testing procedure. An expert will usually be involved in the testing protocols.

Some testing may result in the destruction of all or part of an object. A specific order prior to conducting these destructive tests is usually required. The discretion of the judge or arbitrator in deciding whether to issue an order allowing destructive testing is guided by two factors: (1) the usefulness or need of the discovery to the party requesting it and (2) the prejudice that will occur to the party opposed to destructive testing.

The terms of a testing protective order frequently include: a testing plan, an opportunity prior to testing for all parties to examine and photograph the object to be tested, notice of the testing, the right of any party to be present at the testing with their experts, thorough recording of the test, the availability of test results and written reports for all parties, and the right of other parties to take additional samples for similar testing.

14.10 WHAT ARE AVAILABLE OBJECTIONS TO PRODUCTION DEMANDS?

A responding party may object to part or all of a request for production and may withhold these materials from discovery. All objections must be bona fide and be supported by sufficient reasons. The most common grounds for objection to production of materials sought pursuant to document production requests include:

- Irrelevant and beyond the scope of proper discovery.

- Not in the possession, custody, or control of the responding party.

- Privilege, trial preparation, or attorney mental impression materials.

- Materials sought are from experts who will not testify at trial.

- Imposes an undue burden or expense.

- Costs disproportional to disputed issues and resources of party.

- Request is vague, ambiguous, or overly broad.

- Public records equally available to the requesting party.

The responding party should consider whether there is any tactical advantage in disclosing materials that are supported by a proper ground for an objection. If the disclosure of the information supports the responding party's case or weakens the opponent's case, it is usually wise to disclose the information.

Think Twice

"These explanations are exhausting me. There must be an easier way." There is, as long as you are working with cooperative and agreeable opposing counsel. Lawyers, even those who are adversaries, recognize that in the short and long run it is easier, cheaper, and saner to reach mutually acceptable agreements on the discoverability of documents and ESI. The when, where, and how the materials will be disclosed can usually be resolved by negotiated stipulations. These stipulations may be self-enforcing or need to be confirmed in a judicial order. It all depends on how well the lawyers can work together.

14.11 HOW DO I OBTAIN DOCUMENTS AND ELECTRONICALLY STORED INFORMATION (ESI) FROM NON–PARTIES?

To obtain documents from a non-party you usually must serve them (and the other parties) with a notice of the non-party's deposition accompanied by a subpoena ordering the non-party to produce the materials at the deposition. Some forums permit the service of a subpoena without a scheduled deposition, hearing or trial. The scope of the obtainable information is the same as the scope of discovery from parties. See Federal Rule of Civil Procedure 45 and similar state court and arbitration rules.

14.12   HOW DO I OBTAIN RECORDS FROM THE GOVERNMENT?

If the government is a party, you can obtain information the same way you obtain information from any party. If the federal government is a non-party, you can obtain information through the Freedom of Information Act, (FOIA) 5 U.S.C. Section 552. If you are seeking information from a non-federal governmental unit, you may be able to obtain information pursuant to state statutes similar to the FOIA.

FOIA allows the broad disclosure of records held by the government and provides that the government agencies must release any records in the agency's possession to any person upon request. Access to the records is provided either by the publication in the federal register, access at the agency's headquarters, or by making copies available upon request. Specific exceptions to disclosure are grounded in privilege, confidentiality, national security concerns, and law enforcement investigation.

Think Twice

As a reminder, you may be able to use a wide variety of investigative sources to obtain this information independently and to confirm the accuracy and completeness of what you receive. Review Chapter 7. While you should expect to trust the other lawyer, it can be useful to make sure you may have received all you requested. It's the opposing parties who may not always provide their lawyers with the available information, especially if it's quite damaging.

C.   GETTING INFORMATION

14.13   WHAT ARE INTERROGATORIES?

Interrogatories are prepared questions submitted to another party who has to respond with a written answer. Interrogatories can be an effective and efficient way to obtain objective, specific information from parties regarding their claims or defenses, the existence of documents, financial data, damage computations, expert information, and other relevant objective data. Interrogatories can also be ineffective and relatively useless if they seek general or subjective information or allow the other party to respond with self-serving responses. Interrogatories cannot be served on non-parties.

14.13.1 When Can I Submit Them?

You can serve interrogatories when you need the information. You can often serve interrogatories with or soon after the service of litigation pleadings and arbitration documents, or serve them later in a case to obtain information to help draft a document/ESI production request or to prepare for a deposition or hearing. The responding party usually has a minimum of 30 days to respond.

14.13.2 What Information Can I Seek?

You are most likely to obtain useful information when you seek specific types of information that cannot be obtained more effectively, efficiently, or economically through other discovery devices. Information based upon testimony or narrative explanations and information depending upon the demeanor and credibility of a person is usually better sought through depositions. Information regarding the content of documents and electronically stored information is better left to material production requests. Examples of useful information sought through interrogatories are:

The identity (name, address, email, and telephone number) of individuals likely to have discoverable relevant information and a summary of this information.

Specific information a party has to support an allegation in a specific claim or defense stated in a complaint or answer.

The existence, description, location, and condition of relevant documents, ESI, tangible things, witness statements, property, and objects.

Specific information about damages sought, the computation of damages, and a description of any documents and material supporting the damage computations, if not previously disclosed.

The existence and coverage of liability or other insurance, if not disclosed at the outset.

The identities of expert witnesses who will testify at trial, or who are employees of a party, or who have been retained or specially employed.

Specific information about expert trial witnesses including their opinions, bases of opinions, prepared reports, authored publications, paid compensation, qualifications, and the other cases in which the expert has testified at a trial or deposition, if not already disclosed

Business and corporate information concerning the principal place of business, date and state of incorporation, and states that license the business.

Summary financial information or summary technical or statistical information.

Opinions, conclusions, and legal contentions can be inquired about in addition to factual information, though typically, other methods of discovery, including requests for admissions, are more effective ways to obtain this information.

Think Twice

Interrogatories should be used with precision and specificity. If you seek broad categories of information, you may well be disappointed because the answers are too broad. If you seek information ambiguously described (because you are uncertain what is out there), you'll likely receive unhelpful information. Because interrogatories are an inexpensive way to seek information, the temptation is to overuse them or to seek elusive information. Instead, it's usually better to be focused and selective in their use.

14.14   HOW DO I DRAFT INTERROGATORIES?

There are three parts to the interrogatory request:

- Instructions
- Definitions
- Questions

14.14.1   Instructions

Interrogatories usually include a prefatory statement and a variety of instructions.

Preface: Plaintiff requests that the defendant answer the following interrogatories in writing and under oath pursuant to Rule 33 of the Rules of Civil Procedure and that answers be served on the plaintiff within thirty (30) days after service of these interrogatories.

Procedural instructions: In answering these interrogatories, furnish all information, however obtained, including hearsay, if it is available to you and information known by or in possession of yourself, your agents, and your attorneys, or appearing in your records.

Response instructions: If you cannot answer the following interrogatories in full after exercising due diligence to secure the information, answer to the extent possible, specifying your inability to answer the remainder, stating whatever information or knowledge you have concerning the unanswered portion, and detailing what you did in attempting to secure the unknown information.

Document/ESI production instructions: A question that seeks information contained in or information about or identification of a document or electronically stored information may be answered by providing a copy of these materials for inspection and reproduction.

Supplementary answer instructions: These interrogatories shall be deemed to be continuing until and during the course of trial. Information sought by these interrogatories that you obtain after you submit your answers must be disclosed to the plaintiff by supplementary answers.

Identification instruction: The person or persons who provide information and answers to the following interrogatories will each identify which answers have been provided and furnish their name, address, and title.

14.14.2   Definitions

Definitions may precede interrogatories defining certain words used in the questions to make certain the responding party will use the same definition, to identify a word that is peculiar to the interrogatories, to shorten questions by avoiding the need to repeat the meaning of a term, and to ensure complete responses. Examples of definitions are:

Describe: This word means to specify in detail an answer to the question and not just to answer in a summary or outline fashion.

August 15 contract: This term refers to the contract signed by both the plaintiff and the defendant on August 15, 2010, attached as exhibit A to the complaint.

Identify: The word "identify" means to state the name, address, email, telephone number, employment, and title of all persons identified in a response.

14.14.3 Questions

The following section 14.15 explains how to compose questions.

Think Twice

And you already know, as with other discovery requests, there are samples and examples of effective interrogatories that are tried and true. All you need do is search for them or call a colleague, and then conform them to the specific needs of your case.

14.15 HOW DO I EFFECTIVELY DRAFT QUESTIONS?

Interrogatories should contain clear, precise, direct questions. They should not be vague or broad. The questions should have the other attorney thinking: "Yes, I understand what they want to know." Such thinking comes easier for some lawyers than others. After you draft your interrogatories you can review their effectiveness by asking:

- Can the question be redrafted in a simpler, less complex manner?

- Will the answer to the interrogatory provide me with the information I want?

- Should some questions be eliminated or consolidated?

- Can the other side reasonably avoid answering all or part of a question?

An effective drafting technique is to use the "branching" approach. A broad question is asked and then followed by specific questions relating to one or more of the possible responses. For example:

> State whether defendant is a corporation or a partnership. If a corporation, identify the members of the board of directors. If a partnership, identify all the partners.

14.16　HOW MANY QUESTIONS CAN I ASK?

Most jurisdictions limit the number of interrogatories. Federal Rule of Civil Procedure 33(a) limits interrogatories to 25 in number including subparts. The rules of many state courts and arbitration organizations limit the number of interrogatories to no more than 20 or 50 interrogatories. A question is counted as one interrogatory if it is one question or if it includes subdivisions that directly relate to the initial question. For example, one interrogatory will be:

> State whether the plaintiff owns an automobile. If the answer is yes, describe the make and model, its current market value, the state in which it is licensed, and whether it has manual or power seats.

You can use drafting techniques that help reduce the number of interrogatories asked. For example:

Use discrete subparts, and avoid prefacing them with letters or numbers. Ask:

> See the automobile question above.

Do not separate the sub-topics conspicuously, with conjunctive or disjunctive words or with unnecessary punctuation. Avoid using and, or, the, semicolons, and colons. Ask:

> Please identify all schools that plaintiff has attended, beginning with high school.

Reduce a clause or lengthy phrase to one word or a concise phrase. Ask:

> Describe in detail defendant's job duties.

Include necessary specifications or exact details by using subtopics. Ask:

> *Please describe plaintiff's hair, including, but not limit-*
> *ed to the color, style, number of gray hairs, approximate*
> *length of sideburns, color of the roots, and the curvature*
> *and degrees of the cowlick.*

Ask simple questions. Ask:

> *Identify all members of the baseball team and name their*
> *positions.*

Employ questions that seek only one possible response from a list of alternative suggested answers, unless you do not want to suggest the answer. Ask:

> *State whether the attorney for plaintiff prefers to be*
> *called by the name of lawyer, attorney, attorney at law,*
> *counselor, or something else.*

Use definitions with your interrogatories.

> Reread Section 14.14.2.

Compare your interrogatories with others that have been used in other cases.

There are many examples of effective interrogatories appearing in cases similar to yours and on internet websites and in form books. These sample and example questions should be reviewed to determine their usefulness and edited to apply to your case.

Think Twice

"So when are interrogatories used most efficiently and affordably?" When they meet the needs of the requesting party, when the case involves obtaining information best suited to an interrogatory, and when the requesting law-yer knows how to use them effectively. Interrogatories produce useful information if the opposing side responds properly. That being said, the drafter of interrogatories needs to remember that the drafter of the answers will ultimately be the opposing lawyer. That is the primary reason that interrogatories almost always work best when the information sought is objective, factual information.

14.17 HOW ARE INTERROGATORIES RESPONDED TO?

A responding party may:

- Answer the questions.

- Assert objections.

- Provide documents and electronically stored information instead of answers that contain the information sought.

- Seek an extension of time to answer

14.17.1　How Are Questions Answered?

A party must provide complete, accurate, and responsive answers to interrogatories that are not objectionable.

14.17.2　What Is an Appropriate Answer?

Answers must answer the question asked. All information known to the answering party must be disclosed, whether it is helpful, neutral, or harmful. Three factors influence the drafting of answers:

- Interpreting questions

- Gathering information

- Drafting answers

Interpreting questions. Questions must be interpreted reasonably. If a reasonable person can understand the question, the responding attorney must answer the question. Unreasonable extrapolations, quibbling, and stretched interpretations have no place in responding to an interrogatory.

Gathering information. A party has a duty to conduct a reasonable investigation to obtain information for the response. Parties must reveal whatever information they or their employees, offices, or managing agents know personally, learn through hearsay, believe to be true, appear in their documents, or have in their possession or control. A party must make a conscientious effort to obtain all information that does not require undue labor or expense.

Drafting answers. Interrogatory answers must be in writing and under oath and signed by the party providing the information, and usually the attorney. The rules of most jurisdictions require that the question be repeated in full before each answer.

While the lawyer will ultimately draft the answers, the client needs to take an active role in reviewing the questions, gathering the information, and helping to prepare the answers. In most cases, it is the client and not the attorney who will know the answer. In most cases, the client will gather information and materials that will be reviewed by the attorney in drafting answers. It is important to involve clients directly because it is their case, because they have to sign the answers under oath, and because the answers may be used later in the trial for substantive and impeachment evidence.

The attorney can and should take an active role in preparing and drafting answers. The party can provide the information or create a first draft, and the attorney can shape the information into an appropriate response. Answers can be phrased in the best possible way to support the position of a party as long as they are full and complete responses. More information than asked for can be provided if it is useful for the party serving the interrogatories to know specific information helpful to your case.

Answers cannot be evasive, incomplete, or deceptive. Situations may arise when a response can legitimately be qualified. These situations include:

> When a party is unable to answer a question because of a lack of information or some other reason the party must indicate those reasons.

> If a party does not know an answer at the time the response is due but later learns the information, the information can be provided in a supplementary answer.

> A party may answer one interrogatory by referring to a previous response, as long as the previous response fully answers that interrogatory.

Think Twice

"It sounds like there could be a conflict between avoiding answering questions and providing full and complete answers." There ought not be a conflict. It's the clear duty of the responding lawyer to answer properly phrased questions. And it's an available option to object to and decline to answer improperly drafted questions.

14.18 WHAT OBJECTIONS MAY BE MADE TO INTER-ROGATORIES?

Objections must be stated with specificity and must usually include all grounds to support the objection. If an interrogatory is only objectionable in part, the non-objectionable part of the interrogatory must be answered. Grounds for objections that may be applicable to interrogatories include:

- Irrelevant and beyond the scope of discoverable information.

- Privilege, trial preparation, or attorney mental impression information.

- Unduly burdensome and requiring extensive cost and time.

- Excessive number.

- Seeks legal research.

The party objecting to an interrogatory has the burden in any subsequent proceeding to establish the validity of the specific objection. It is not enough to suspect there might be an objection, there must be an actual legal or factual basis for the objection. Unfounded objections subject a party and the attorney to sanctions.

Questions that are objectionable on legitimate grounds should still be answered in some situations. If the answer will help a client's case, then the answer should be provided. If an easily-made response will provide information that does not prejudice a client's case, the response should be given to avoid wasting time and money objecting and facing the prospects of a motion to compel a response. If a question can be modified to avoid an objectionable feature, it may be advisable to submit a responsive answer.

14.19 WHAT CAN I DO IF I DON'T GET WHAT I WANT FROM MY INTERROGATORIES?

You can contact the other attorney and negotiate a compromise solution. You may be able to redraft the interrogatory to make it acceptable. The other side may be willing to provide some but not all information. This may satisfy you. If not, you can seek an order enforcing your discovery request.

D. GETTING ADMISSIONS

14.20 WHAT ARE REQUESTS FOR ADMISSIONS?

As you might suspect, requests for admissions are written statements submitted by one party to another seeking admissions. The purpose of these requests is to seek the agreement of the other side to a relevant fact, opinion, conclusion, authentication of a document, content of an ESI, or other useful information. This approach narrows undisputed issues and also obtains some discoverable information.

Admission requests are usually submitted in the latter stages of a case, near the end of discovery, and can be helpful in determining what issues need to be decided and what evidence needs to be introduced in a hearing or trial. Lawyers will sometimes, however, use requests for admission to attempt to narrow issues at the beginning of discovery. Parties may be allowed to change or amend responses, however, provided that an admission has not prejudiced the requesting party. See section 14.24.

14.21 HOW DO I DRAFT REQUESTS FOR ADMIS-SIONS?

Requests should be concise and understandable statements. The format of a request looks like:

Plaintiff MG requests defendant CL within 30 days of the service of this request to make the following admissions for the purposes of this action only and subject to all objections to admissibility which may be interposed at the trial:

Each of the following statements is true:

   1. You said, "The sky is falling" when you saw the sky falling on February 2.

   2. The color of the sky you saw falling was blue.

   3. A one foot square piece of sky hit your school desk on February 2.

Each of the following documents, exhibited with this request, is genuine:

1.   Exhibit 1 to this request is the written statement you signed with your claw mark on February 3.

Additional instructions and definitions of some of the words used in the statements may also be included.

Think Twice

"Why don't I just copy those forms out there to draft admission requests?" For one reason, we keep reminding you that you have to customize the samples and examples. For another reason, admission requests are usually quite case specific and borrowing from other cases won't meet your particular needs.

14.22   WHAT ARE RESPONSES TO REQUESTS?

A party receiving a request for admission may:

Admit the statement. A party must respond to a request in a truthful, specific, and unconditional way. Honesty determines how to respond. A party admits something by responding yes or by some other specific affirmative response.

Deny the statement. A party can deny a statement if it is untrue. The responding party should ask: "Can I in good faith, honestly, and unconditionally deny all or part of this request?" To be effective, a denial must deny the truth of the matter.

Qualify the answer. If part of a statement is true and part untrue, the party can admit the true part and deny the untrue part. If a party cannot admit or deny a statement, the party must set forth in detail the reasons why an admission or denial cannot be made. A party, for example, may be uncertain or have some reasonable doubt about a factual matter that is the subject of a request. If so, the party must explain why the request cannot be answer with a yes or no response to the statement. A party should not attempt to be evasive or to avoid direct responses by using qualified answers. A party can add more information in response than the request seeks. It is appropriate for an attorney to include information supportive of a case in a response.

Object to the request. A party has a right to object to inappropriate requests for admissions. The same types of objections applicable to interrogatories and requests for production apply to requests for admissions and evidentiary objections. See sections 14.10 and 14.18. The grounds for an objection must be specifically stated.

Obtain an agreement or order. A party can obtain an agreement from the requesting party or an order from the court or hearing officer extending the time to respond. The applicable rules usually provide that an untimely response to the request for admission deems the requests to be admitted. Consequently, the agreement of the other side or judge or arbitrator is critical to obtaining an effective extension of time.

Do nothing. This is the worst choice because the statements will be admitted, as just explained.

Think Twice

Because of the impact that an admission can have in a case, it can be tempting to do your very best to avoid responding in any meaningful way. You will have to respond to avoid adverse consequences, but in so doing you'll have an urge to avoid conceding obvious, outcome determinative facts. Your obligations under the rules and your ethical responsibilities will help you resist this urge and respond appropriately.

14.23   CAN I CHALLENGE A RESPONSE?

The rules typically allow a requesting party to challenge the sufficiency of any response through a motion and hearing. If the response is an otherwise appropriate objection or explanation, you may obtain an order requiring the other side to respond fully. If the response is a non-response or an unacceptable response, the request may automatically become an admission after the time runs to respond. In some forums, you may still need to seek a ruling from the judge or arbitrator declaring this statement to be an admission.

14.24   CAN A RESPONSE BE CHANGED?

A party may be able to withdraw an admission and substitute an amended response. This may be permitted when the other party will not be substantially prejudiced by such a reversal. If the admission was a genuine mistake and should not have been made, a withdrawal will likely be allowed. If the request for the withdrawal occurs late in a case and should have been interposed earlier, the request will usually be denied.

14.25 WHAT IS THE EFFECT OF AN ADMISSION?

Admissions are conclusive proof of the matter asserted for purposes of a pending action. The admission has the same effect as a pleading admission or a stipulation of facts. The fact finder must accept the admission as true and cannot disbelieve it. The party that made the admissions cannot contradict or rebut the admissions at the trial or hearing. Admissions are readily admissible in a case, and a party need only offer them as evidence.

Think Twice

"So, are admission requests used often? Are they really effective" They can be. Some lawyers use them frequently with good results. Other lawyers dislike having to use them and avoid them. Still other lawyers sometimes use them and sometimes not. It does depend on the type of case and the nature of the issues in dispute, in addition to the preferences of the lawyer.

E. GETTING AN EXAMINATION

14.26 WHY WOULD I WANT TO REQUEST AN EXAMINATION?

You may want to have an adverse party examined by a medical doctor or psychiatrist because the party's condition is in issue and in controversy. Federal Rule of Civil Procedure 35 and similar state and arbitration rules apply broadly to any case in which there is a controversy about the physical, mental, or blood condition of the person to be examined. Examinations are common in personal injury cases, and may also be involved in parentage, harassment, incompetence, and undue influence cases.

14.26.1 What Are the Grounds for an Examination?

The physical, mental, or blood condition of a party must be *in controversy and good cause must exist* to support an examination. Parties should be involuntarily examined by a doctor only if they have voluntarily placed their physical or mental condition at issue in a case. An opposing party has the right to have an examination conducted if other parties seek a remedy, such as damages, for their physical or mental condition. The most common example of an appropriate occasion for an examination is when a plaintiff seeks damages for physical injuries or emotional distress. Non-parties cannot be examined involuntarily.

14.26.2   What Examination Documents Are Needed?

Examinations are usually conducted pursuant to a stipulation between the parties. Parties can mutually agree to the terms of the examination. If there is a disagreement, the party seeking the examination will need to serve and file a notice of motion, motion, affidavit, proposed order, and legal memorandum and schedule a hearing before the judge or arbitrator. The stipulation or order for examination typically covers the following provisions of the examination: time, location, manner of examination, person conducting the examination, scope of the examination, who may be present during the examination, and any conditions restricting or relating to the procedures.

14.27   WHAT HAPPENS AT THE EXAMINATION?

The examination typically takes place at the office of the doctor conducting the examination. Obviously, the person to be examined is there, and sometimes the person's attorney. The extent and nature of the examination is limited by the specific issues relevant in the case.

14.28   WHAT HAPPENS AFTER THE EXAMINATION?

The examining doctor ordinarily prepares a report of the examination. This document is a detailed statement of the doctor's examination, specific findings, and overall conclusions. A copy of the report is ordinarily forwarded to the party examined and to other parties.

Think Twice

"Will I really have to know these procedures when I become a real lawyer." Many of you may not. It depends upon your area of practice. If you are a plaintiff's lawyer representing injured parties, Rule 35 will be a regular part of your life. If you are a defense lawyer in these cases, Rule 35 exams will be an essential discovery method for you. Time will tell.

EPILOGUE

And now the end is near ... of this book, but it is only the beginning of your work as a lawyer. One of our primary goals was to provide you with the information and knowledge you need to become a competent and confident professional. We encourage you to use what you have learned to help others and to enhance our civil justice system.

We trust that our explanation of lawyering theories, skills, strategies, approaches, and tactics has provided you with the foundation to begin to learn to be the best practitioner you can be. We hope that your review of the available videos has helped you understand how lawyers use these skills and approaches to do their work effectively. And we expect that your tolerance towards our modest attempts at humor have made you a more understanding person.

Becoming an excellent lawyer is work that never ends. You will need to constantly analyze and critique what you do and what other lawyers do to in an effort to improve continually. This is a reasonable goal for a professional, and more important-ly, this is what our clients and the community expect. We can eloquently explain why we should maintain high standards for our work, but the expectations that clients and the public have for us should alone motivate us to do our best.

We conclude this book with our sincere wishes that you will delight in being a lawyer. For those of you who practice, we hope you will experience the joys, challenges, frustrations, and feelings of accomplishment that come from representing clients. For the rest of you, we hope you will apply your lawyering skills to be a better professional. To all of you, we wish the very best.

This book covers much of the work of the lawyer, but not all. Companion books provide additional information about the work of the advocate:

Fundamentals of Pretrial Litigation, 8th Edition 2011, by Roger S. Haydock, David F. Herr, and Jeffrey W. Stempel (West). This book explains pretrial practice from the initiation of a lawsuit, arbitration, and administra-

tive hearing to its completion. Major topics include pleadings, discovery, motions, ADR, and settlement.

Trial: Advocacy Before Judges, Jurors, and Arbitrators, 4th Edition 2011, by Roger S. Haydock and John O. Sonsteng (West). This text explains how to try bench trials, arbitrations, administrative hearings, and jury trials and includes descriptions and examples of effective strategies, tactics, and techniques.

Index

INDEX

†